12 Reasons
Why I Love Her

By

Jamie S. Rich

and

Joëlle Jones

Published by Oni Press, Inc.

Portland, OR, USA

Lettered by *Douglas E. Sherwood*

Edited by *James Lucas Jones*

Cover colors by *Lee Loughridge*

Book design by *Steven Birch @ Servo Graphics*

Thanks to Stephanie Donnelly and Maryanne Snell for their last-minute eyeballs

Published by *Oni Press, Inc.*

Joe Nozemack publisher

Randal C. Jarrell managing editor

Douglas E. Sherwood editorial assistant

Oni Press, Inc.

1305 SE Martin Luther King Jr. Blvd.

Suite A

Portland, OR 97214

www.onipress.com

www.confessions123.com

www.ooglygoogly.sandwich.net/joelle

First Edition: October 2006

ISBN 1-932664-51-3

1 3 5 7 9 10 8 6 4 2

Printed in Canada

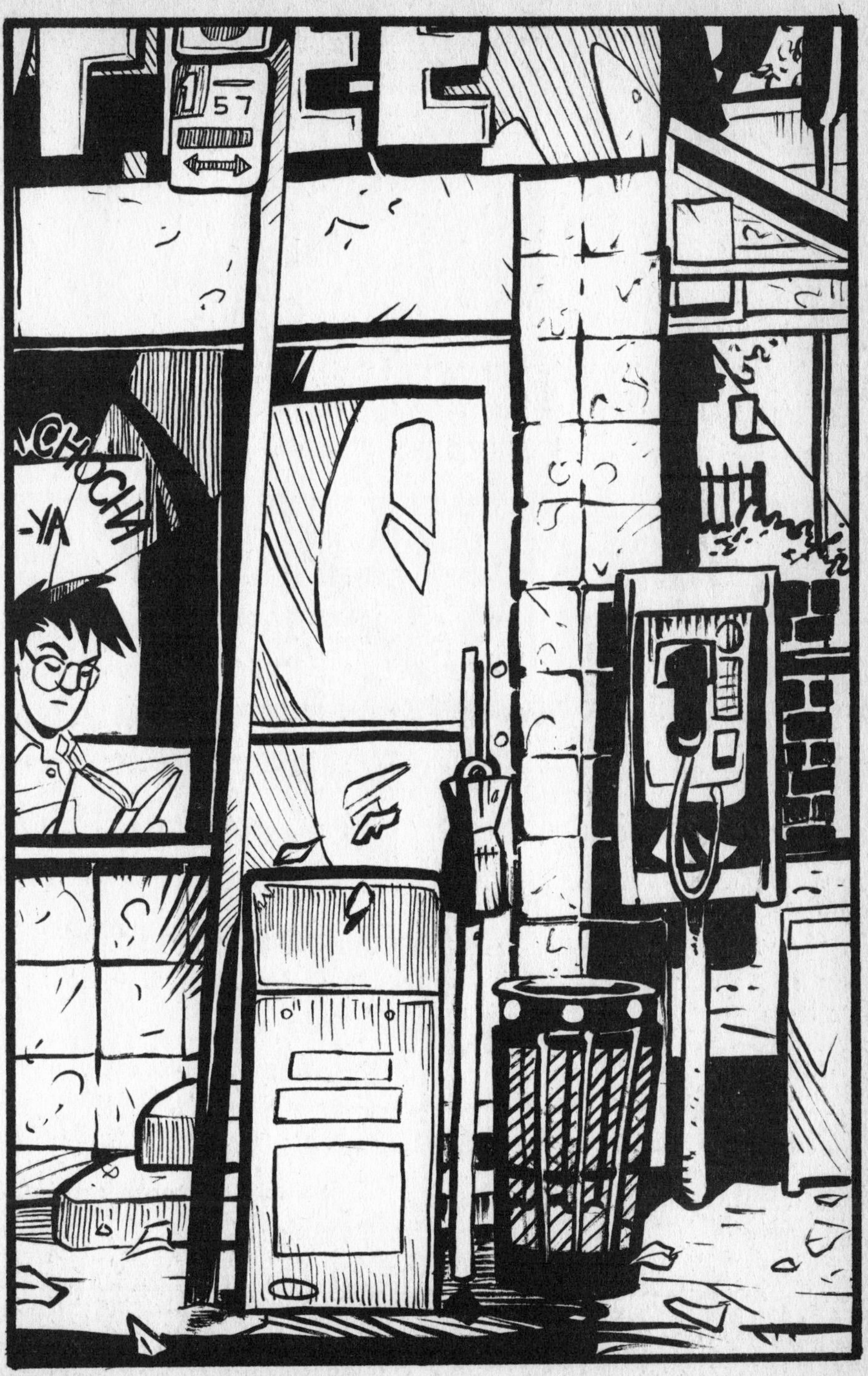
57
CHOCHA
-YA

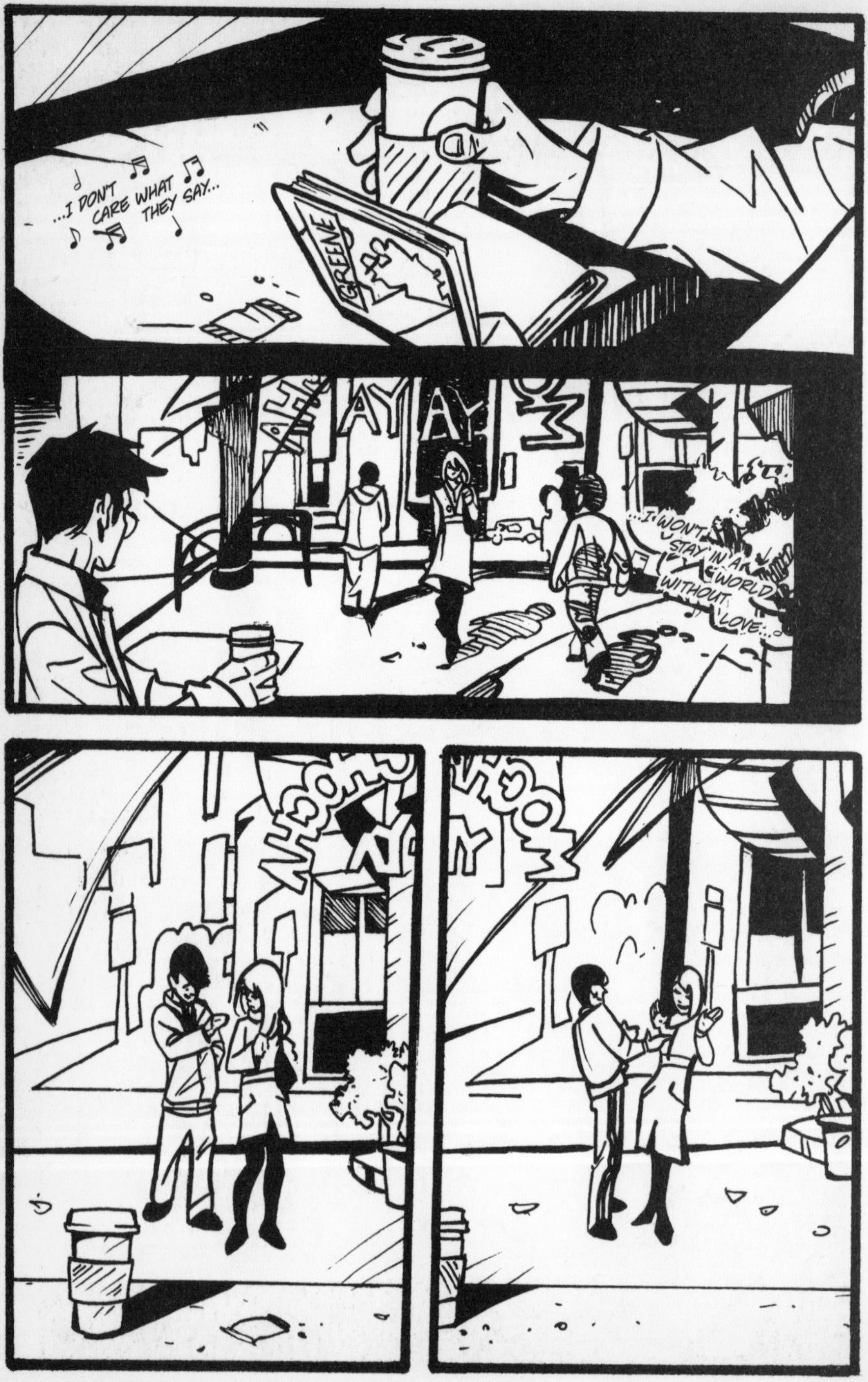
...I DON'T CARE WHAT THEY SAY...
GREENE
...I WON'T STAY IN A WORLD WITHOUT LOVE...

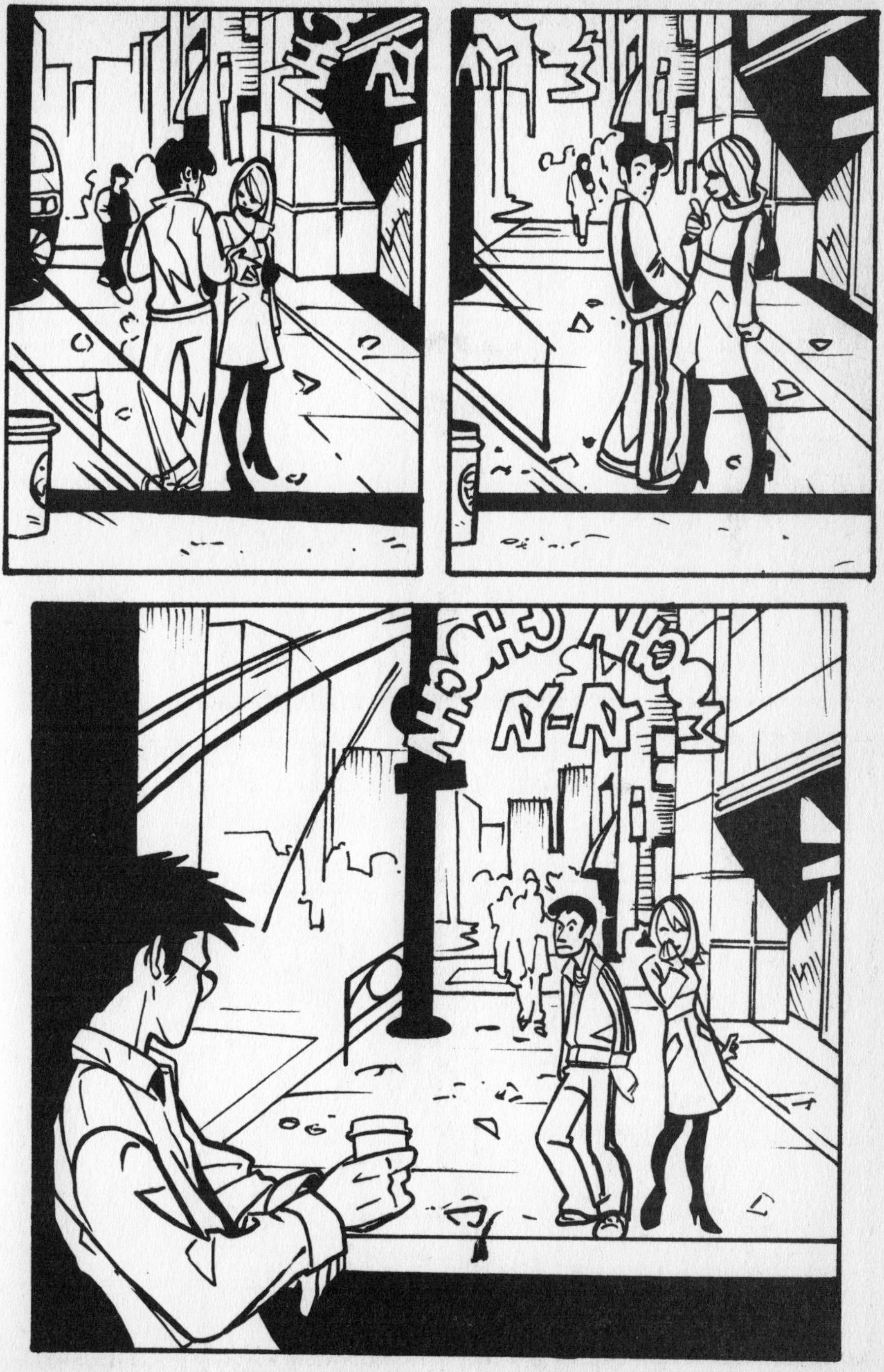

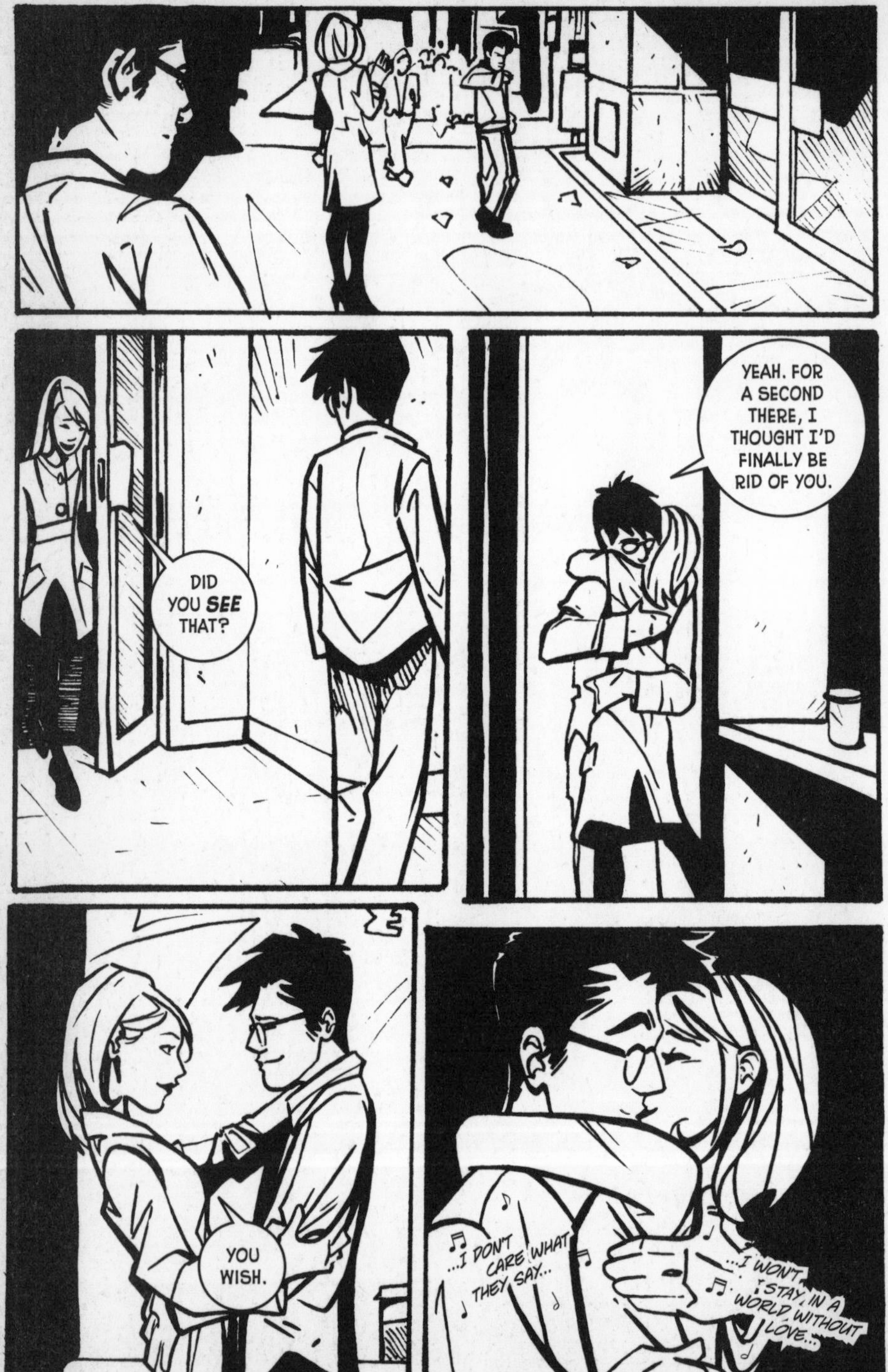
DID YOU SEE THAT?
YEAH. FOR A SECOND THERE, I THOUGHT I'D FINALLY BE RID OF YOU.
YOU WISH.
...I DON'T CARE WHAT THEY SAY...
...I WON'T STAY IN A WORLD WITHOUT LOVE...

One

SONG

Nancy Sinatra
"Let Me Kiss You"

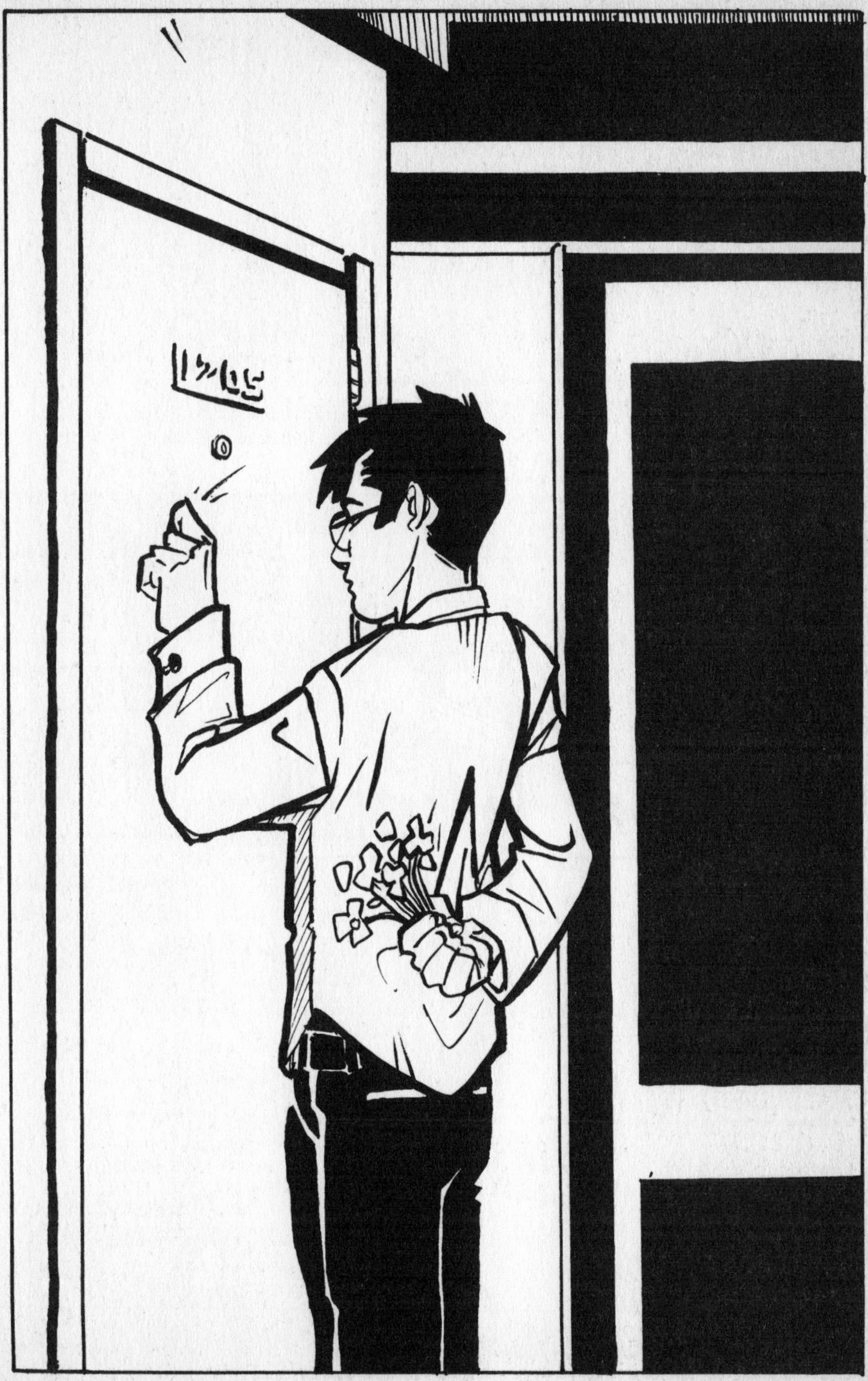

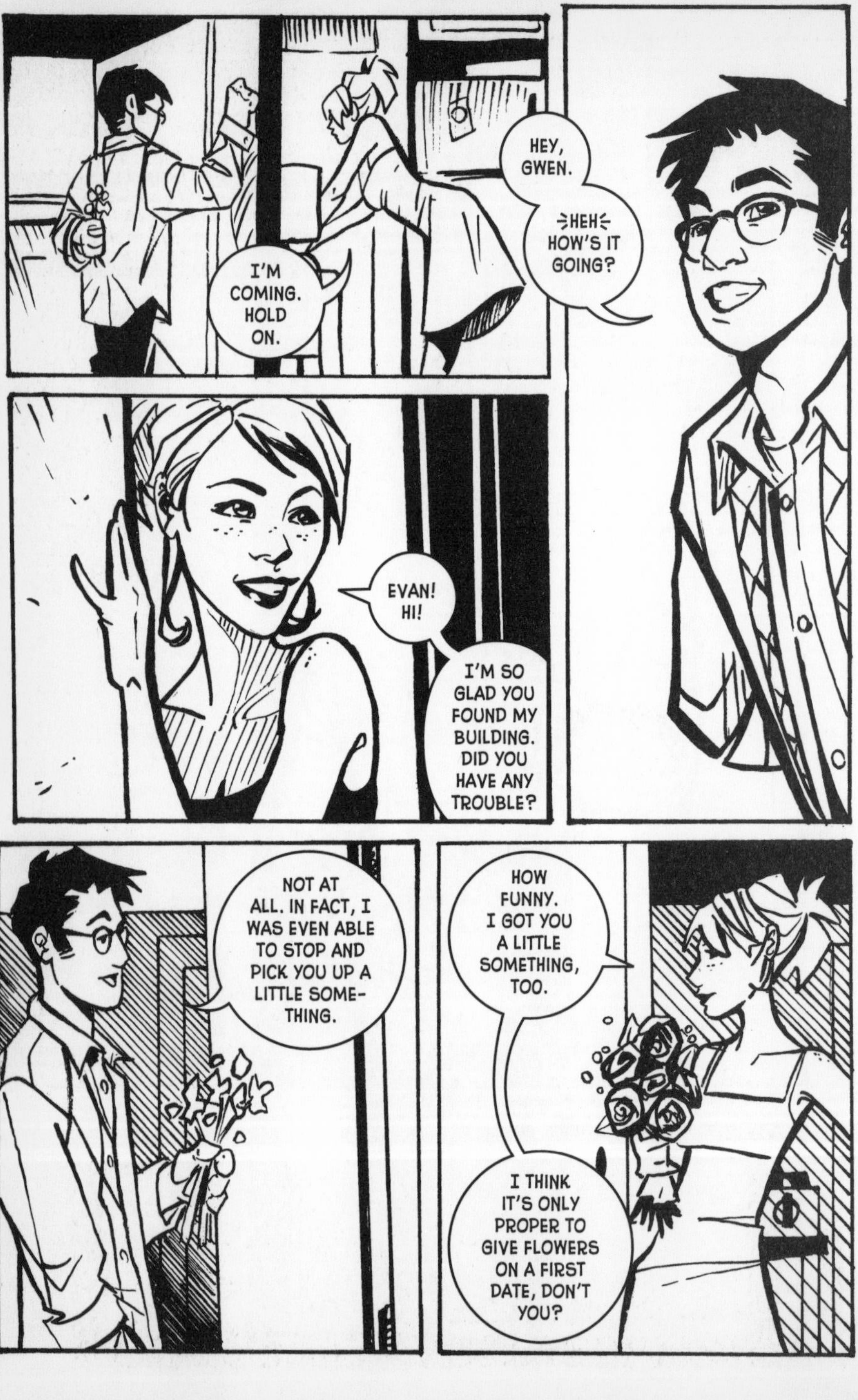
I'M COMING. HOLD ON.
HEY, GWEN.
=HEH= HOW'S IT GOING?
EVAN! HI!
I'M SO GLAD YOU FOUND MY BUILDING. DID YOU HAVE ANY TROUBLE?
NOT AT ALL. IN FACT, I WAS EVEN ABLE TO STOP AND PICK YOU UP A LITTLE SOME-THING.
HOW FUNNY. I GOT YOU A LITTLE SOMETHING, TOO.
I THINK IT'S ONLY PROPER TO GIVE FLOWERS ON A FIRST DATE, DON'T YOU?

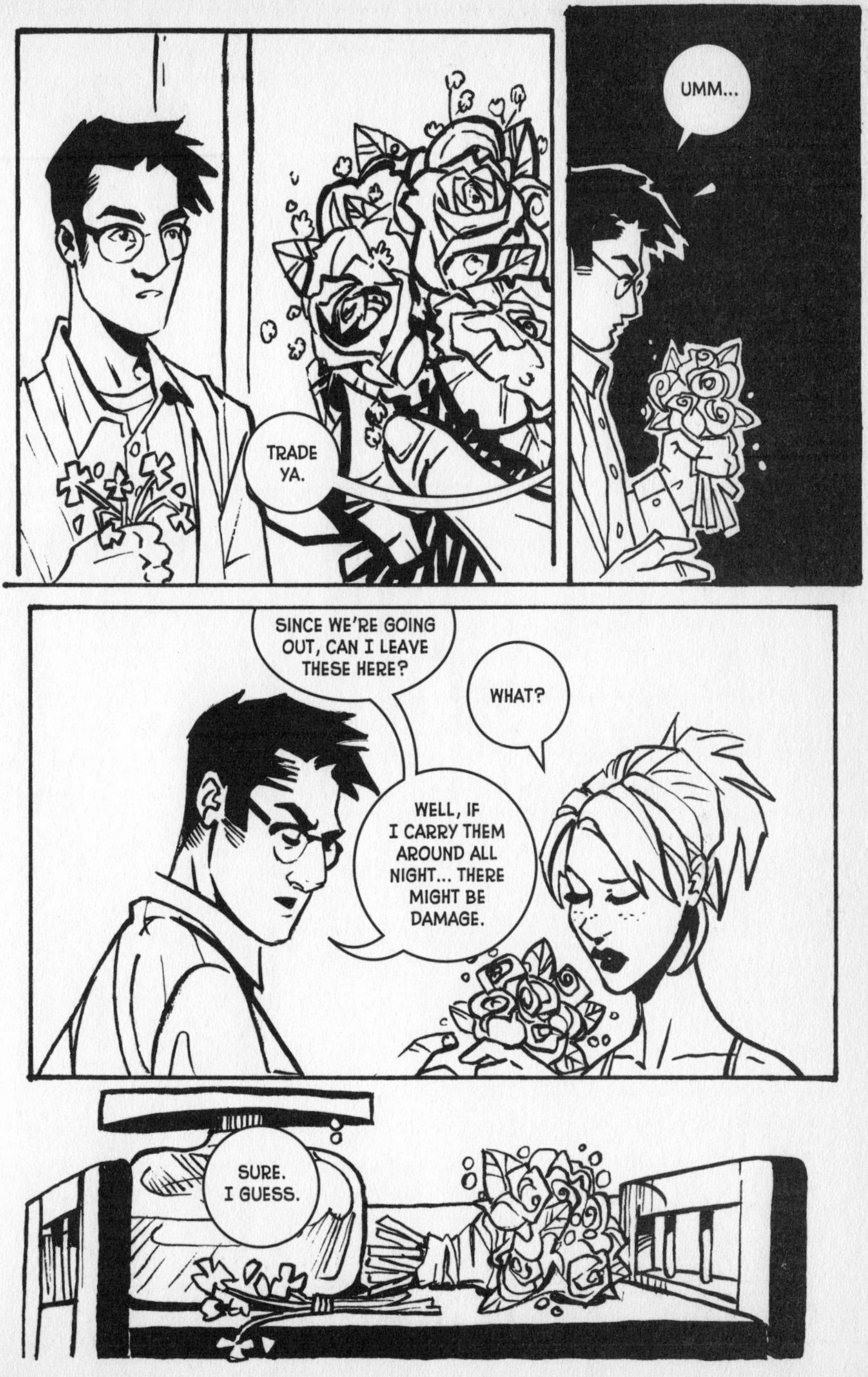
TRADE YA.
UMM...
SINCE WE'RE GOING OUT, CAN I LEAVE THESE HERE?
WHAT?
WELL, IF I CARRY THEM AROUND ALL NIGHT... THERE MIGHT BE DAMAGE.
SURE. I GUESS.

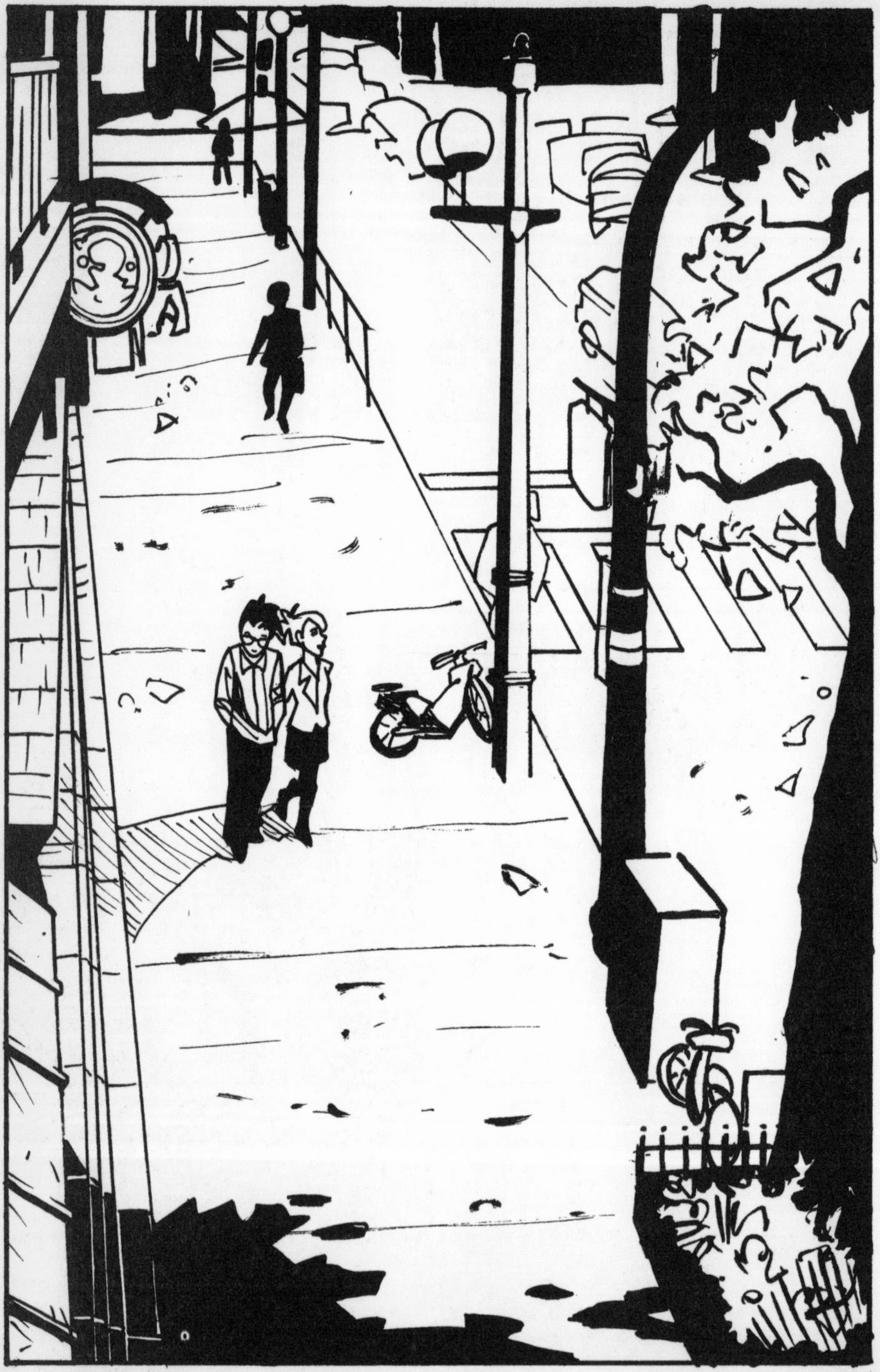

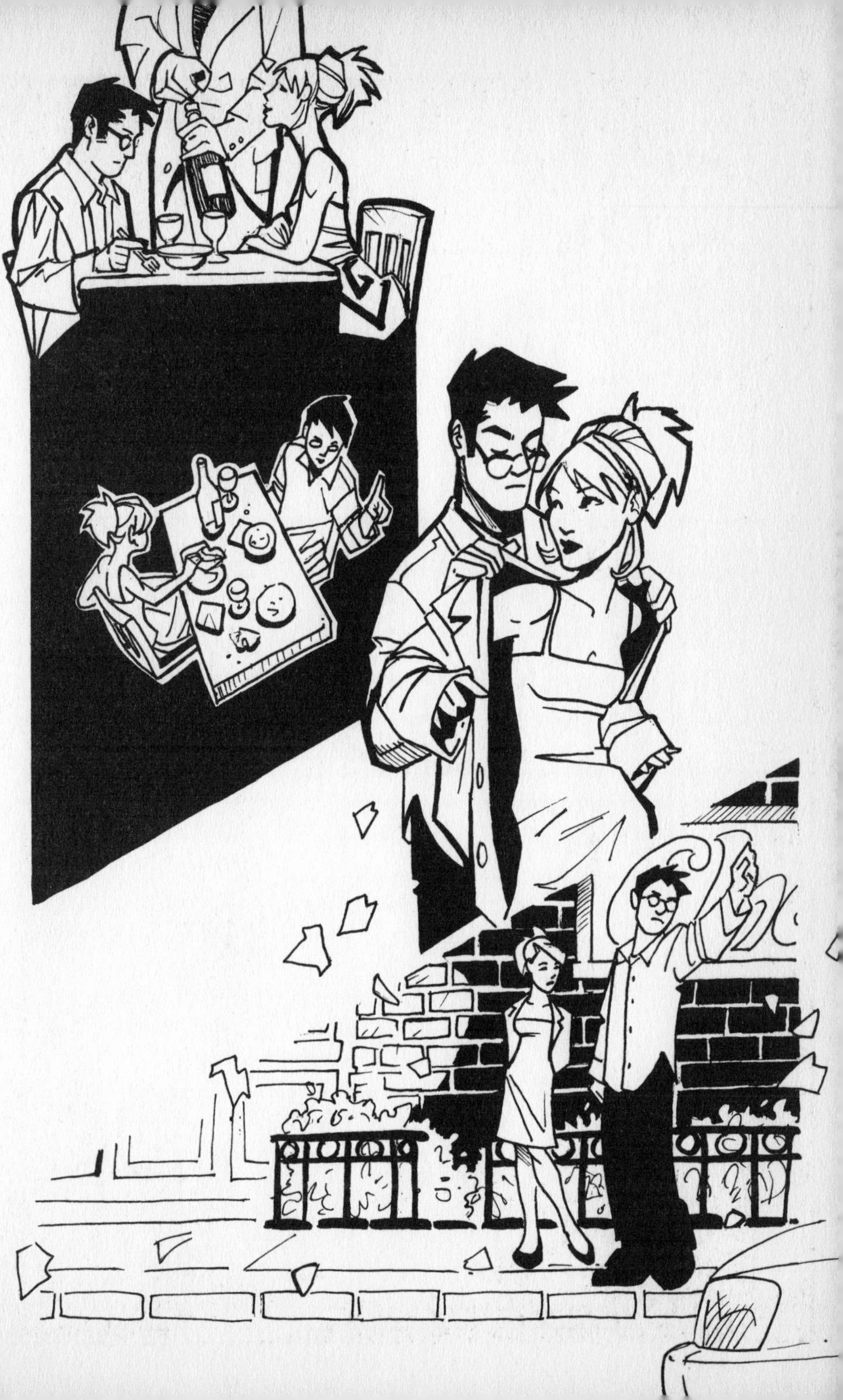

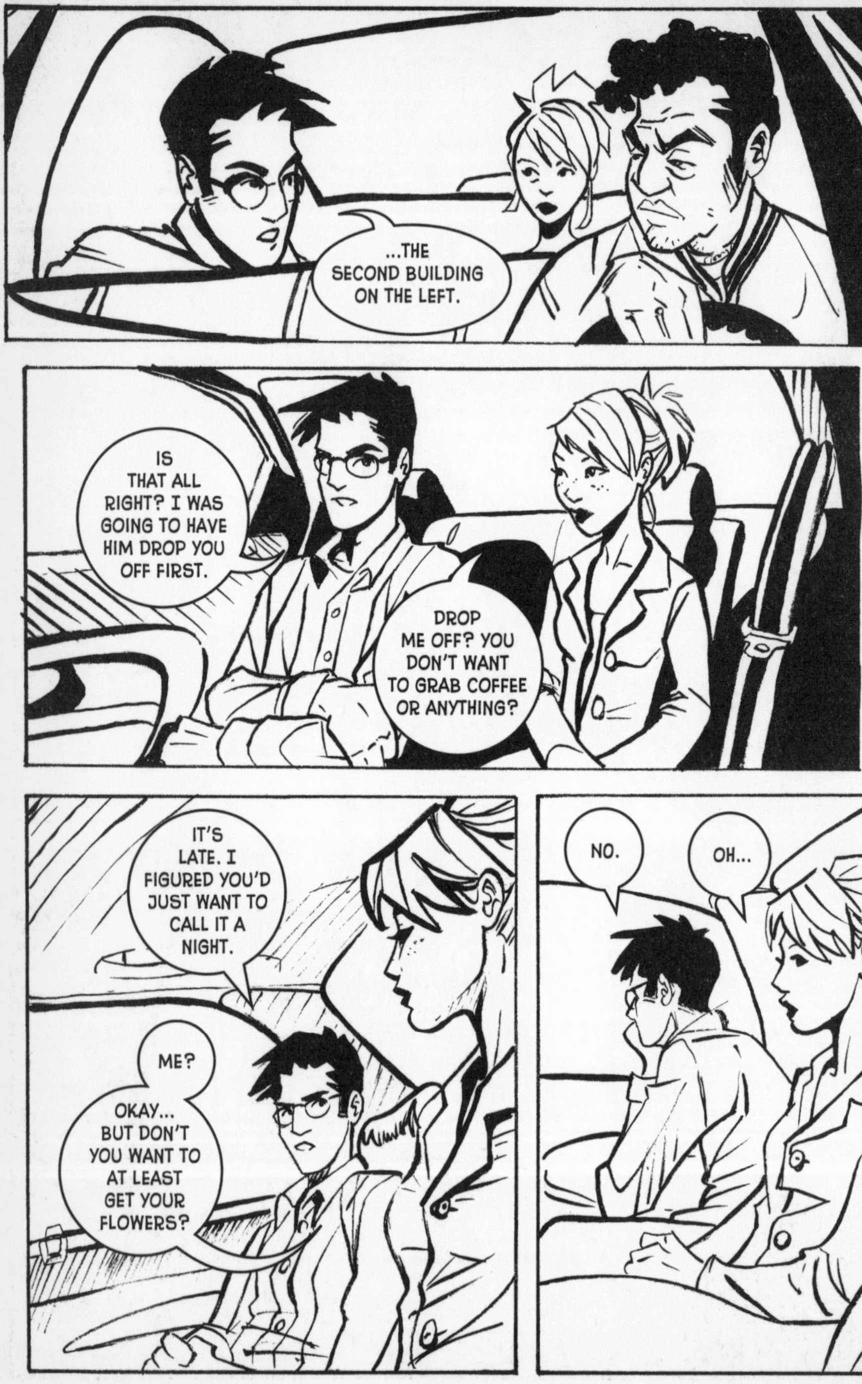

...THE SECOND BUILDING ON THE LEFT.
IS THAT ALL RIGHT? I WAS GOING TO HAVE HIM DROP YOU OFF FIRST.
DROP ME OFF? YOU DON'T WANT TO GRAB COFFEE OR ANYTHING?
IT'S LATE. I FIGURED YOU'D JUST WANT TO CALL IT A NIGHT.
ME?
OKAY... BUT DON'T YOU WANT TO AT LEAST GET YOUR FLOWERS?
NO.
OH...

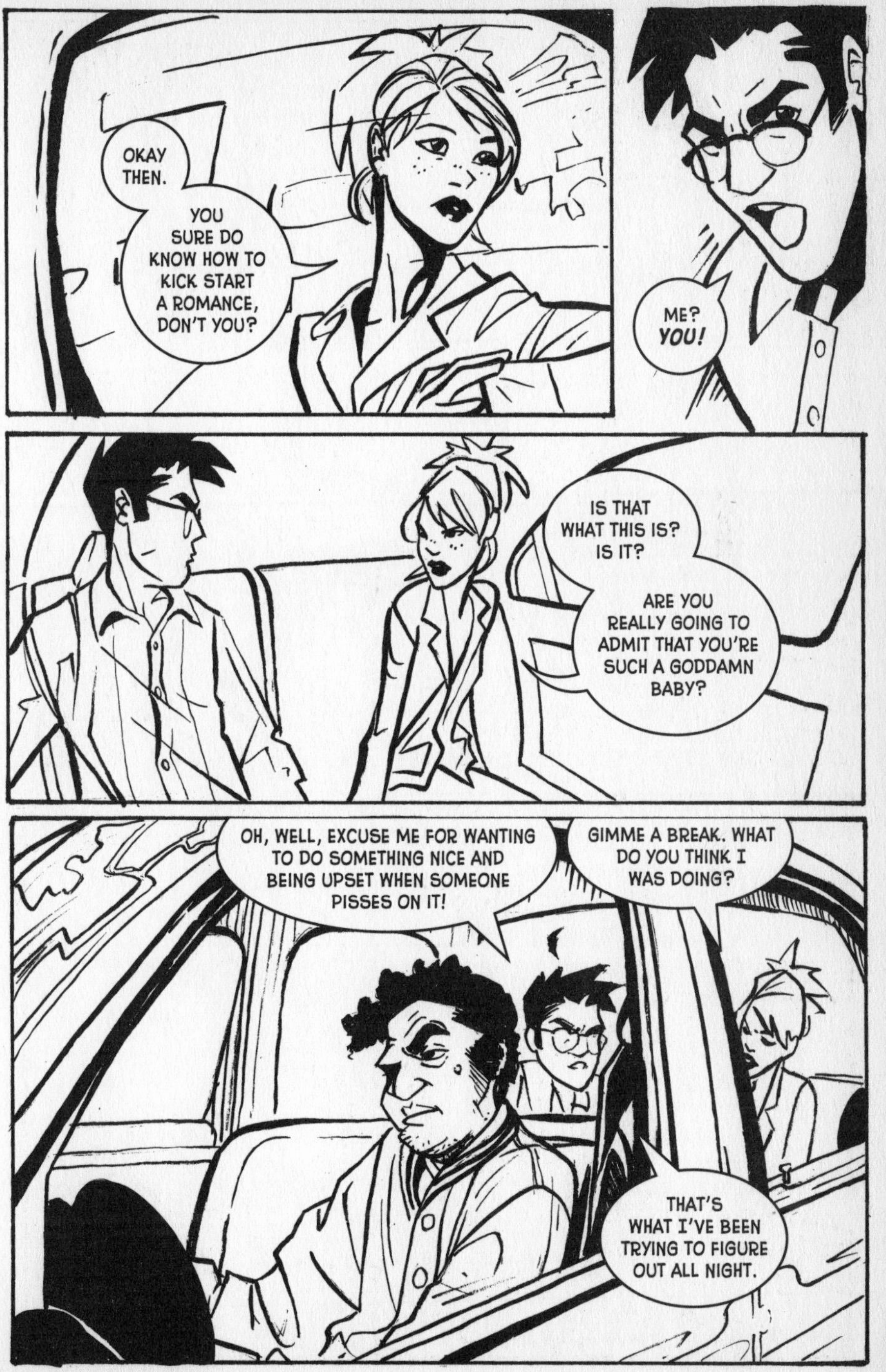

OKAY THEN.
YOU SURE DO KNOW HOW TO KICK START A ROMANCE, DON'T YOU?
ME? *YOU!*
IS THAT WHAT THIS IS? IS IT?
ARE YOU REALLY GOING TO ADMIT THAT YOU'RE SUCH A GODDAMN BABY?
OH, WELL, EXCUSE ME FOR WANTING TO DO SOMETHING NICE AND BEING UPSET WHEN SOMEONE PISSES ON IT!
GIMME A BREAK. WHAT DO YOU THINK I WAS DOING?
THAT'S WHAT I'VE BEEN TRYING TO FIGURE OUT ALL NIGHT.

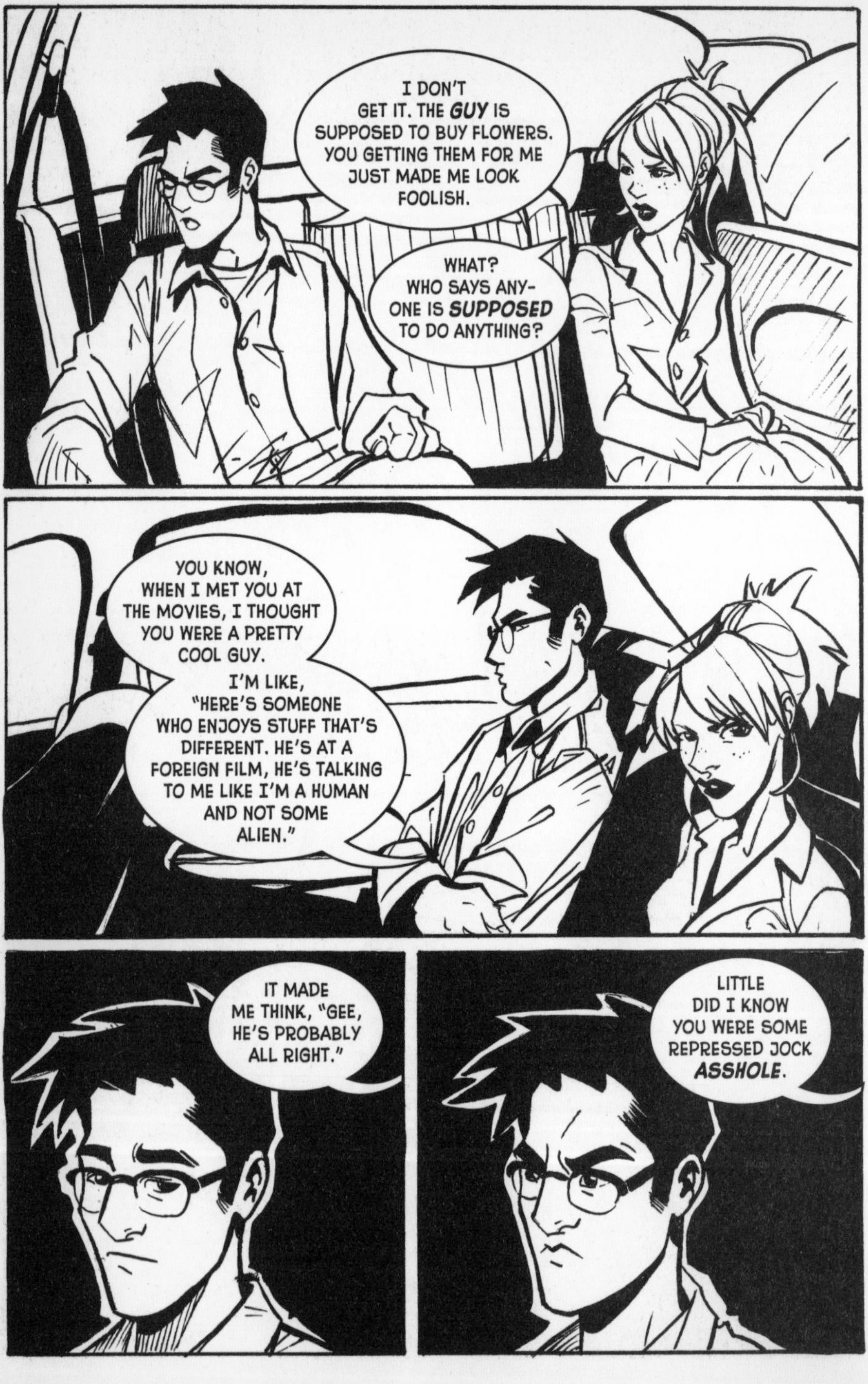
I DON'T GET IT. THE GUY IS SUPPOSED TO BUY FLOWERS. YOU GETTING THEM FOR ME JUST MADE ME LOOK FOOLISH.
WHAT? WHO SAYS ANY-ONE IS SUPPOSED TO DO ANYTHING?
YOU KNOW, WHEN I MET YOU AT THE MOVIES, I THOUGHT YOU WERE A PRETTY COOL GUY.
I'M LIKE, "HERE'S SOMEONE WHO ENJOYS STUFF THAT'S DIFFERENT. HE'S AT A FOREIGN FILM, HE'S TALKING TO ME LIKE I'M A HUMAN AND NOT SOME ALIEN."
IT MADE ME THINK, "GEE, HE'S PROBABLY ALL RIGHT."
LITTLE DID I KNOW YOU WERE SOME REPRESSED JOCK ASSHOLE.

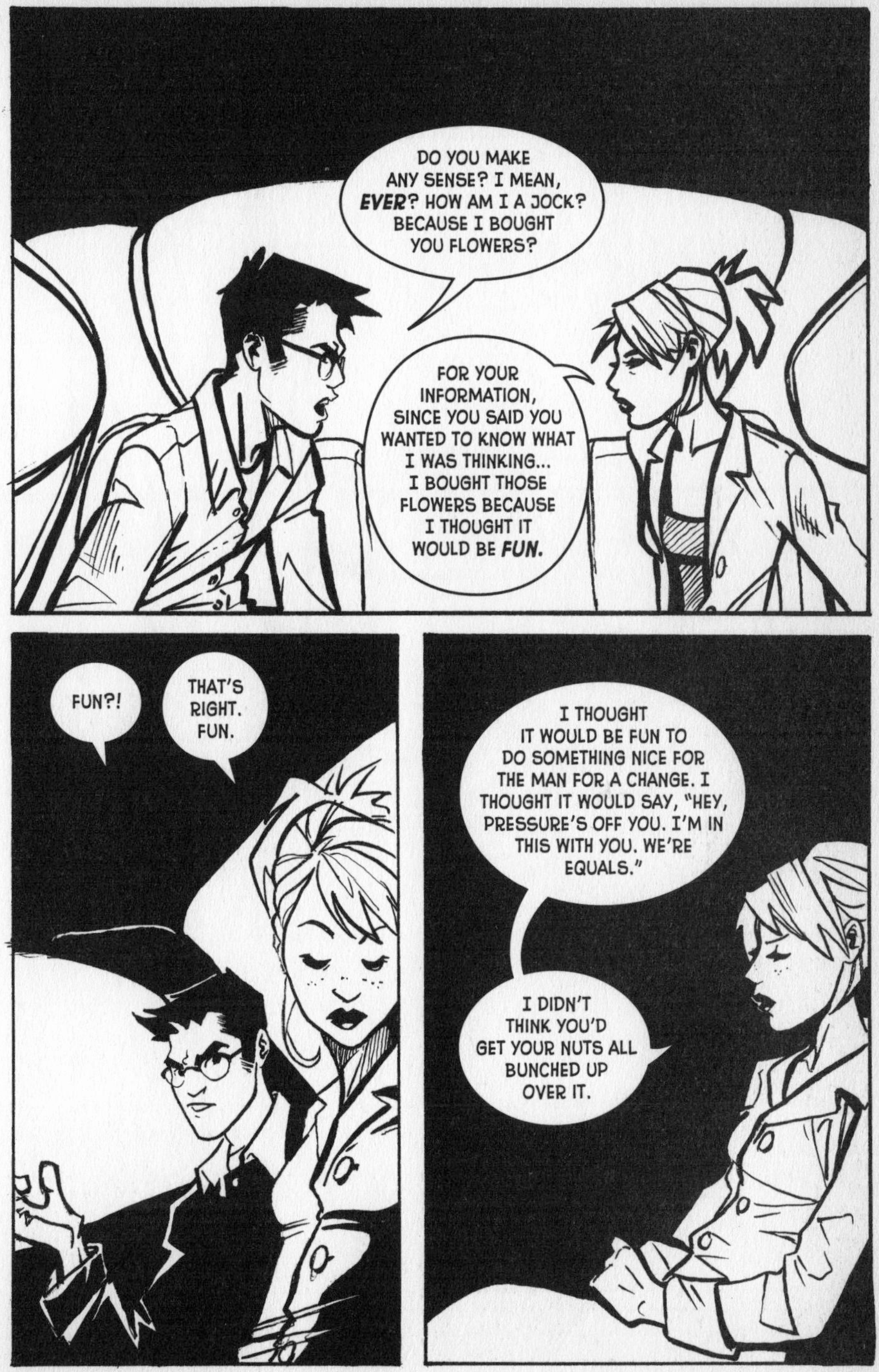
DO YOU MAKE ANY SENSE? I MEAN, EVER? HOW AM I A JOCK? BECAUSE I BOUGHT YOU FLOWERS?
FOR YOUR INFORMATION, SINCE YOU SAID YOU WANTED TO KNOW WHAT I WAS THINKING... I BOUGHT THOSE FLOWERS BECAUSE I THOUGHT IT WOULD BE FUN.
FUN?!
THAT'S RIGHT. FUN.
I THOUGHT IT WOULD BE FUN TO DO SOMETHING NICE FOR THE MAN FOR A CHANGE. I THOUGHT IT WOULD SAY, "HEY, PRESSURE'S OFF YOU. I'M IN THIS WITH YOU. WE'RE EQUALS."
I DIDN'T THINK YOU'D GET YOUR NUTS ALL BUNCHED UP OVER IT.

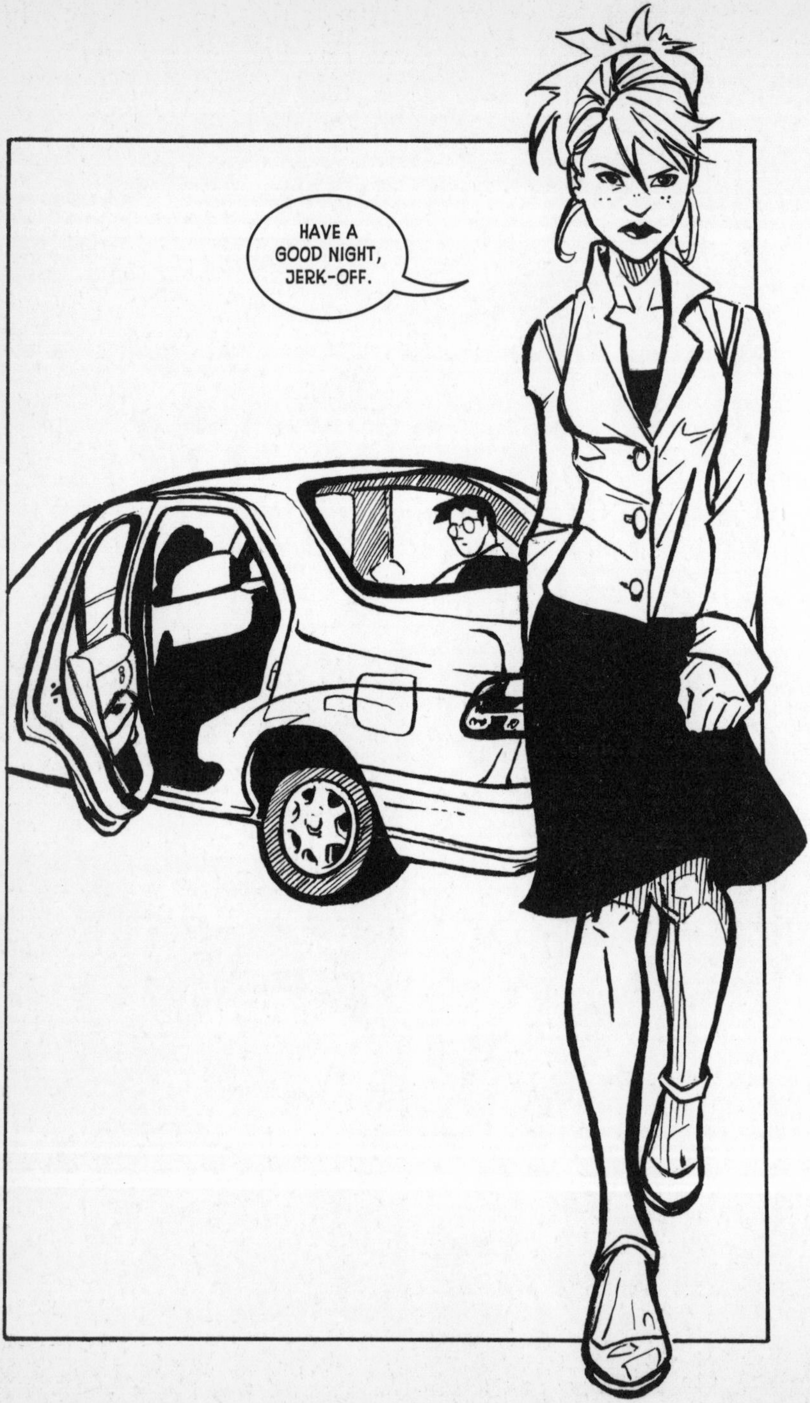
HAVE A GOOD NIGHT, JERK-OFF.

Two

SONG

Beth Gibbons & Rustin Mann
"Mysteries"

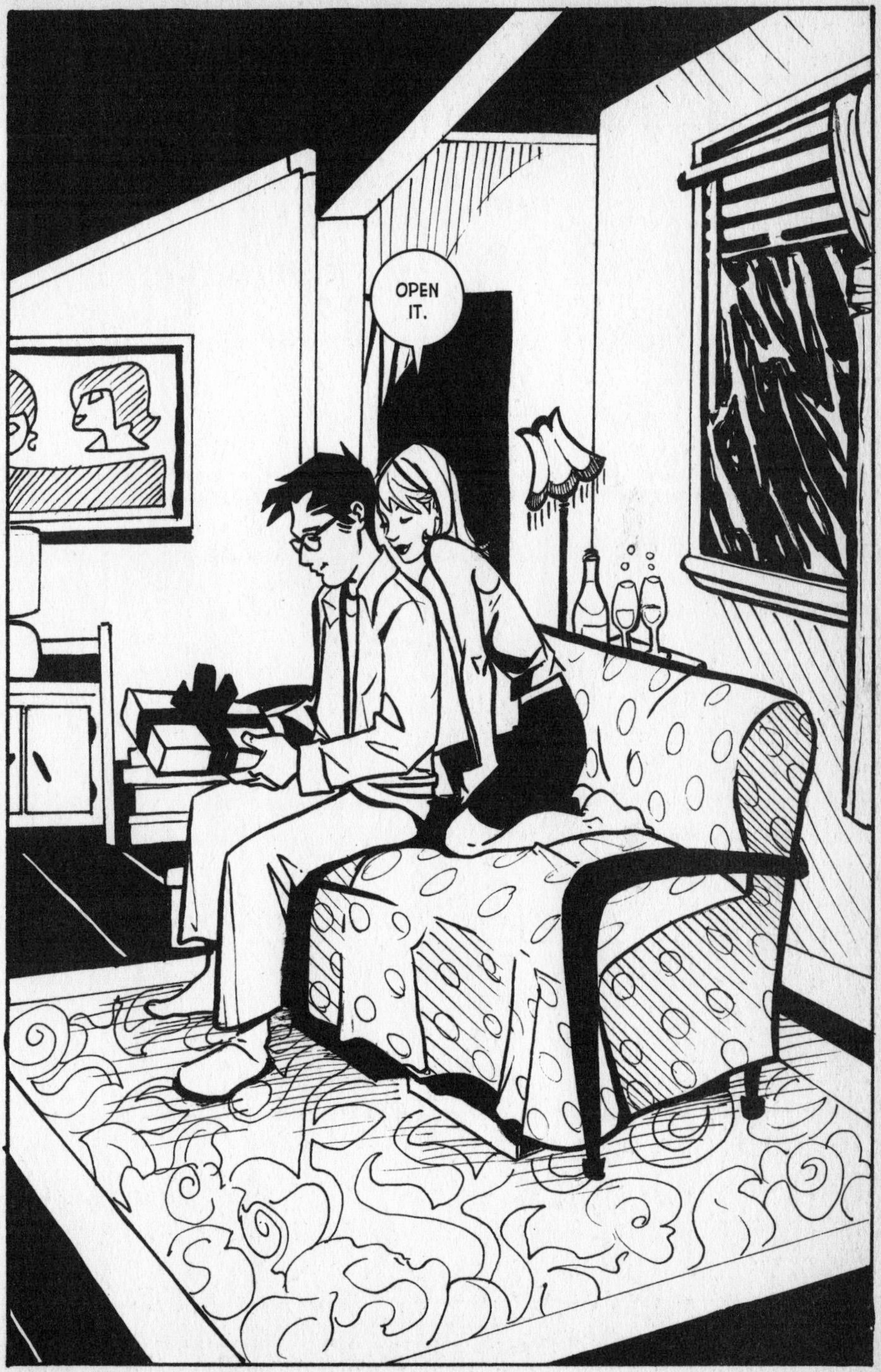
OPEN IT.

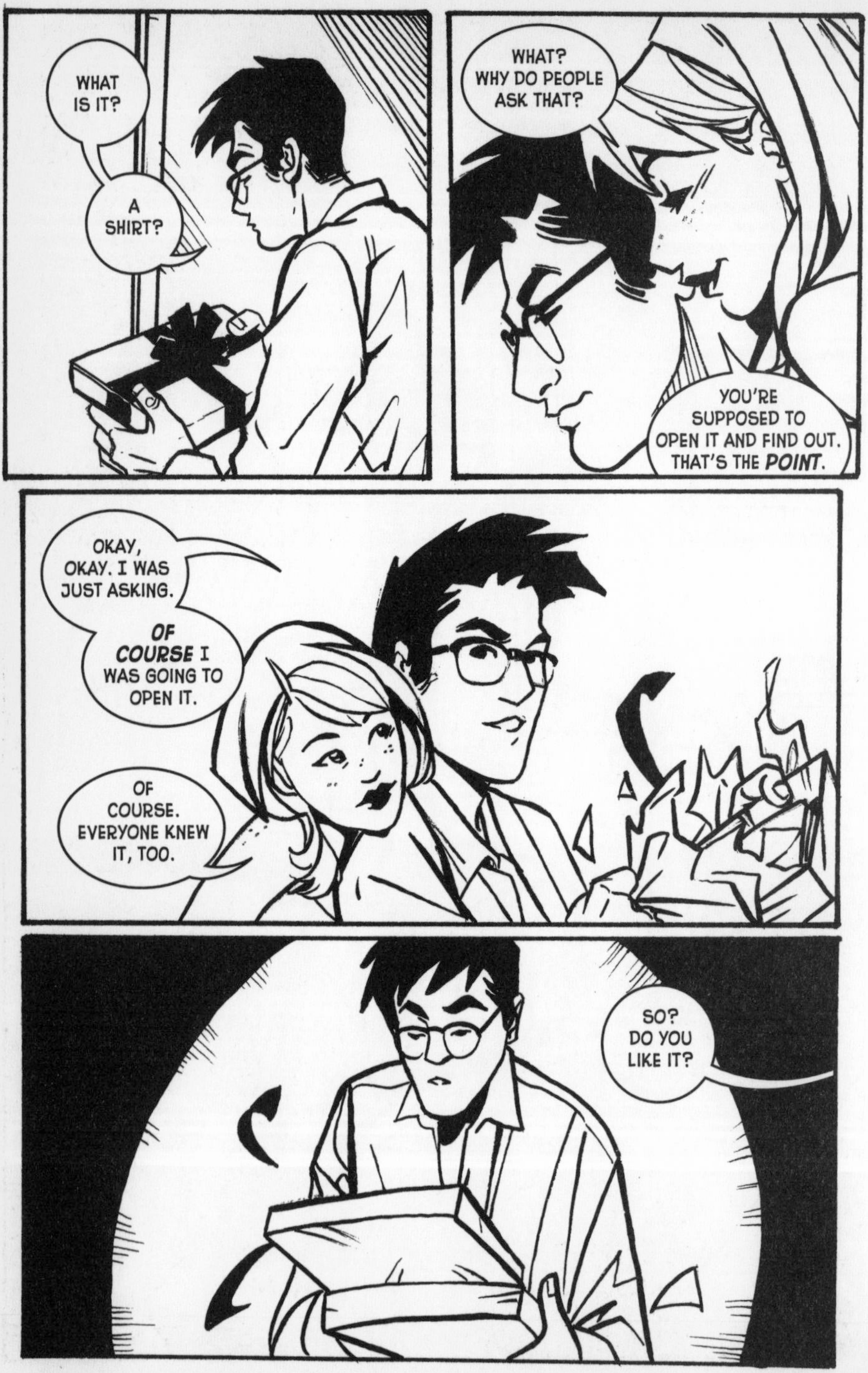
WHAT IS IT?
A SHIRT?
WHAT? WHY DO PEOPLE ASK THAT?
YOU'RE SUPPOSED TO OPEN IT AND FIND OUT. THAT'S THE *POINT*.
OKAY, OKAY. I WAS JUST ASKING.
OF COURSE I WAS GOING TO OPEN IT.
OF COURSE. EVERYONE KNEW IT, TOO.
SO? DO YOU LIKE IT?

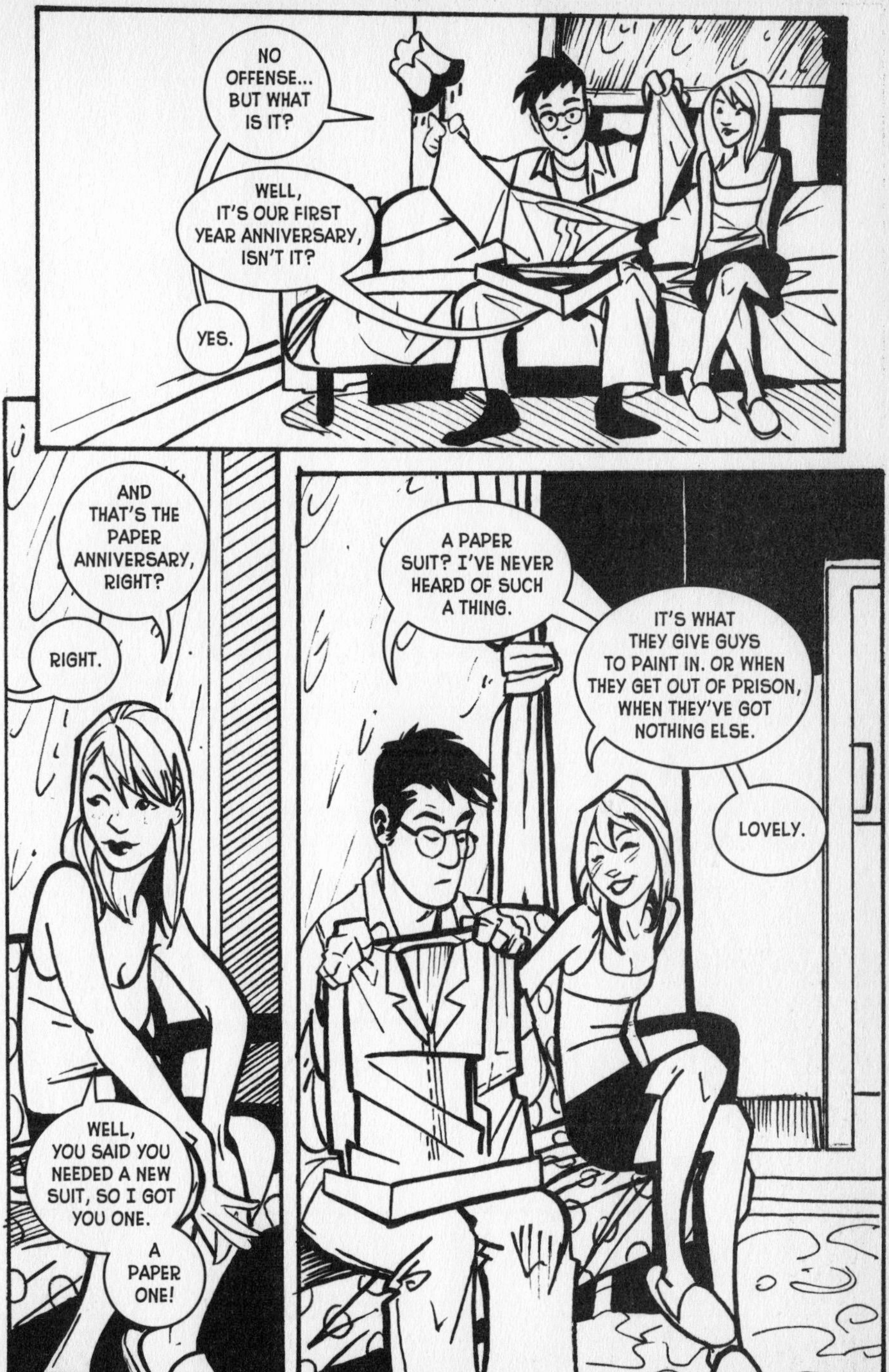
NO OFFENSE... BUT WHAT IS IT?
WELL, IT'S OUR FIRST YEAR ANNIVERSARY, ISN'T IT?
YES.
AND THAT'S THE PAPER ANNIVERSARY, RIGHT?
RIGHT.
WELL, YOU SAID YOU NEEDED A NEW SUIT, SO I GOT YOU ONE.
A PAPER ONE!
A PAPER SUIT? I'VE NEVER HEARD OF SUCH A THING.
IT'S WHAT THEY GIVE GUYS TO PAINT IN. OR WHEN THEY GET OUT OF PRISON, WHEN THEY'VE GOT NOTHING ELSE.
LOVELY.

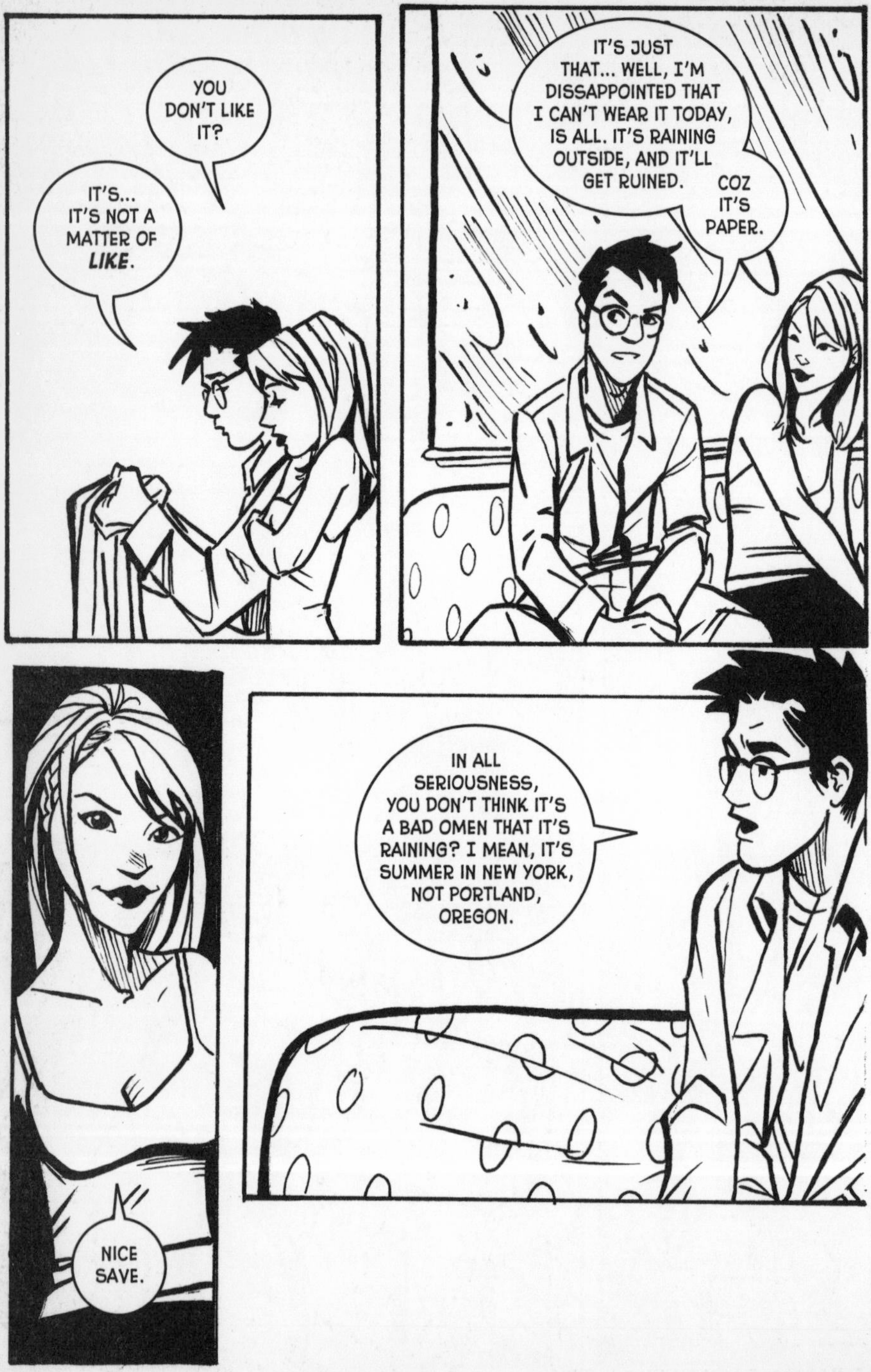
IT'S... IT'S NOT A MATTER OF **LIKE**.
YOU DON'T LIKE IT?
IT'S JUST THAT... WELL, I'M DISSAPPOINTED THAT I CAN'T WEAR IT TODAY, IS ALL. IT'S RAINING OUTSIDE, AND IT'LL GET RUINED.
COZ IT'S PAPER.
NICE SAVE.
IN ALL SERIOUSNESS, YOU DON'T THINK IT'S A BAD OMEN THAT IT'S RAINING? I MEAN, IT'S SUMMER IN NEW YORK, NOT PORTLAND, OREGON.

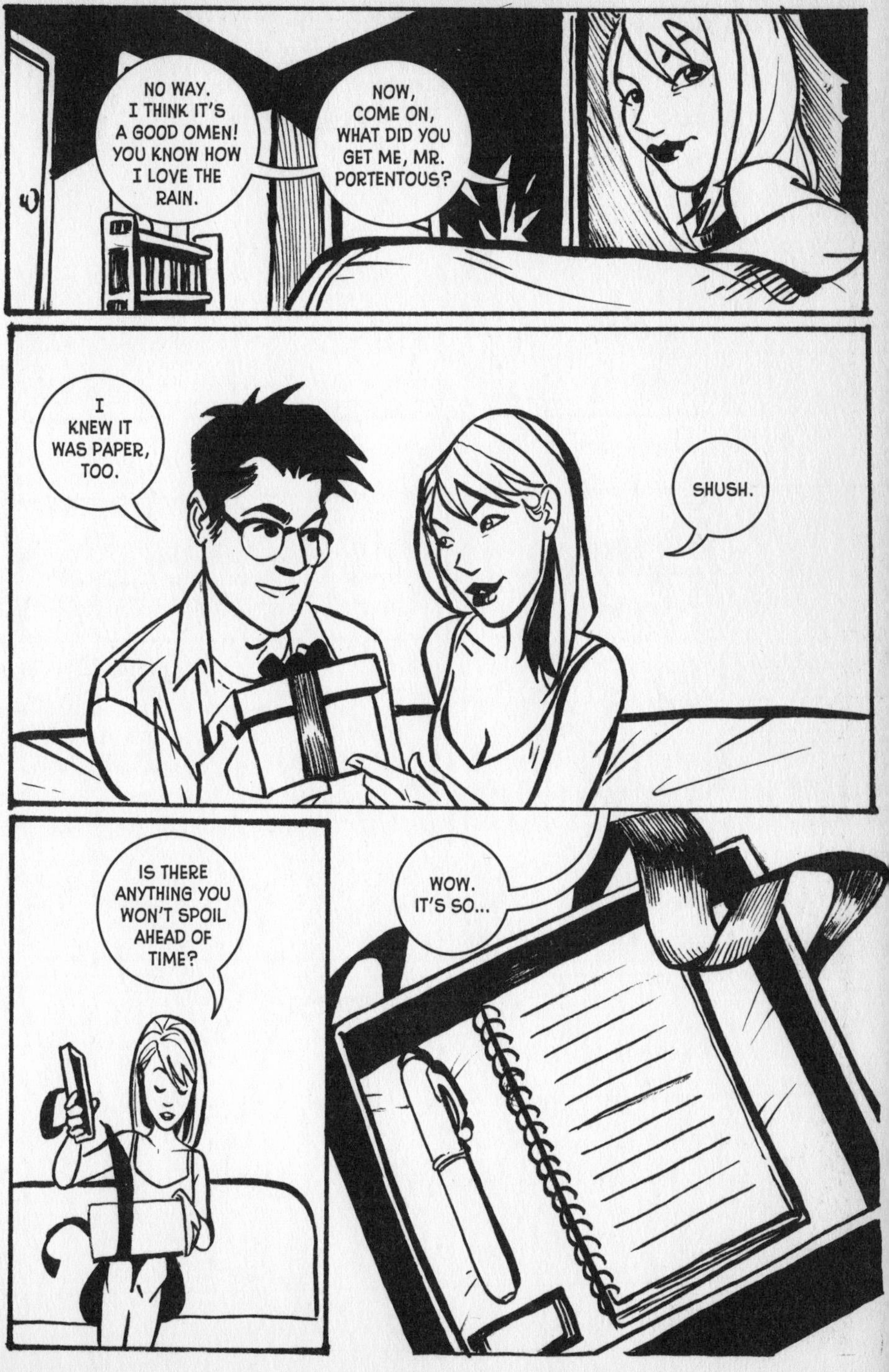
NO WAY. I THINK IT'S A GOOD OMEN! YOU KNOW HOW I LOVE THE RAIN.
NOW, COME ON, WHAT DID YOU GET ME, MR. PORTENTOUS?
I KNEW IT WAS PAPER, TOO.
SHUSH.
IS THERE ANYTHING YOU WON'T SPOIL AHEAD OF TIME?
WOW. IT'S SO...

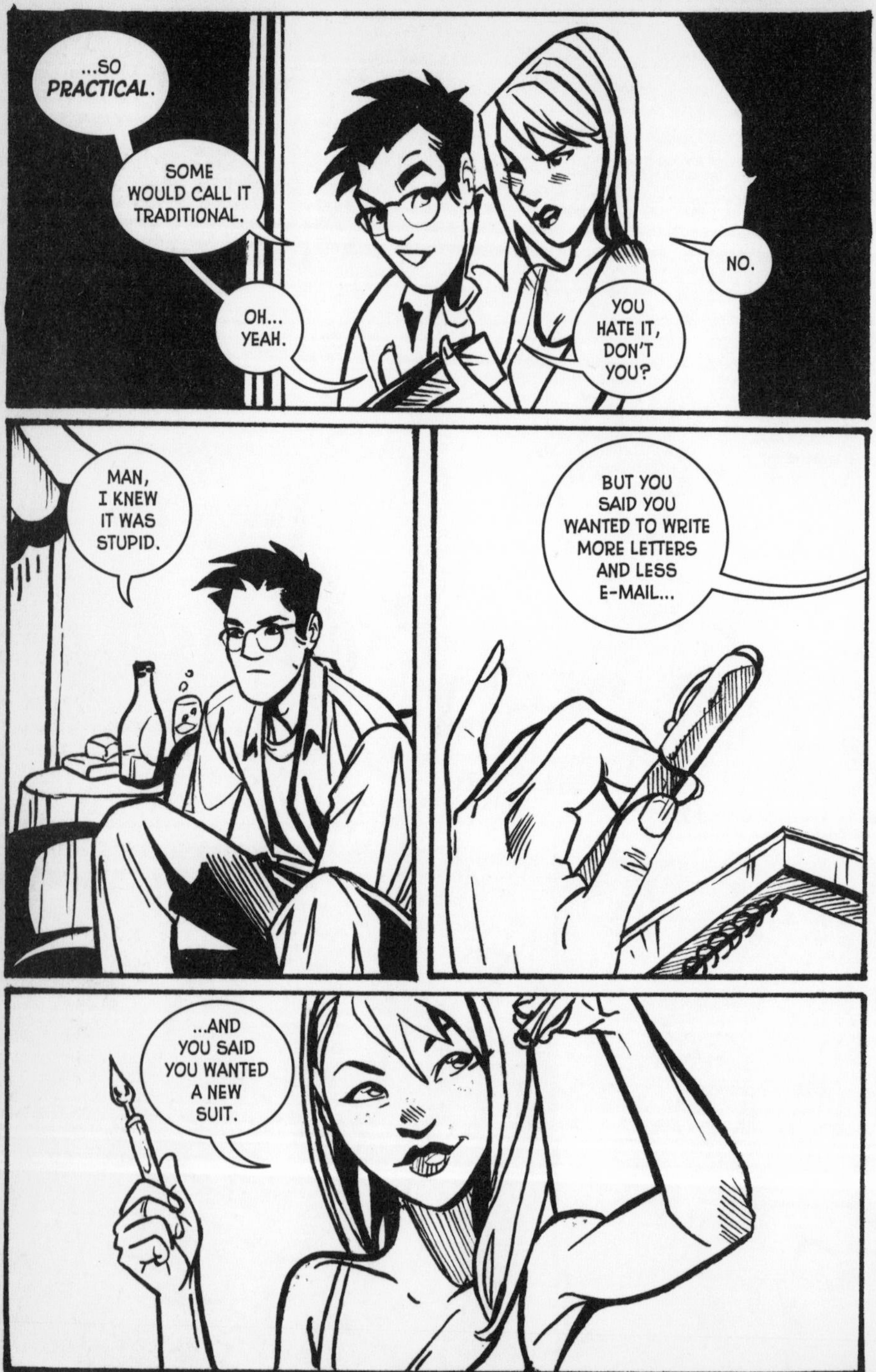
...SO *PRACTICAL*.
SOME WOULD CALL IT TRADITIONAL.
OH... YEAH.
YOU HATE IT, DON'T YOU?
NO.
MAN, I KNEW IT WAS STUPID.
BUT YOU SAID YOU WANTED TO WRITE MORE LETTERS AND LESS E-MAIL...
...AND YOU SAID YOU WANTED A NEW SUIT.

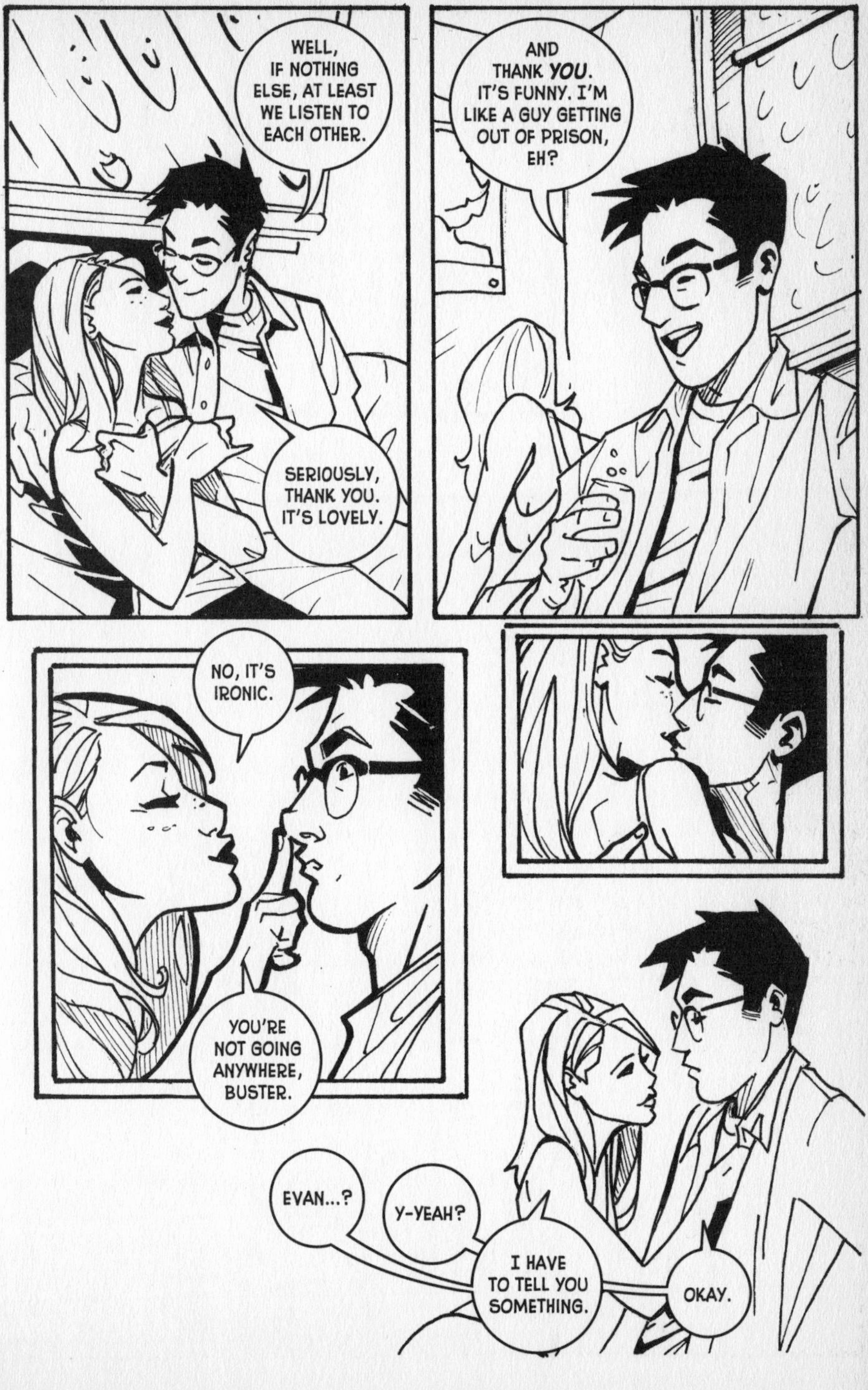
WELL, IF NOTHING ELSE, AT LEAST WE LISTEN TO EACH OTHER.
SERIOUSLY, THANK YOU. IT'S LOVELY.
AND THANK *YOU*. IT'S FUNNY. I'M LIKE A GUY GETTING OUT OF PRISON, EH?
NO, IT'S IRONIC.
YOU'RE NOT GOING ANYWHERE, BUSTER.
EVAN...?
Y-YEAH?
I HAVE TO TELL YOU SOMETHING.
OKAY.

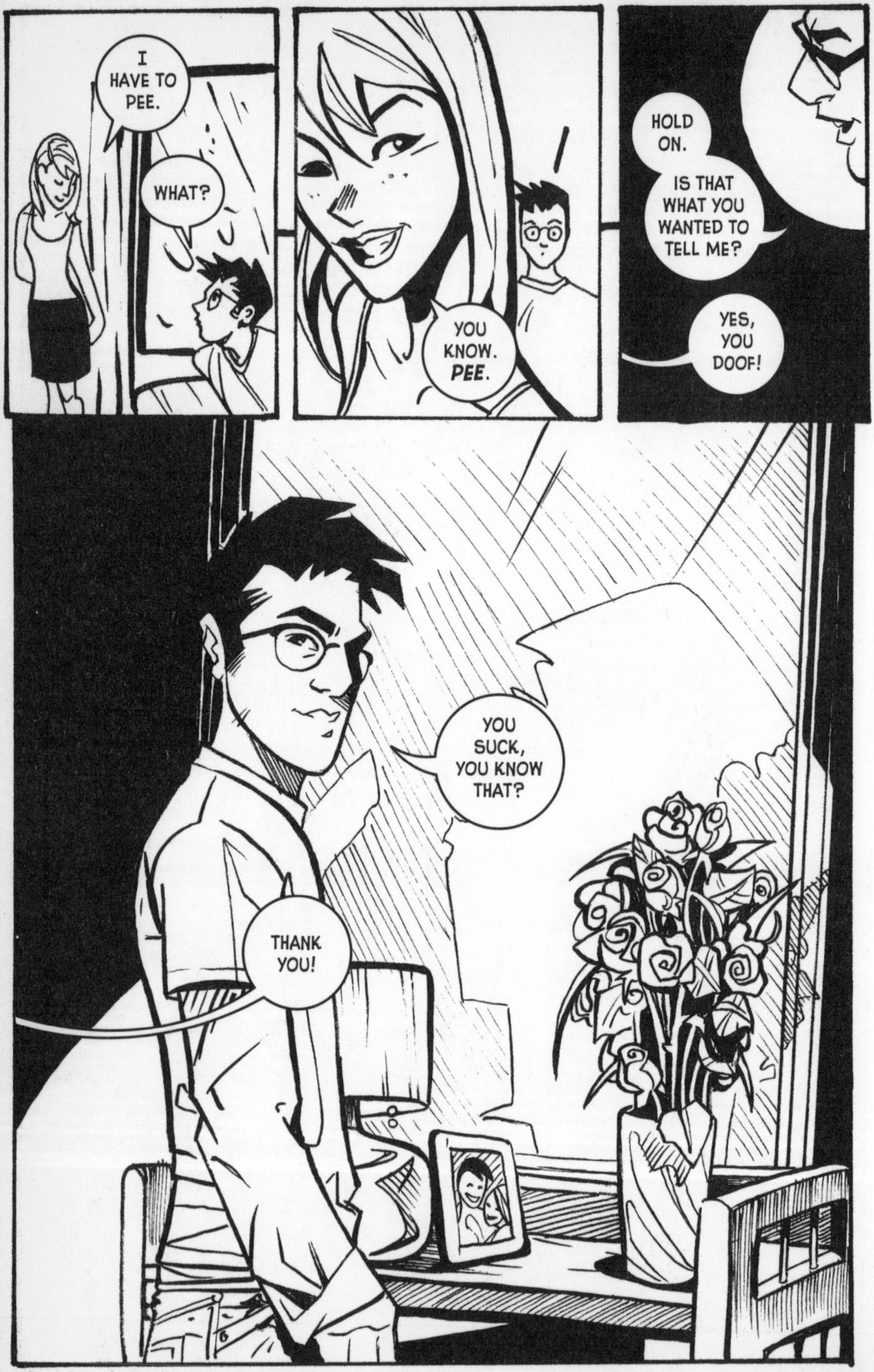
I HAVE TO PEE.
WHAT?
YOU KNOW. PEE.
HOLD ON.
IS THAT WHAT YOU WANTED TO TELL ME?
YES, YOU DOOF!
YOU SUCK, YOU KNOW THAT?
THANK YOU!

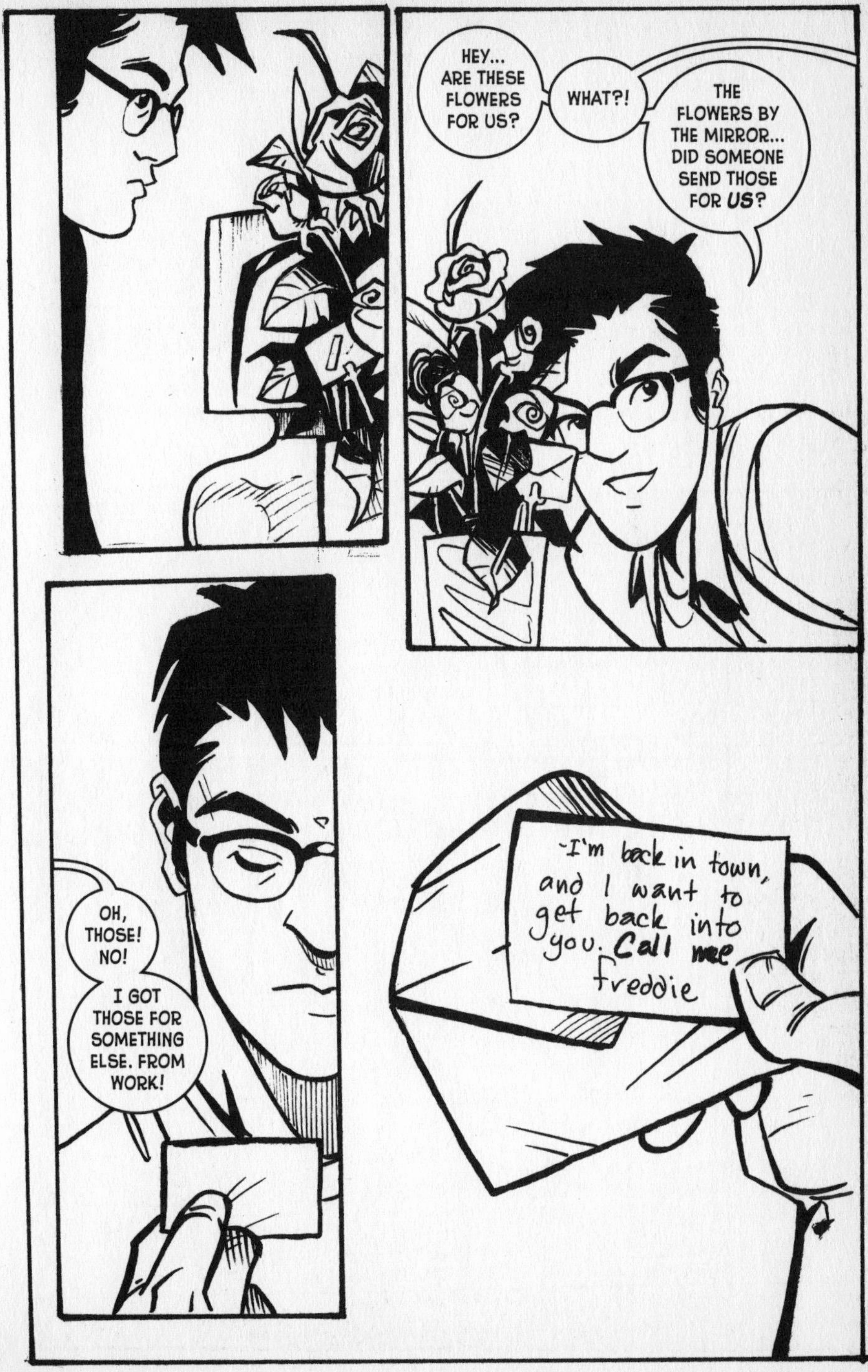
HEY... ARE THESE FLOWERS FOR US?
WHAT?!
THE FLOWERS BY THE MIRROR... DID SOMEONE SEND THOSE FOR US?
OH, THOSE! NO!
I GOT THOSE FOR SOMETHING ELSE. FROM WORK!
-I'm back in town, and I want to get back into you. Call me
freddie

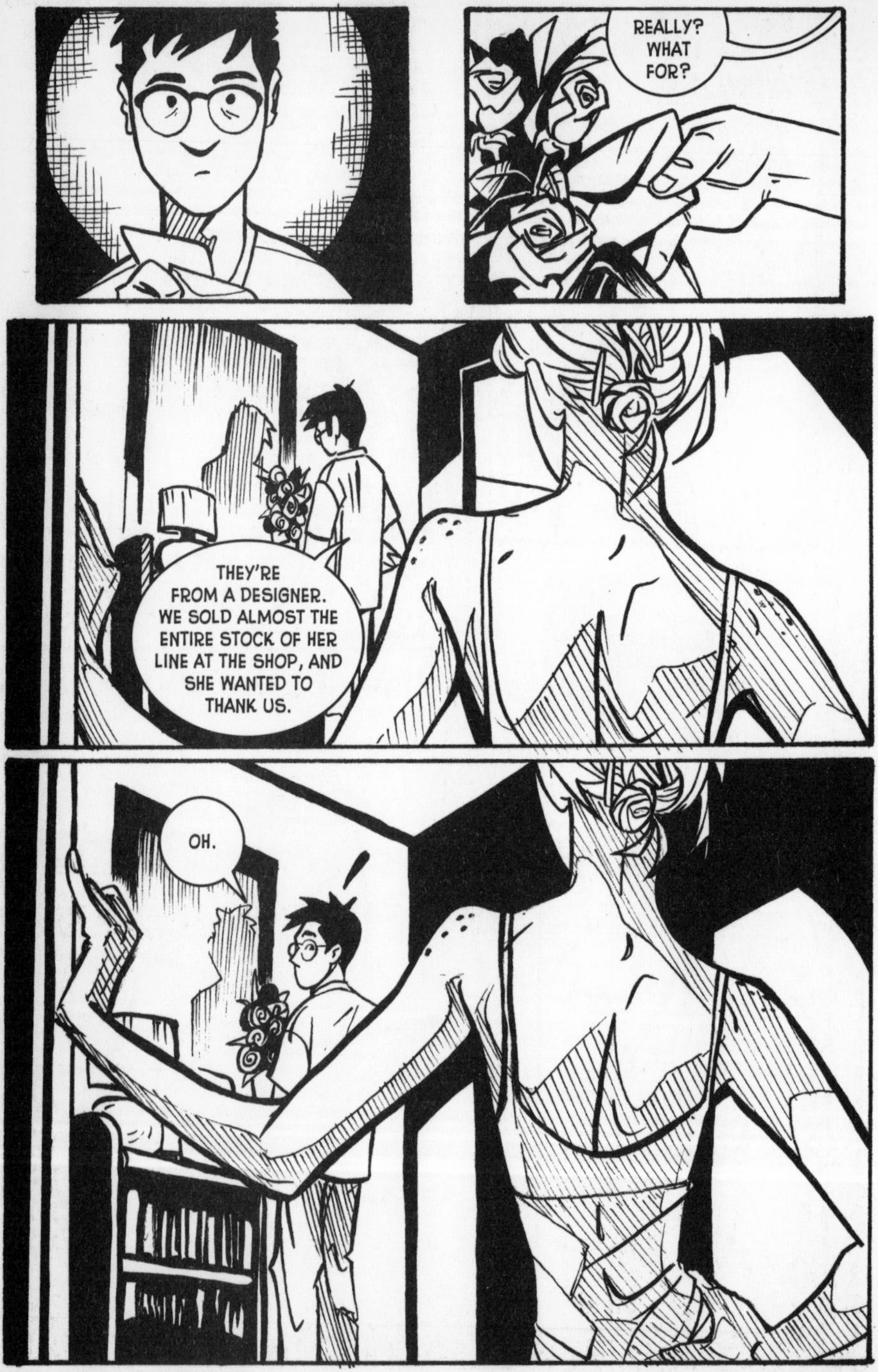
REALLY? WHAT FOR?
THEY'RE FROM A DESIGNER. WE SOLD ALMOST THE ENTIRE STOCK OF HER LINE AT THE SHOP, AND SHE WANTED TO THANK US.
OH.
!

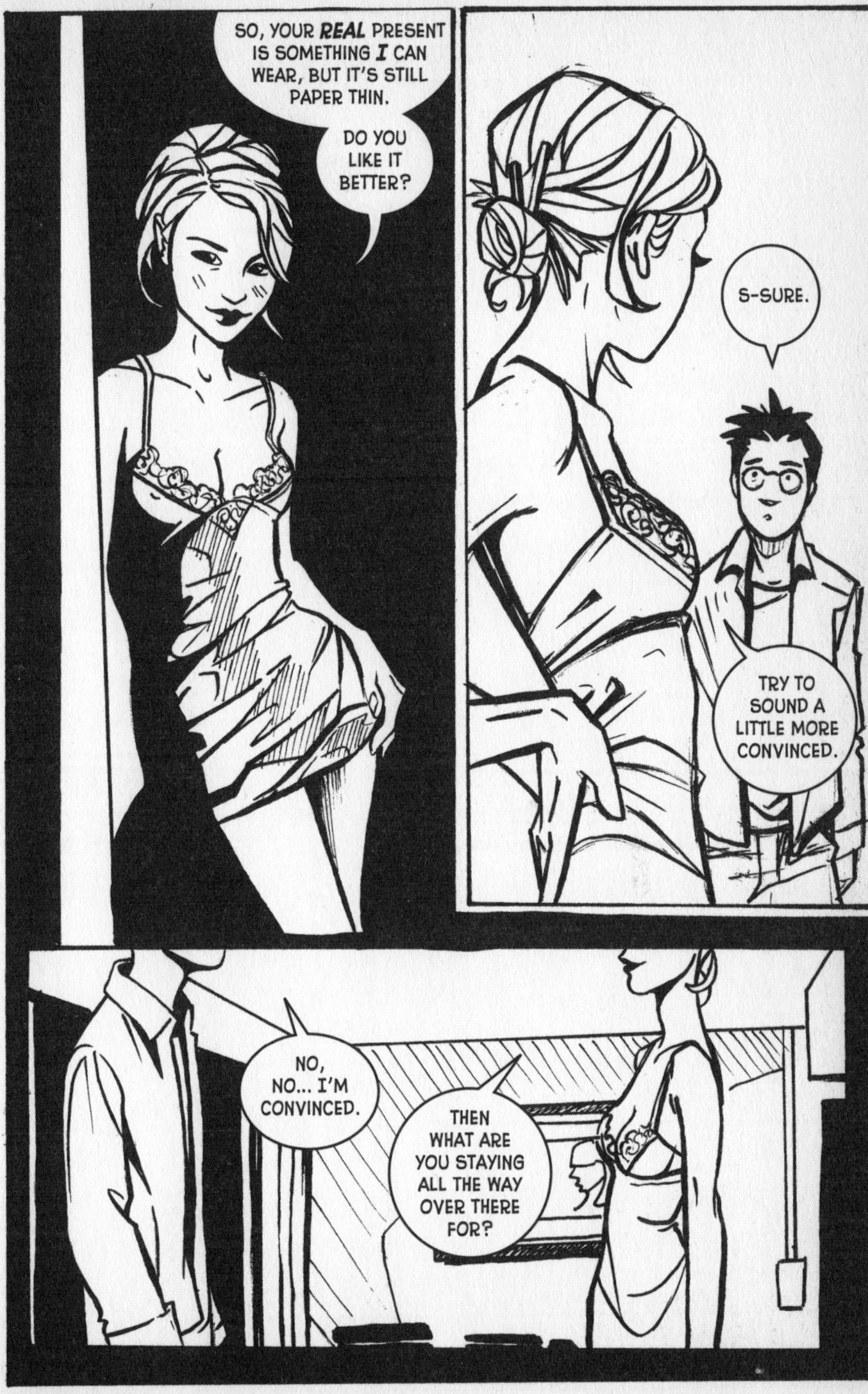
SO, YOUR **REAL** PRESENT IS SOMETHING ***I*** CAN WEAR, BUT IT'S STILL PAPER THIN.
DO YOU LIKE IT BETTER?
S-SURE.
TRY TO SOUND A LITTLE MORE CONVINCED.
NO, NO... I'M CONVINCED.
THEN WHAT ARE YOU STAYING ALL THE WAY OVER THERE FOR?

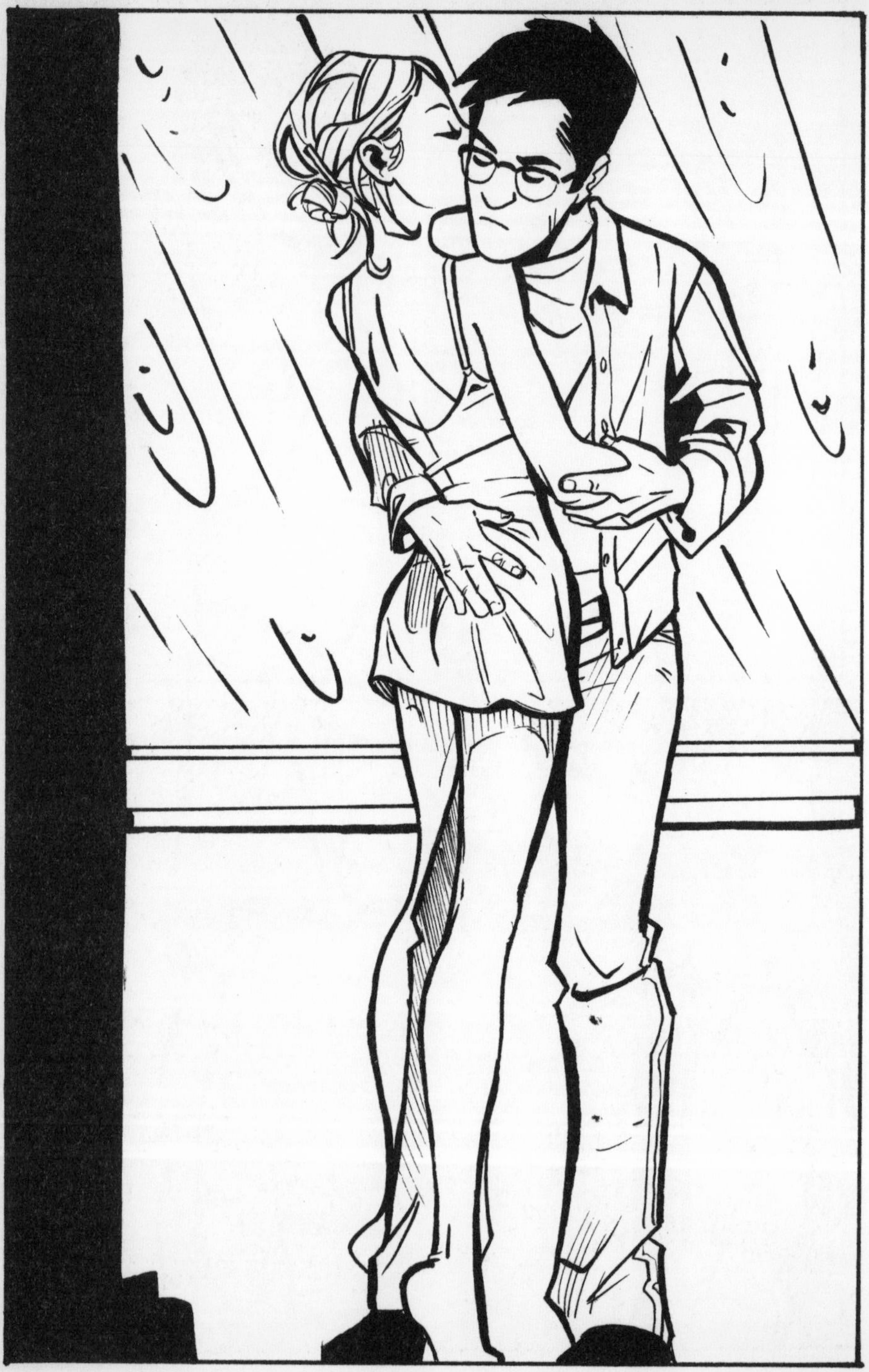

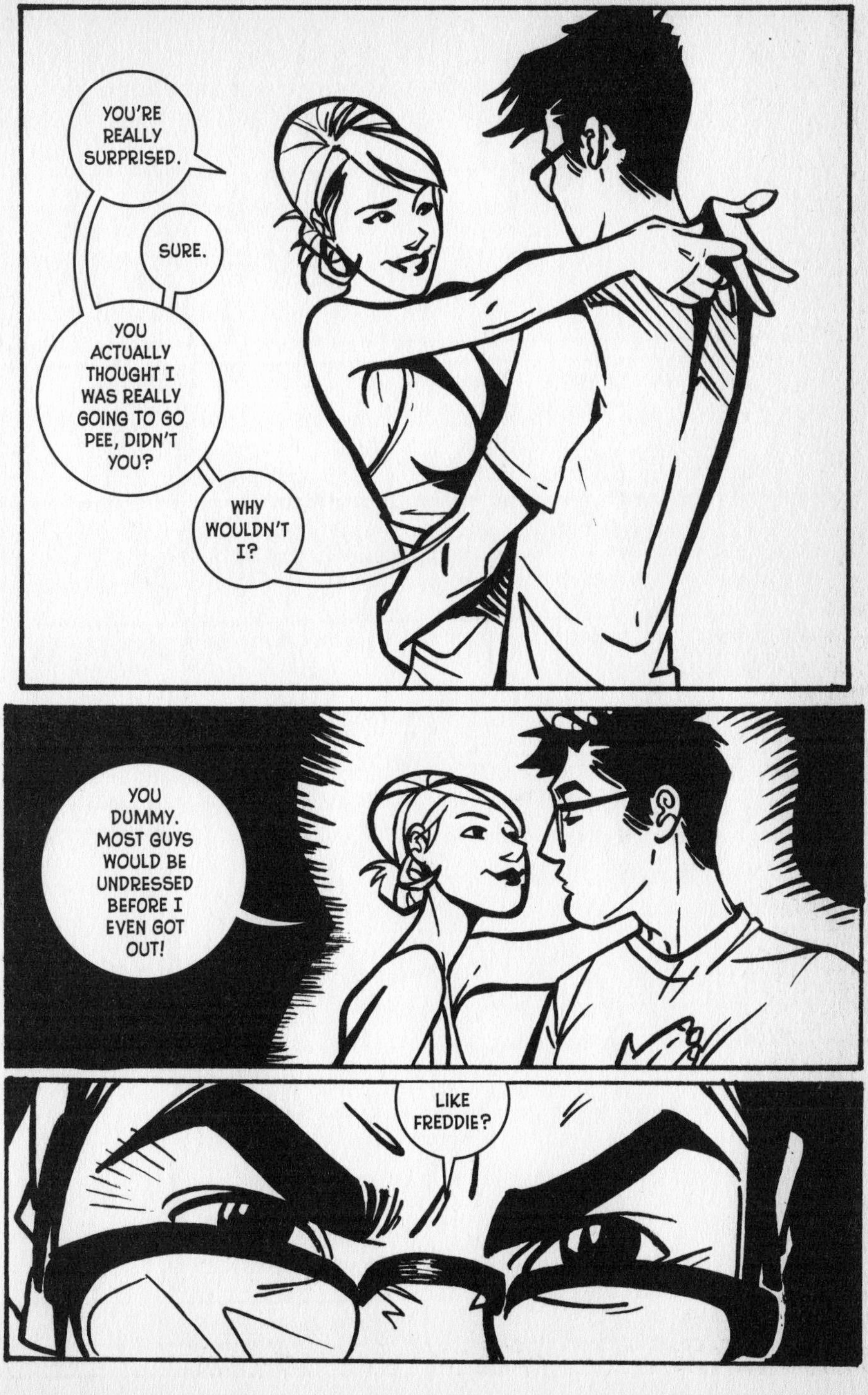
YOU'RE REALLY SURPRISED.
SURE.
YOU ACTUALLY THOUGHT I WAS REALLY GOING TO GO PEE, DIDN'T YOU?
WHY WOULDN'T I?
YOU DUMMY. MOST GUYS WOULD BE UNDRESSED BEFORE I EVEN GOT OUT!
LIKE FREDDIE?

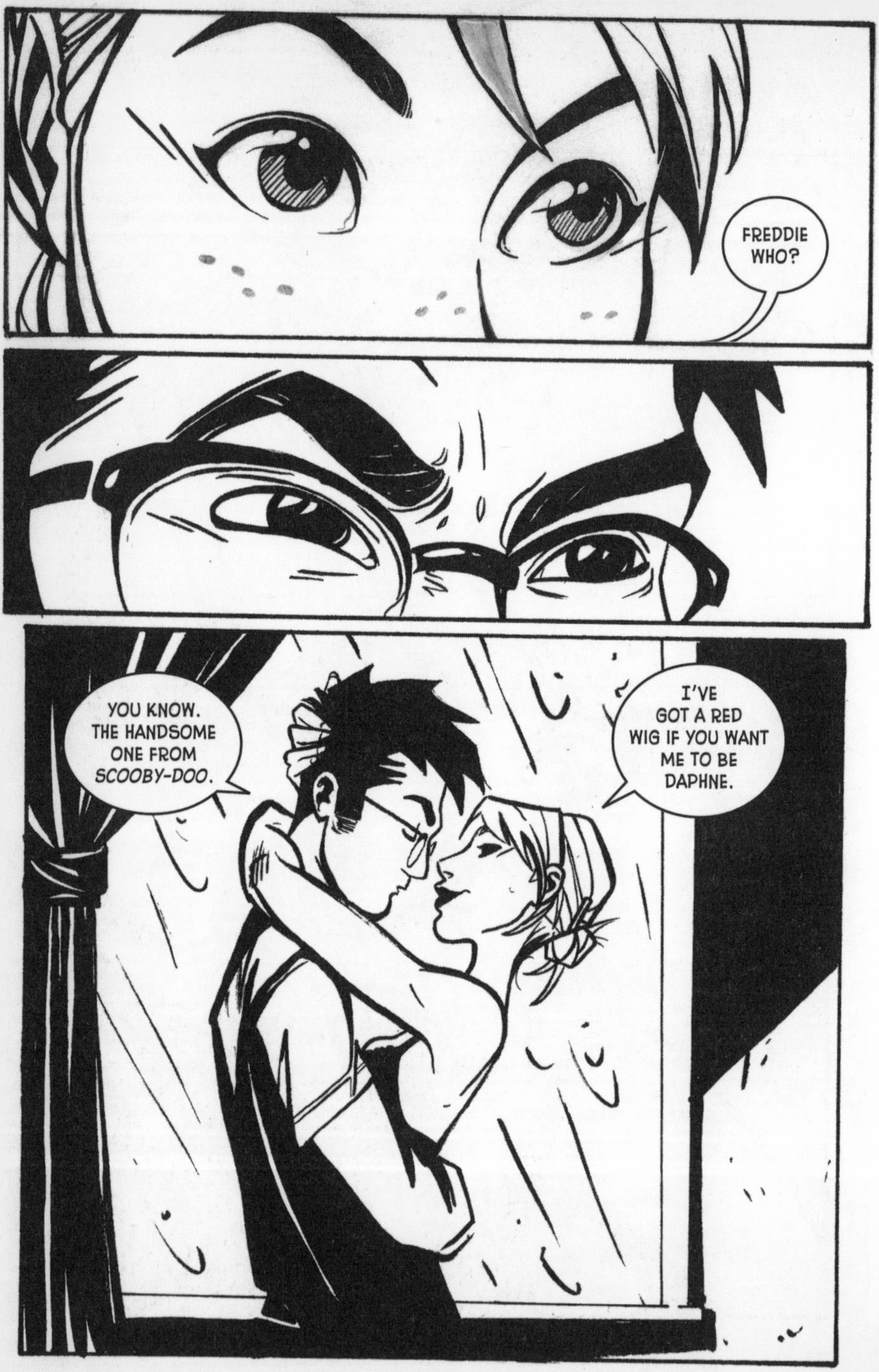
FREDDIE WHO?
YOU KNOW. THE HANDSOME ONE FROM *SCOOBY-DOO*.
I'VE GOT A RED WIG IF YOU WANT ME TO BE DAPHNE.

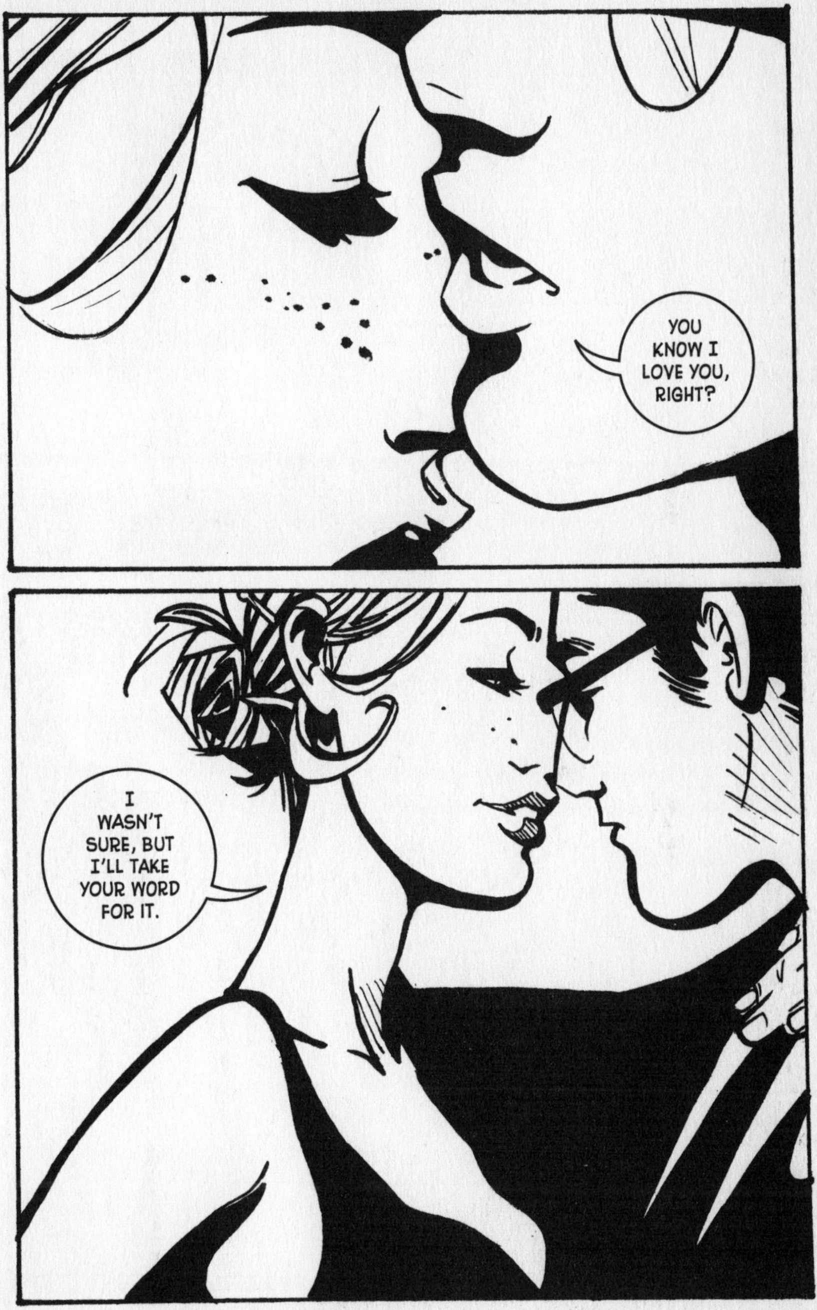
YOU KNOW I LOVE YOU, RIGHT?
I WASN'T SURE, BUT I'LL TAKE YOUR WORD FOR IT.

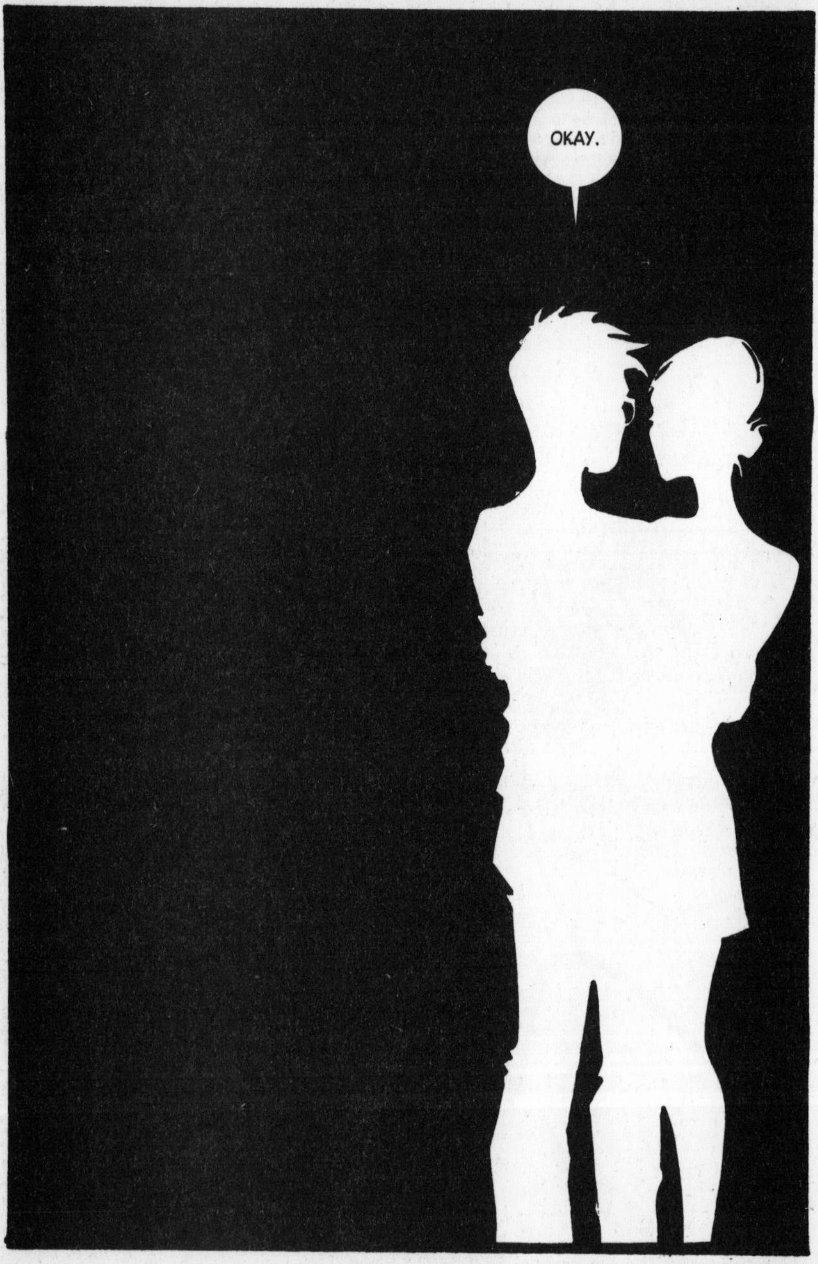
OKAY.

Three

SONG

Pet Shop Boys

"Love Comes Quickly (Blank & Jones Mix)"

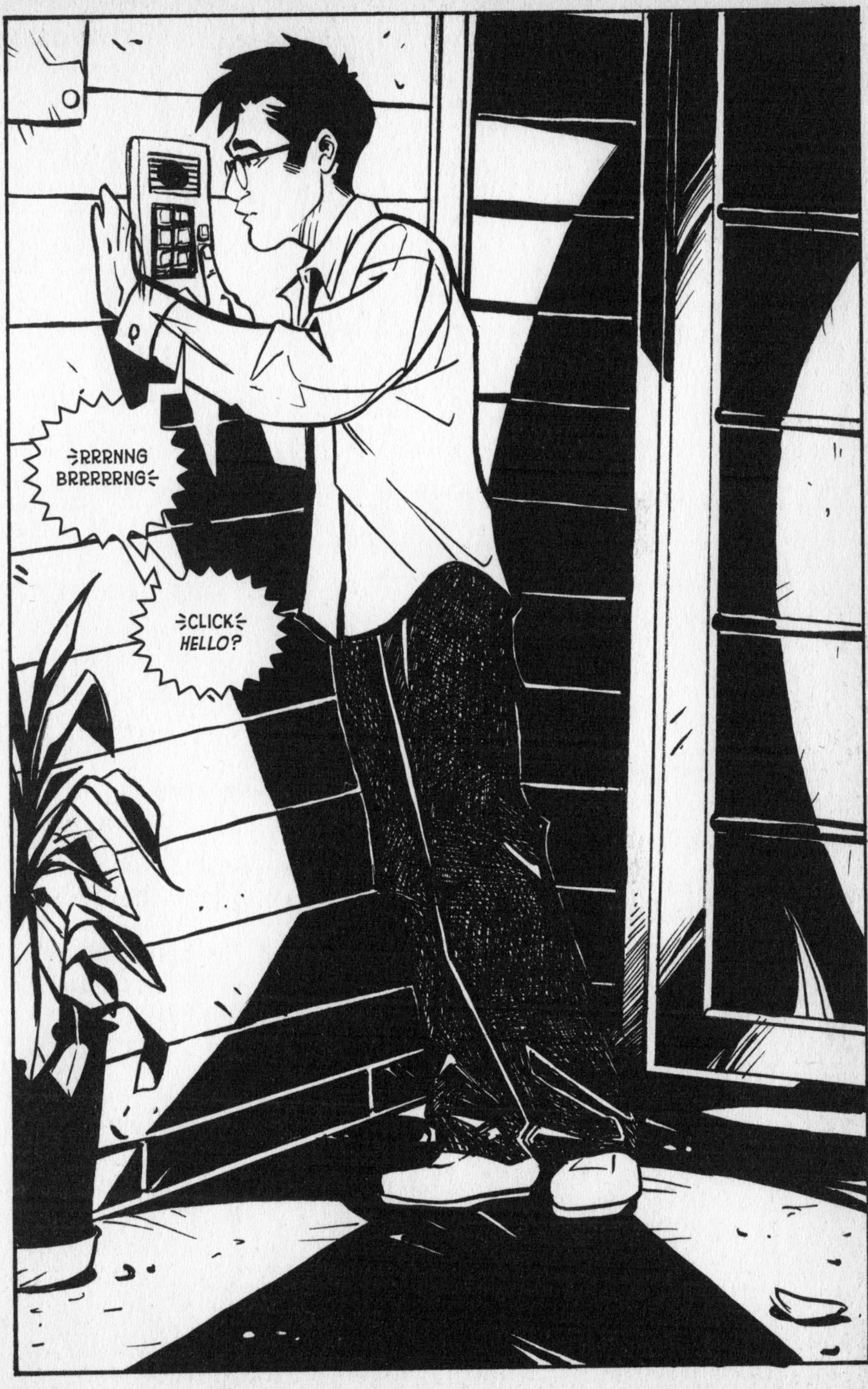
RRRNNG BRRRRRNG
CLICK HELLO?

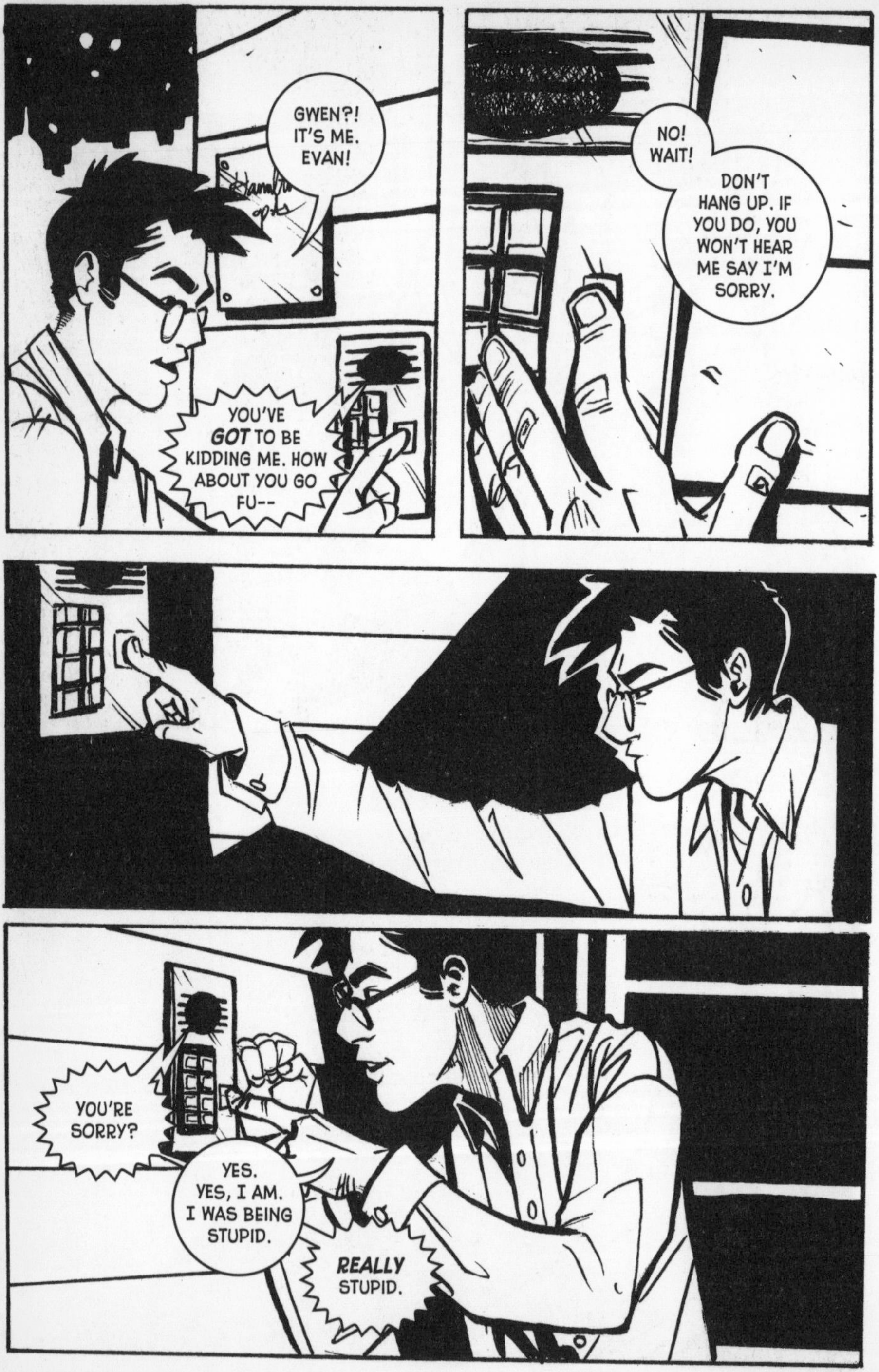
GWEN?! IT'S ME. EVAN!
YOU'VE **GOT** TO BE KIDDING ME. HOW ABOUT YOU GO FU--
NO! WAIT!
DON'T HANG UP. IF YOU DO, YOU WON'T HEAR ME SAY I'M SORRY.
YOU'RE SORRY?
YES. YES, I AM. I WAS BEING STUPID.
REALLY STUPID.

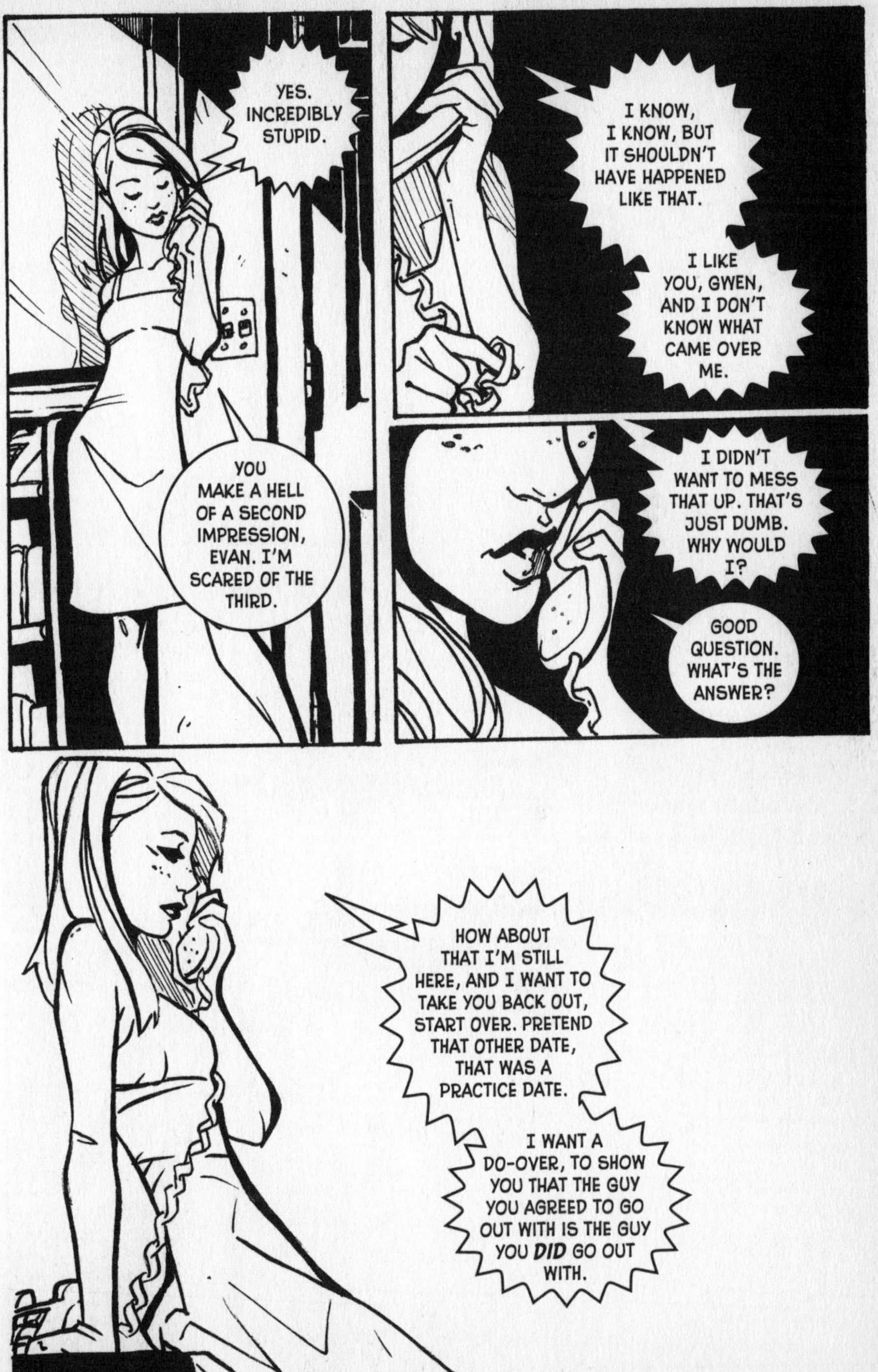
YES. INCREDIBLY STUPID.
YOU MAKE A HELL OF A SECOND IMPRESSION, EVAN. I'M SCARED OF THE THIRD.
I KNOW, I KNOW, BUT IT SHOULDN'T HAVE HAPPENED LIKE THAT.
I LIKE YOU, GWEN, AND I DON'T KNOW WHAT CAME OVER ME.
I DIDN'T WANT TO MESS THAT UP. THAT'S JUST DUMB. WHY WOULD I?
GOOD QUESTION. WHAT'S THE ANSWER?
HOW ABOUT THAT I'M STILL HERE, AND I WANT TO TAKE YOU BACK OUT, START OVER. PRETEND THAT OTHER DATE, THAT WAS A PRACTICE DATE.
I WANT A DO-OVER, TO SHOW YOU THAT THE GUY YOU AGREED TO GO OUT WITH IS THE GUY YOU ***DID*** GO OUT WITH.

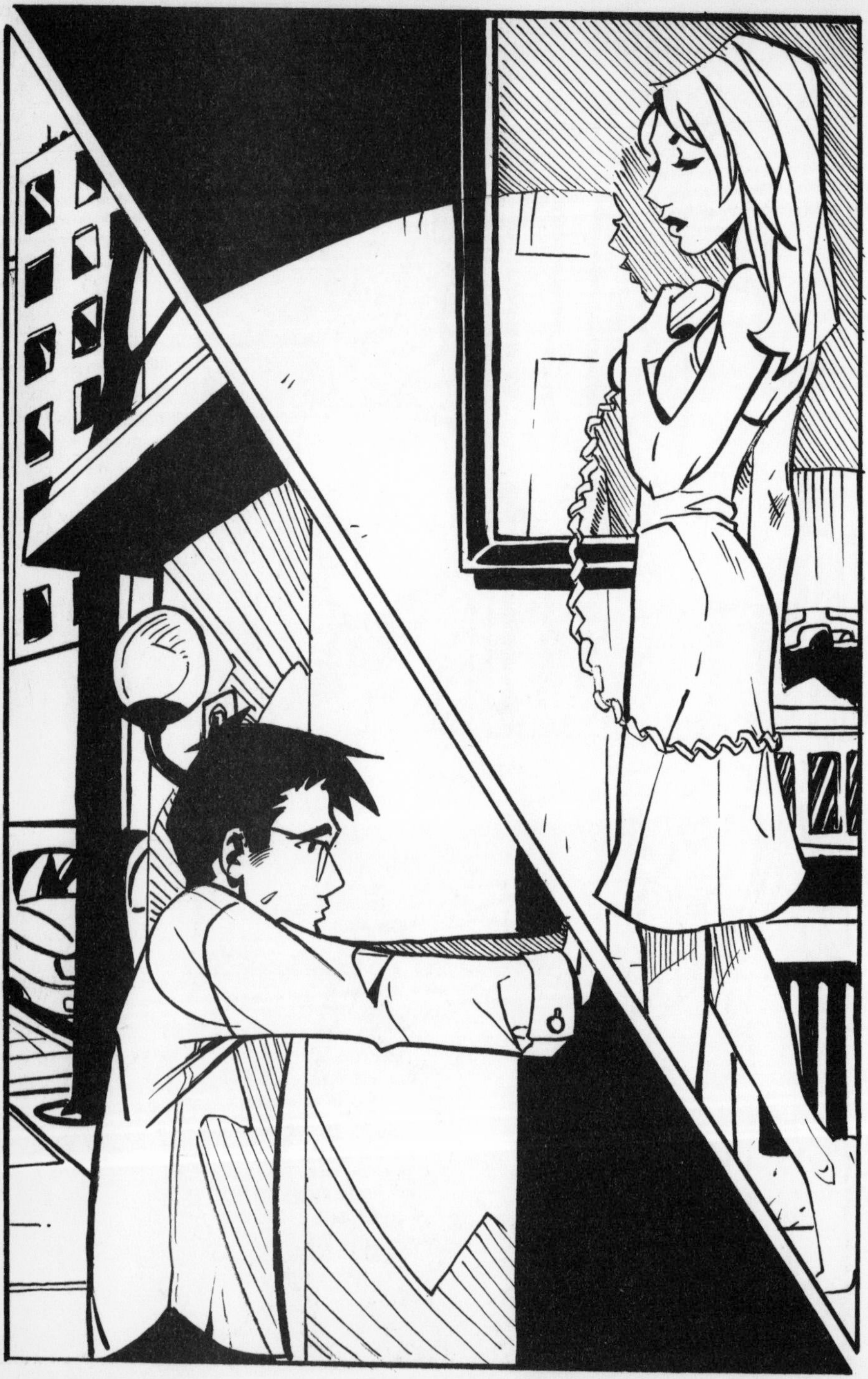

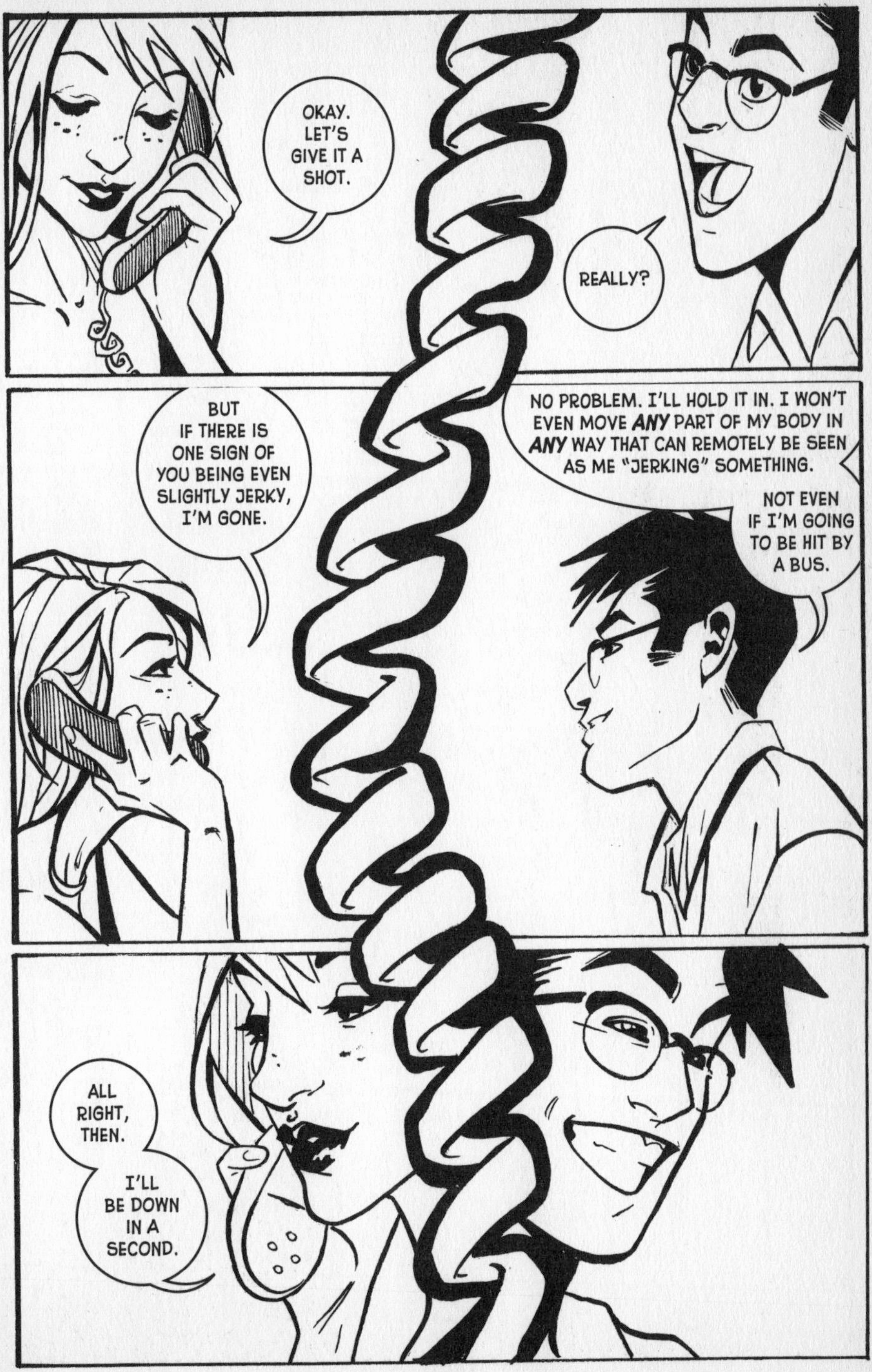
OKAY. LET'S GIVE IT A SHOT.
REALLY?
BUT IF THERE IS ONE SIGN OF YOU BEING EVEN SLIGHTLY JERKY, I'M GONE.
NO PROBLEM. I'LL HOLD IT IN. I WON'T EVEN MOVE ANY PART OF MY BODY IN ANY WAY THAT CAN REMOTELY BE SEEN AS ME "JERKING" SOMETHING.
NOT EVEN IF I'M GOING TO BE HIT BY A BUS.
ALL RIGHT, THEN.
I'LL BE DOWN IN A SECOND.

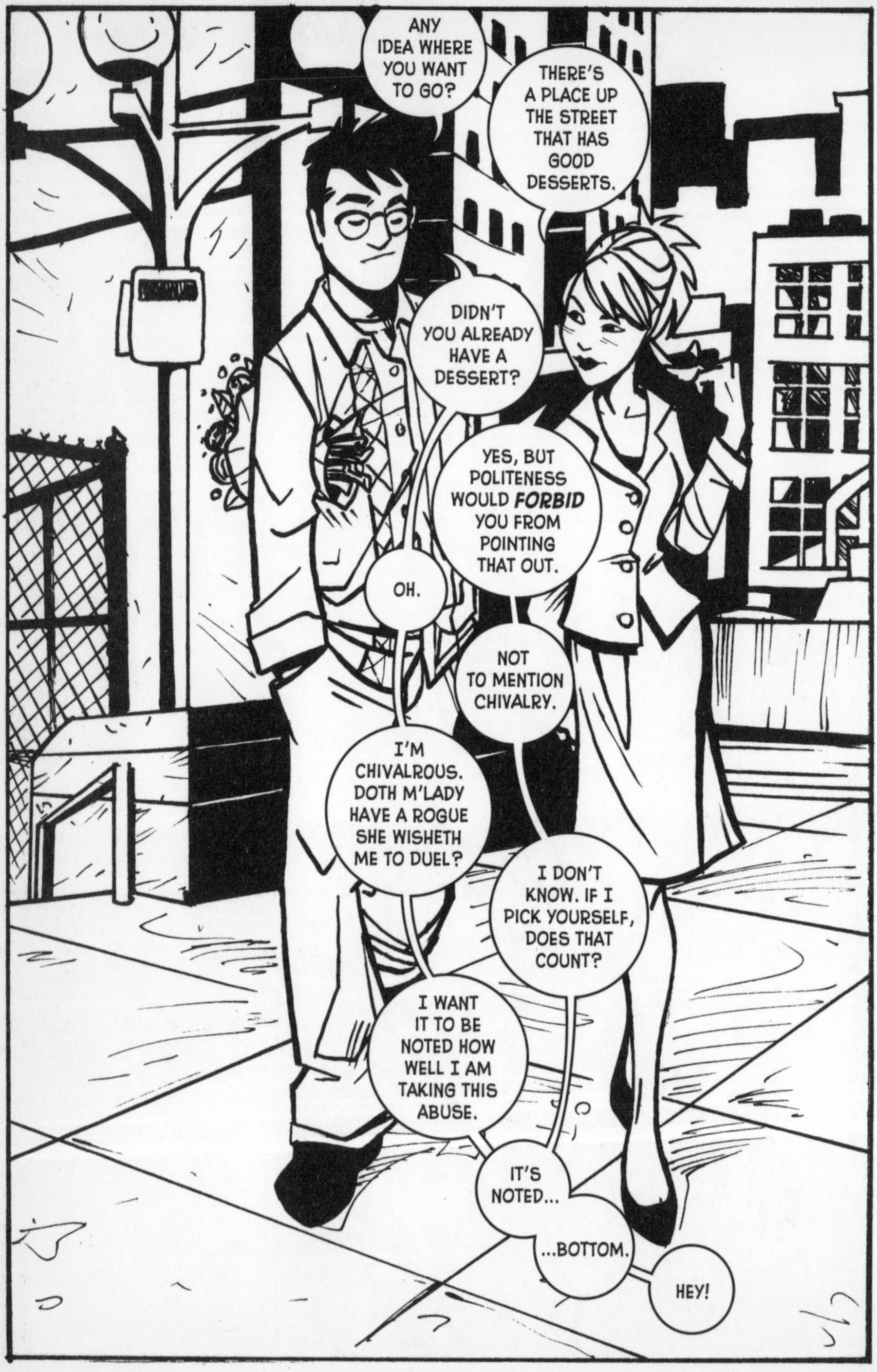
ANY IDEA WHERE YOU WANT TO GO?
THERE'S A PLACE UP THE STREET THAT HAS GOOD DESSERTS.
DIDN'T YOU ALREADY HAVE A DESSERT?
YES, BUT POLITENESS WOULD *FORBID* YOU FROM POINTING THAT OUT.
OH.
NOT TO MENTION CHIVALRY.
I'M CHIVALROUS. DOTH M'LADY HAVE A ROGUE SHE WISHETH ME TO DUEL?
I DON'T KNOW. IF I PICK YOURSELF, DOES THAT COUNT?
I WANT IT TO BE NOTED HOW WELL I AM TAKING THIS ABUSE.
IT'S NOTED...
...BOTTOM.
HEY!

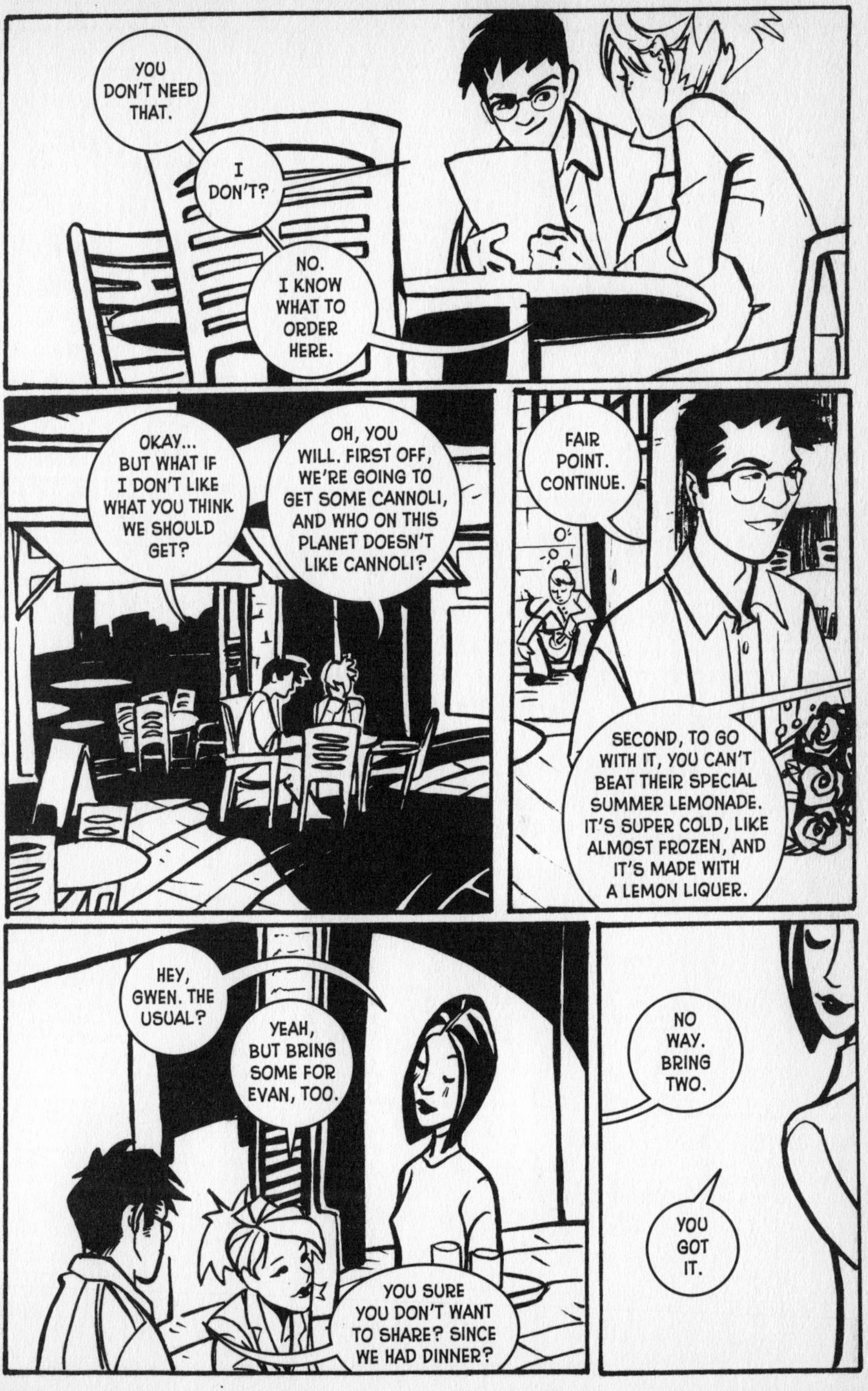
YOU DON'T NEED THAT.
I DON'T?
NO. I KNOW WHAT TO ORDER HERE.
OKAY... BUT WHAT IF I DON'T LIKE WHAT YOU THINK WE SHOULD GET?
OH, YOU WILL. FIRST OFF, WE'RE GOING TO GET SOME CANNOLI, AND WHO ON THIS PLANET DOESN'T LIKE CANNOLI?
FAIR POINT. CONTINUE.
SECOND, TO GO WITH IT, YOU CAN'T BEAT THEIR SPECIAL SUMMER LEMONADE. IT'S SUPER COLD, LIKE ALMOST FROZEN, AND IT'S MADE WITH A LEMON LIQUER.
HEY, GWEN. THE USUAL?
YEAH, BUT BRING SOME FOR EVAN, TOO.
YOU SURE YOU DON'T WANT TO SHARE? SINCE WE HAD DINNER?
NO WAY. BRING TWO.
YOU GOT IT.

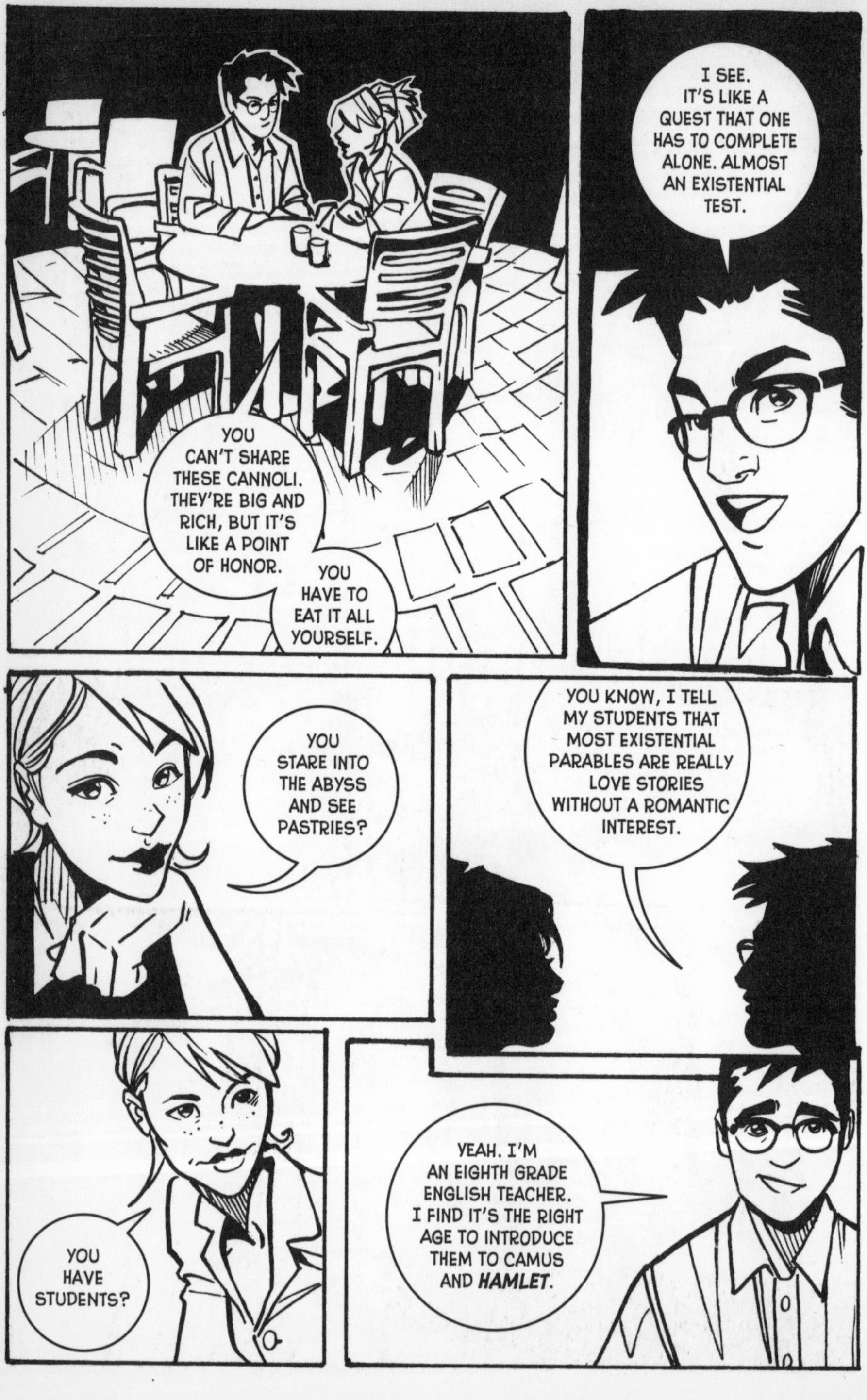
YOU CAN'T SHARE THESE CANNOLI. THEY'RE BIG AND RICH, BUT IT'S LIKE A POINT OF HONOR.
YOU HAVE TO EAT IT ALL YOURSELF.
I SEE. IT'S LIKE A QUEST THAT ONE HAS TO COMPLETE ALONE. ALMOST AN EXISTENTIAL TEST.
YOU STARE INTO THE ABYSS AND SEE PASTRIES?
YOU KNOW, I TELL MY STUDENTS THAT MOST EXISTENTIAL PARABLES ARE REALLY LOVE STORIES WITHOUT A ROMANTIC INTEREST.
YOU HAVE STUDENTS?
YEAH. I'M AN EIGHTH GRADE ENGLISH TEACHER. I FIND IT'S THE RIGHT AGE TO INTRODUCE THEM TO CAMUS AND *HAMLET*.

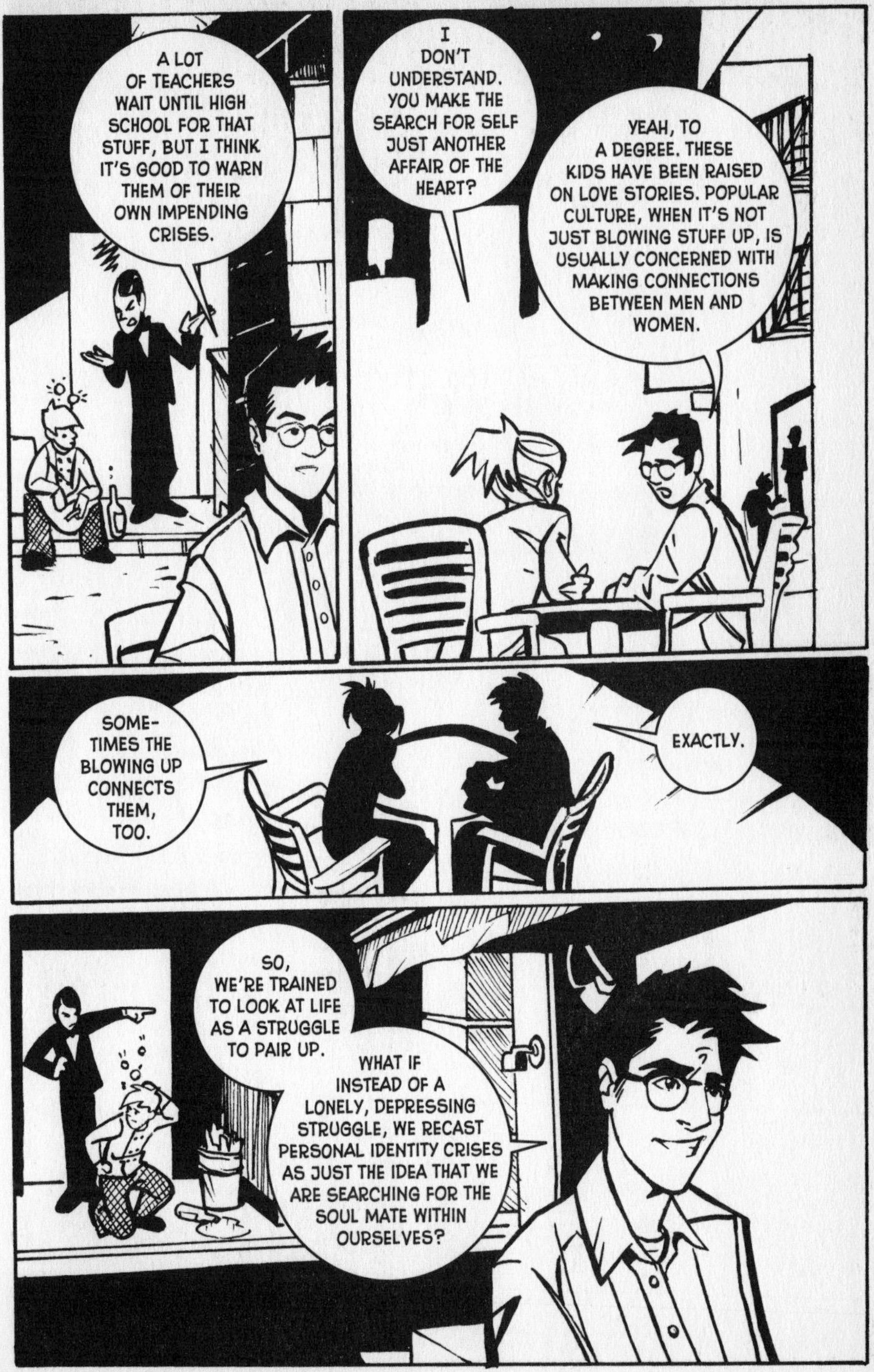
A LOT OF TEACHERS WAIT UNTIL HIGH SCHOOL FOR THAT STUFF, BUT I THINK IT'S GOOD TO WARN THEM OF THEIR OWN IMPENDING CRISES.
I DON'T UNDERSTAND. YOU MAKE THE SEARCH FOR SELF JUST ANOTHER AFFAIR OF THE HEART?
YEAH, TO A DEGREE. THESE KIDS HAVE BEEN RAISED ON LOVE STORIES. POPULAR CULTURE, WHEN IT'S NOT JUST BLOWING STUFF UP, IS USUALLY CONCERNED WITH MAKING CONNECTIONS BETWEEN MEN AND WOMEN.
SOME-TIMES THE BLOWING UP CONNECTS THEM, TOO.
EXACTLY.
SO, WE'RE TRAINED TO LOOK AT LIFE AS A STRUGGLE TO PAIR UP.
WHAT IF INSTEAD OF A LONELY, DEPRESSING STRUGGLE, WE RECAST PERSONAL IDENTITY CRISES AS JUST THE IDEA THAT WE ARE SEARCHING FOR THE SOUL MATE WITHIN OURSELVES?

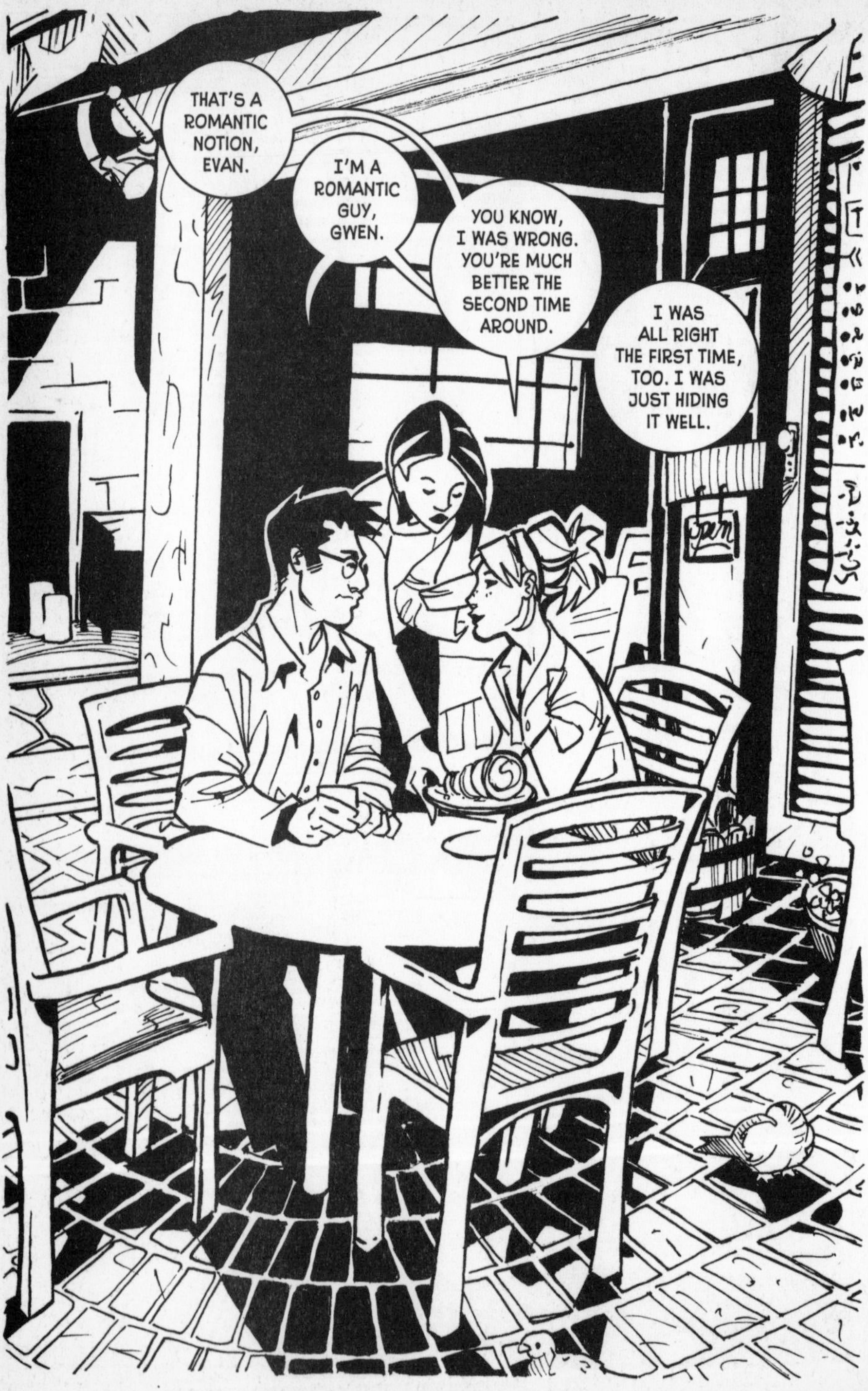
THAT'S A ROMANTIC NOTION, EVAN.
I'M A ROMANTIC GUY, GWEN.
YOU KNOW, I WAS WRONG. YOU'RE MUCH BETTER THE SECOND TIME AROUND.
I WAS ALL RIGHT THE FIRST TIME, TOO. I WAS JUST HIDING IT WELL.

Four

SONG

Bryan Ferry

"September Song"

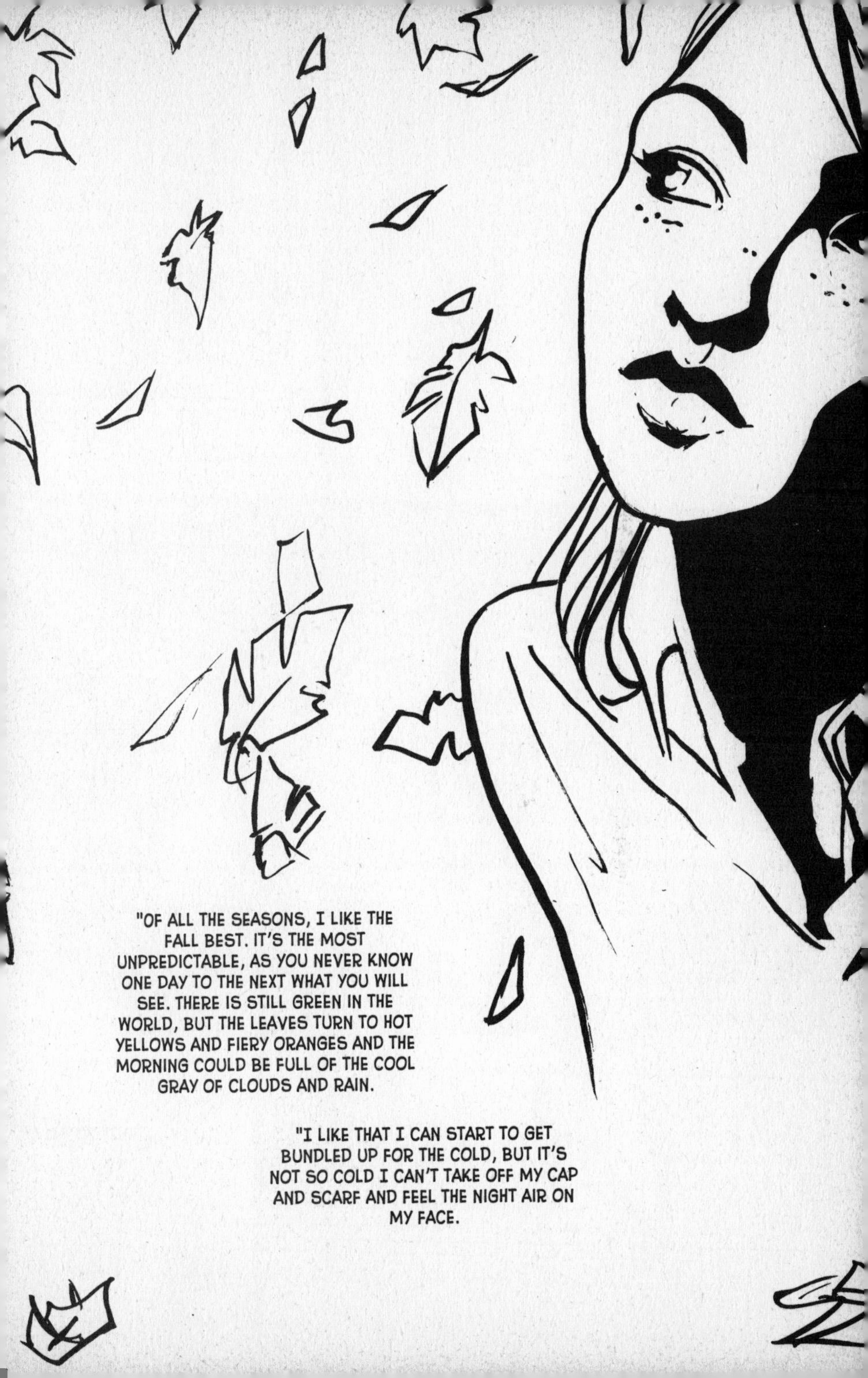
"OF ALL THE SEASONS, I LIKE THE FALL BEST. IT'S THE MOST UNPREDICTABLE, AS YOU NEVER KNOW ONE DAY TO THE NEXT WHAT YOU WILL SEE. THERE IS STILL GREEN IN THE WORLD, BUT THE LEAVES TURN TO HOT YELLOWS AND FIERY ORANGES AND THE MORNING COULD BE FULL OF THE COOL GRAY OF CLOUDS AND RAIN.
"I LIKE THAT I CAN START TO GET BUNDLED UP FOR THE COLD, BUT IT'S NOT SO COLD I CAN'T TAKE OFF MY CAP AND SCARF AND FEEL THE NIGHT AIR ON MY FACE.

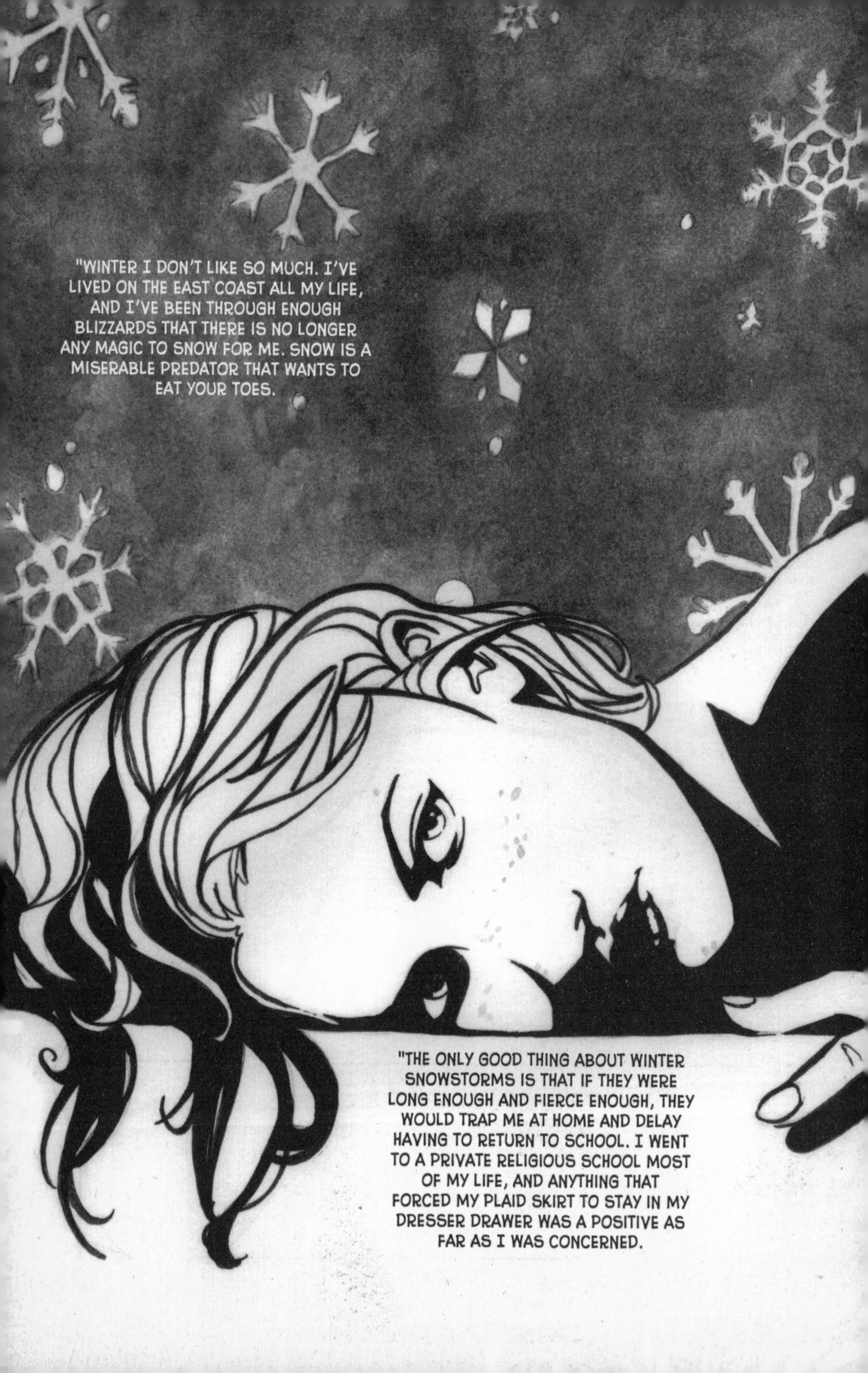
"WINTER I DON'T LIKE SO MUCH. I'VE LIVED ON THE EAST COAST ALL MY LIFE, AND I'VE BEEN THROUGH ENOUGH BLIZZARDS THAT THERE IS NO LONGER ANY MAGIC TO SNOW FOR ME. SNOW IS A MISERABLE PREDATOR THAT WANTS TO EAT YOUR TOES.
"THE ONLY GOOD THING ABOUT WINTER SNOWSTORMS IS THAT IF THEY WERE LONG ENOUGH AND FIERCE ENOUGH, THEY WOULD TRAP ME AT HOME AND DELAY HAVING TO RETURN TO SCHOOL. I WENT TO A PRIVATE RELIGIOUS SCHOOL MOST OF MY LIFE, AND ANYTHING THAT FORCED MY PLAID SKIRT TO STAY IN MY DRESSER DRAWER WAS A POSITIVE AS FAR AS I WAS CONCERNED.

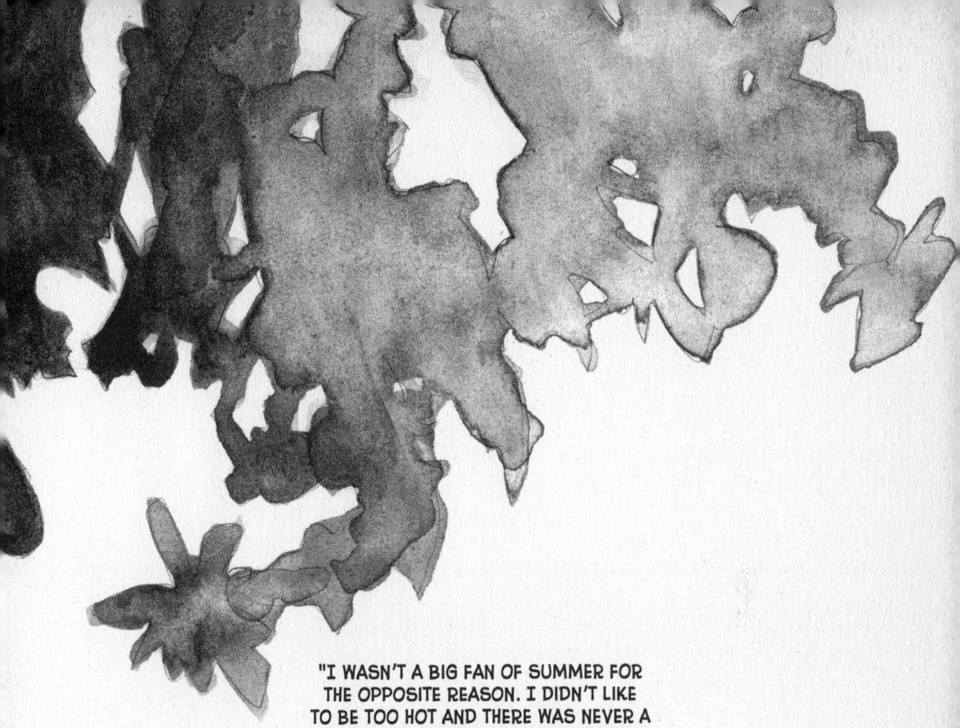

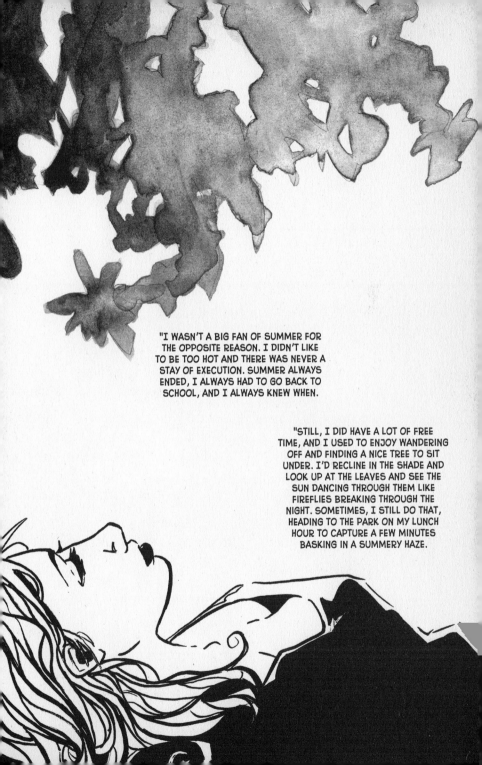

"I WASN'T A BIG FAN OF SUMMER FOR THE OPPOSITE REASON. I DIDN'T LIKE TO BE TOO HOT AND THERE WAS NEVER A STAY OF EXECUTION. SUMMER ALWAYS ENDED, I ALWAYS HAD TO GO BACK TO SCHOOL, AND I ALWAYS KNEW WHEN.

"STILL, I DID HAVE A LOT OF FREE TIME, AND I USED TO ENJOY WANDERING OFF AND FINDING A NICE TREE TO SIT UNDER. I'D RECLINE IN THE SHADE AND LOOK UP AT THE LEAVES AND SEE THE SUN DANCING THROUGH THEM LIKE FIREFLIES BREAKING THROUGH THE NIGHT. SOMETIMES, I STILL DO THAT, HEADING TO THE PARK ON MY LUNCH HOUR TO CAPTURE A FEW MINUTES BASKING IN A SUMMERY HAZE.

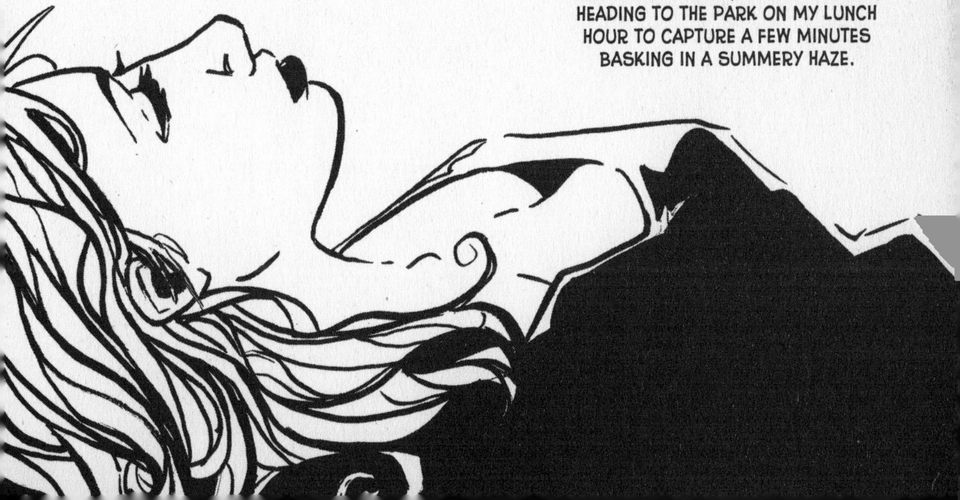

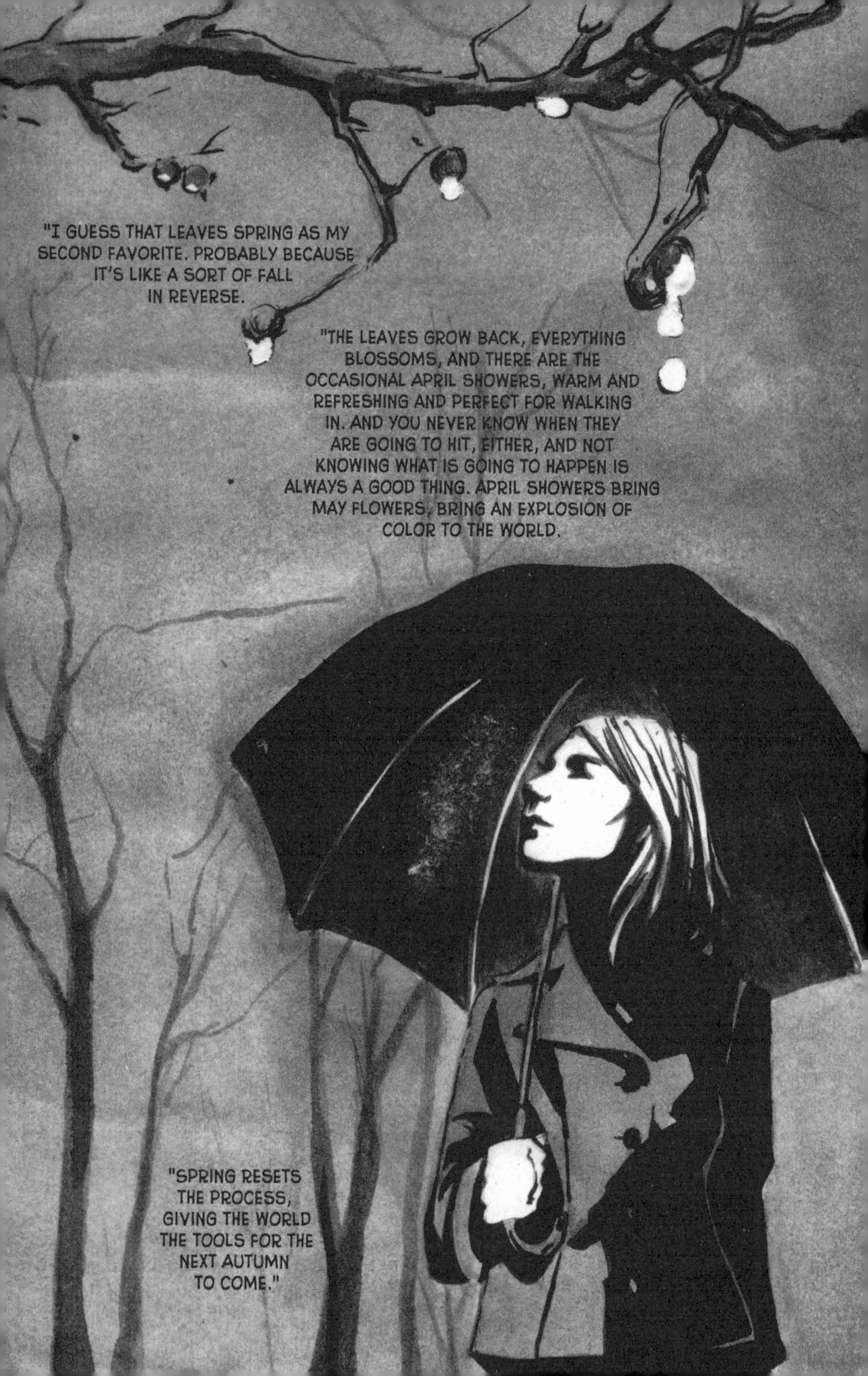
"I GUESS THAT LEAVES SPRING AS MY SECOND FAVORITE. PROBABLY BECAUSE IT'S LIKE A SORT OF FALL IN REVERSE.
"THE LEAVES GROW BACK, EVERYTHING BLOSSOMS, AND THERE ARE THE OCCASIONAL APRIL SHOWERS, WARM AND REFRESHING AND PERFECT FOR WALKING IN. AND YOU NEVER KNOW WHEN THEY ARE GOING TO HIT, EITHER, AND NOT KNOWING WHAT IS GOING TO HAPPEN IS ALWAYS A GOOD THING. APRIL SHOWERS BRING MAY FLOWERS, BRING AN EXPLOSION OF COLOR TO THE WORLD.
"SPRING RESETS THE PROCESS, GIVING THE WORLD THE TOOLS FOR THE NEXT AUTUMN TO COME."

Five

SONG

The Trash Can Sinatras
"A Boy and a Girl"

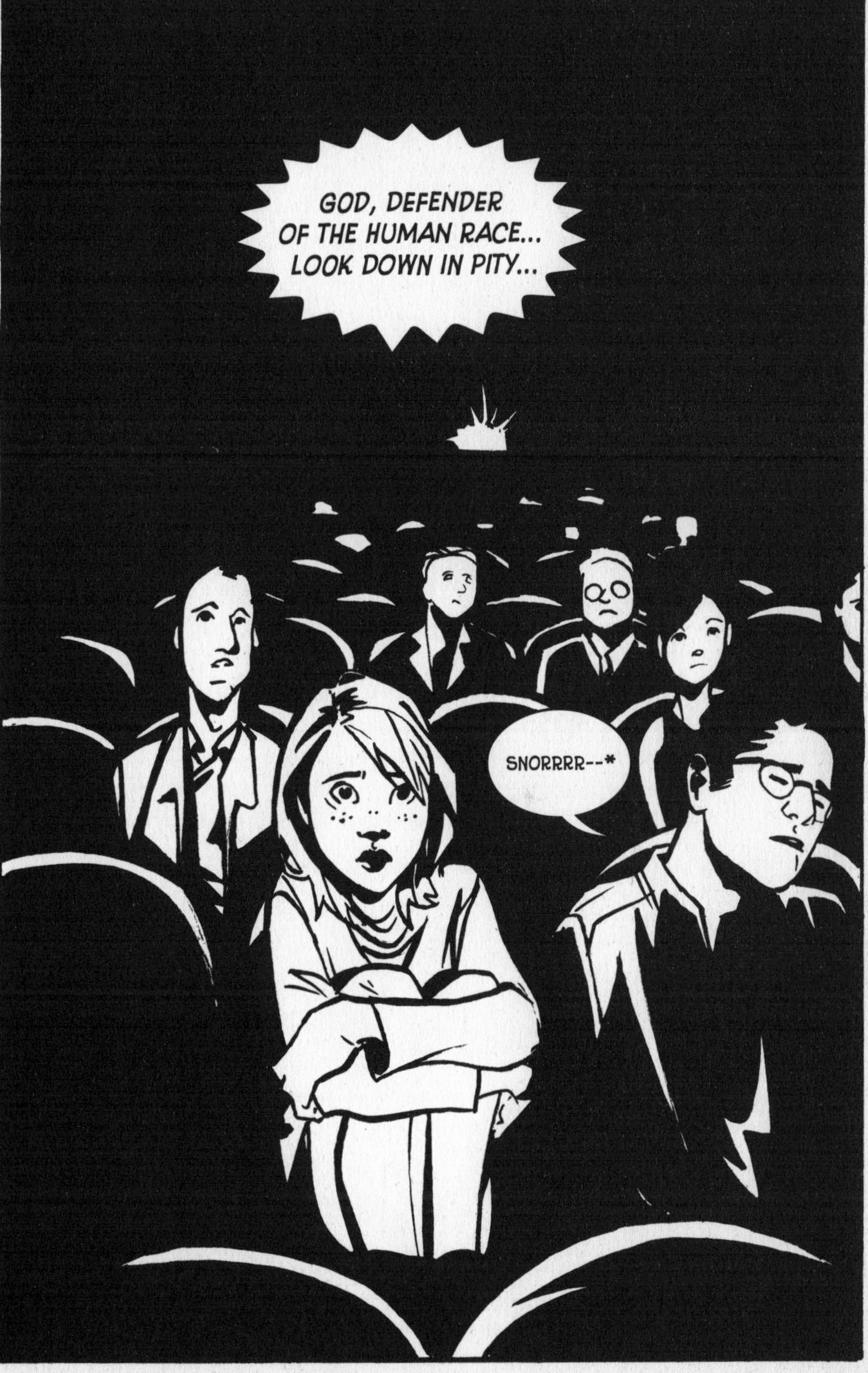
GOD, DEFENDER OF THE HUMAN RACE... LOOK DOWN IN PITY...
SNORRRR--*

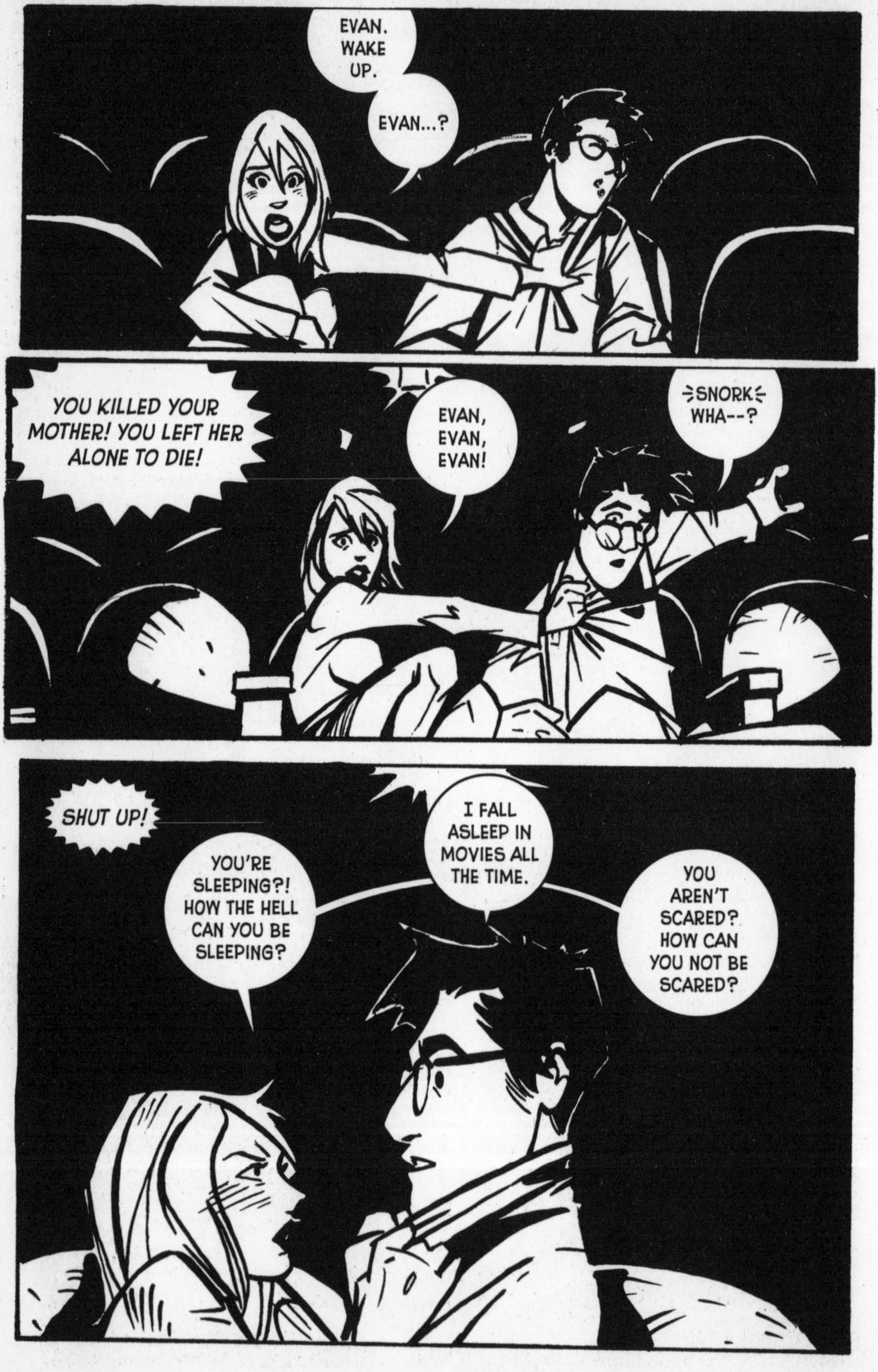
EVAN. WAKE UP.
EVAN...?
YOU KILLED YOUR MOTHER! YOU LEFT HER ALONE TO DIE!
EVAN, EVAN, EVAN!
SNORK WHA--?
SHUT UP!
YOU'RE SLEEPING?! HOW THE HELL CAN YOU BE SLEEPING?
I FALL ASLEEP IN MOVIES ALL THE TIME.
YOU AREN'T SCARED? HOW CAN YOU NOT BE SCARED?

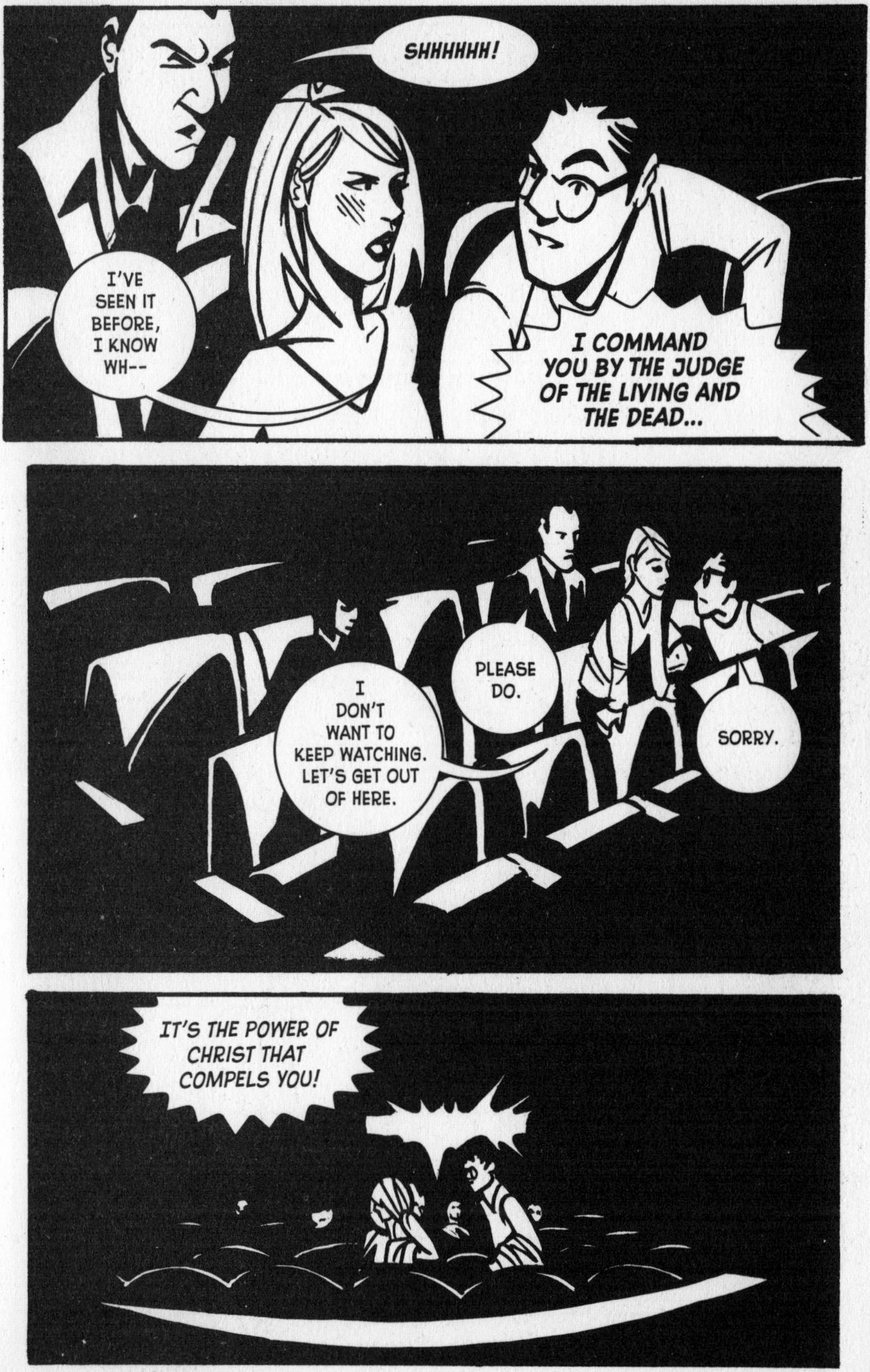
SHHHHHH!
I'VE SEEN IT BEFORE, I KNOW WH--
I COMMAND YOU BY THE JUDGE OF THE LIVING AND THE DEAD...
I DON'T WANT TO KEEP WATCHING. LET'S GET OUT OF HERE.
PLEASE DO.
SORRY.
IT'S THE POWER OF CHRIST THAT COMPELS YOU!

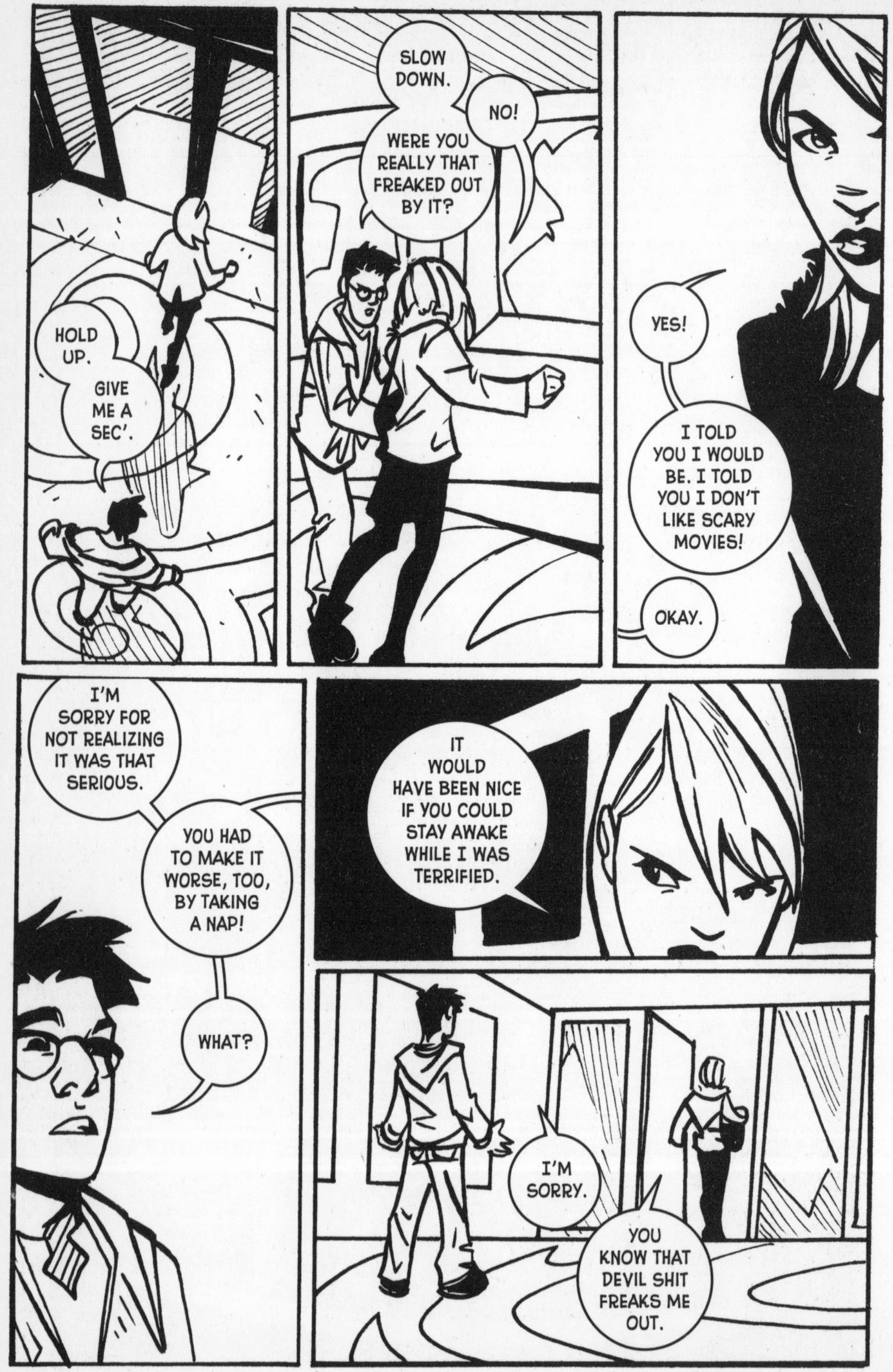
HOLD UP.
GIVE ME A SEC'.
SLOW DOWN.
NO!
WERE YOU REALLY THAT FREAKED OUT BY IT?
YES!
I TOLD YOU I WOULD BE. I TOLD YOU I DON'T LIKE SCARY MOVIES!
OKAY.
I'M SORRY FOR NOT REALIZING IT WAS THAT SERIOUS.
YOU HAD TO MAKE IT WORSE, TOO, BY TAKING A NAP!
WHAT?
IT WOULD HAVE BEEN NICE IF YOU COULD STAY AWAKE WHILE I WAS TERRIFIED.
I'M SORRY.
YOU KNOW THAT DEVIL SHIT FREAKS ME OUT.

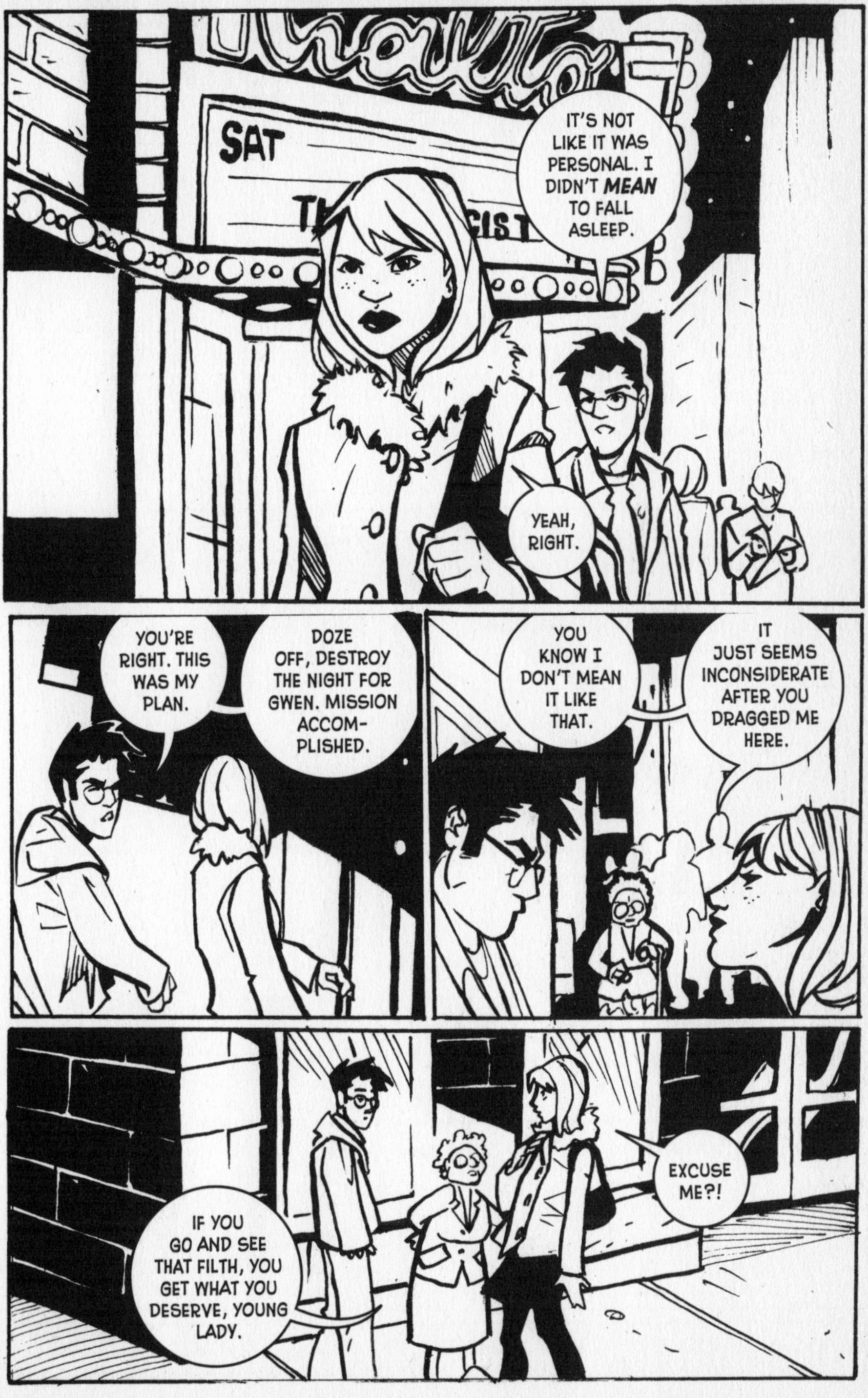
SAT
IT'S NOT LIKE IT WAS PERSONAL. I DIDN'T *MEAN* TO FALL ASLEEP.
YEAH, RIGHT.
YOU'RE RIGHT. THIS WAS MY PLAN.
DOZE OFF, DESTROY THE NIGHT FOR GWEN. MISSION ACCOM-PLISHED.
YOU KNOW I DON'T MEAN IT LIKE THAT.
IT JUST SEEMS INCONSIDERATE AFTER YOU DRAGGED ME HERE.
EXCUSE ME?!
IF YOU GO AND SEE THAT FILTH, YOU GET WHAT YOU DESERVE, YOUNG LADY.

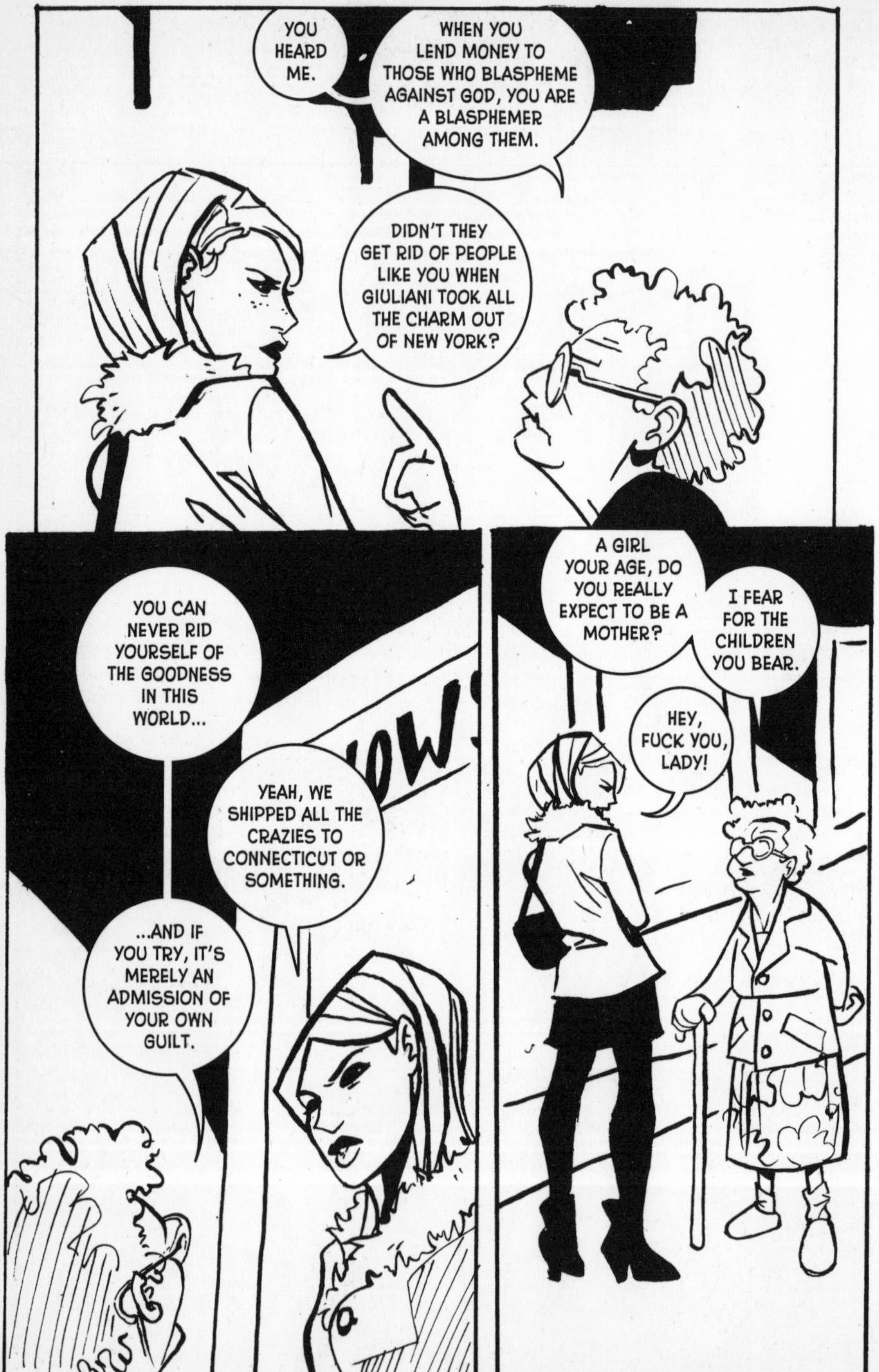
YOU HEARD ME.
WHEN YOU LEND MONEY TO THOSE WHO BLASPHEME AGAINST GOD, YOU ARE A BLASPHEMER AMONG THEM.
DIDN'T THEY GET RID OF PEOPLE LIKE YOU WHEN GIULIANI TOOK ALL THE CHARM OUT OF NEW YORK?
YOU CAN NEVER RID YOURSELF OF THE GOODNESS IN THIS WORLD...
YEAH, WE SHIPPED ALL THE CRAZIES TO CONNECTICUT OR SOMETHING.
...AND IF YOU TRY, IT'S MERELY AN ADMISSION OF YOUR OWN GUILT.
A GIRL YOUR AGE, DO YOU REALLY EXPECT TO BE A MOTHER?
I FEAR FOR THE CHILDREN YOU BEAR.
HEY, FUCK YOU, LADY!

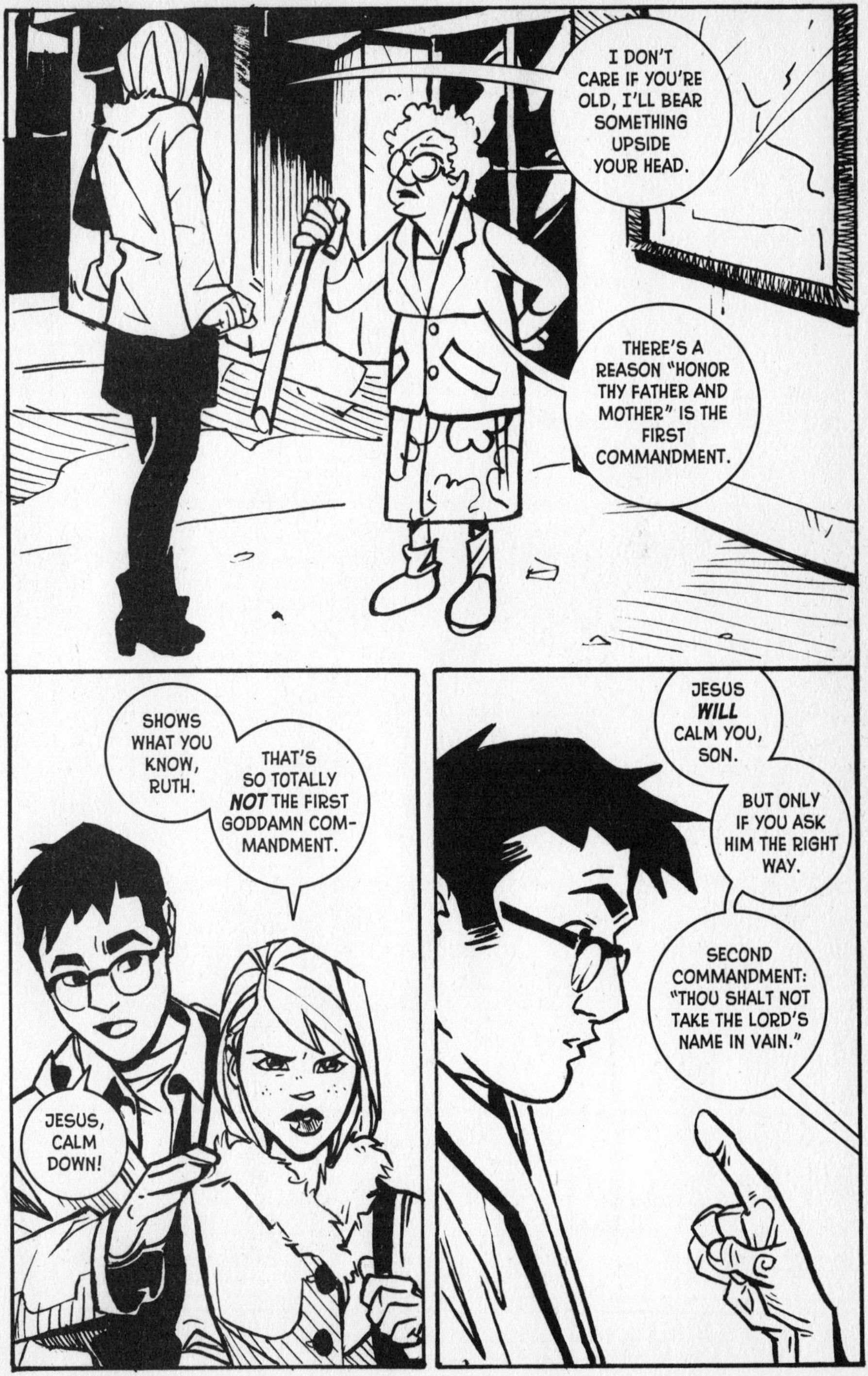
I DON'T CARE IF YOU'RE OLD, I'LL BEAR SOMETHING UPSIDE YOUR HEAD.
THERE'S A REASON "HONOR THY FATHER AND MOTHER" IS THE FIRST COMMANDMENT.
SHOWS WHAT YOU KNOW, RUTH.
THAT'S SO TOTALLY ***NOT*** THE FIRST GODDAMN COM-MANDMENT.
JESUS, CALM DOWN!
JESUS ***WILL*** CALM YOU, SON.
BUT ONLY IF YOU ASK HIM THE RIGHT WAY.
SECOND COMMANDMENT: "THOU SHALT NOT TAKE THE LORD'S NAME IN VAIN."

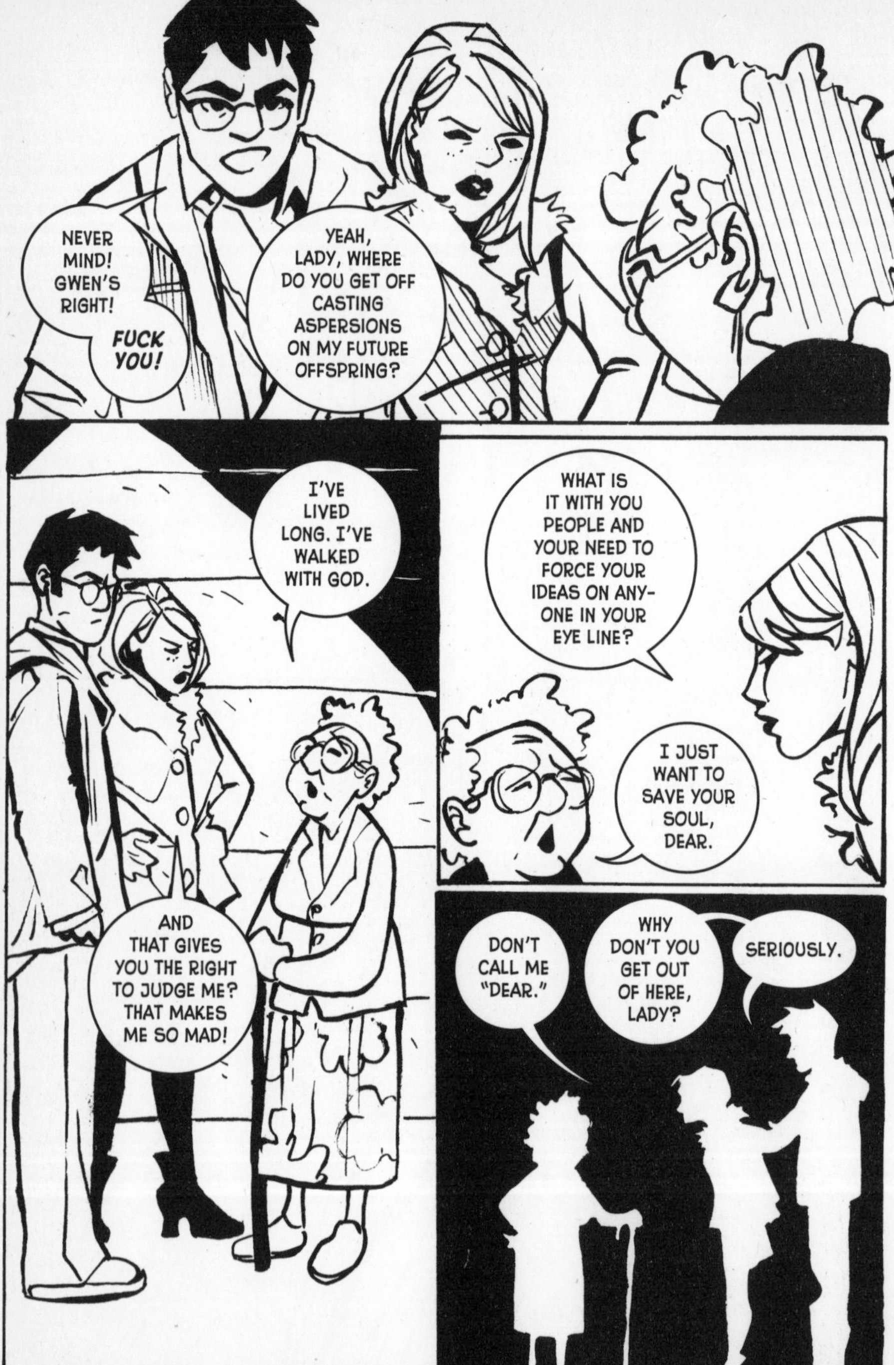
NEVER MIND! GWEN'S RIGHT!
FUCK YOU!
YEAH, LADY, WHERE DO YOU GET OFF CASTING ASPERSIONS ON MY FUTURE OFFSPRING?
I'VE LIVED LONG. I'VE WALKED WITH GOD.
AND THAT GIVES YOU THE RIGHT TO JUDGE ME? THAT MAKES ME SO MAD!
WHAT IS IT WITH YOU PEOPLE AND YOUR NEED TO FORCE YOUR IDEAS ON ANY-ONE IN YOUR EYE LINE?
I JUST WANT TO SAVE YOUR SOUL, DEAR.
DON'T CALL ME "DEAR."
WHY DON'T YOU GET OUT OF HERE, LADY?
SERIOUSLY.

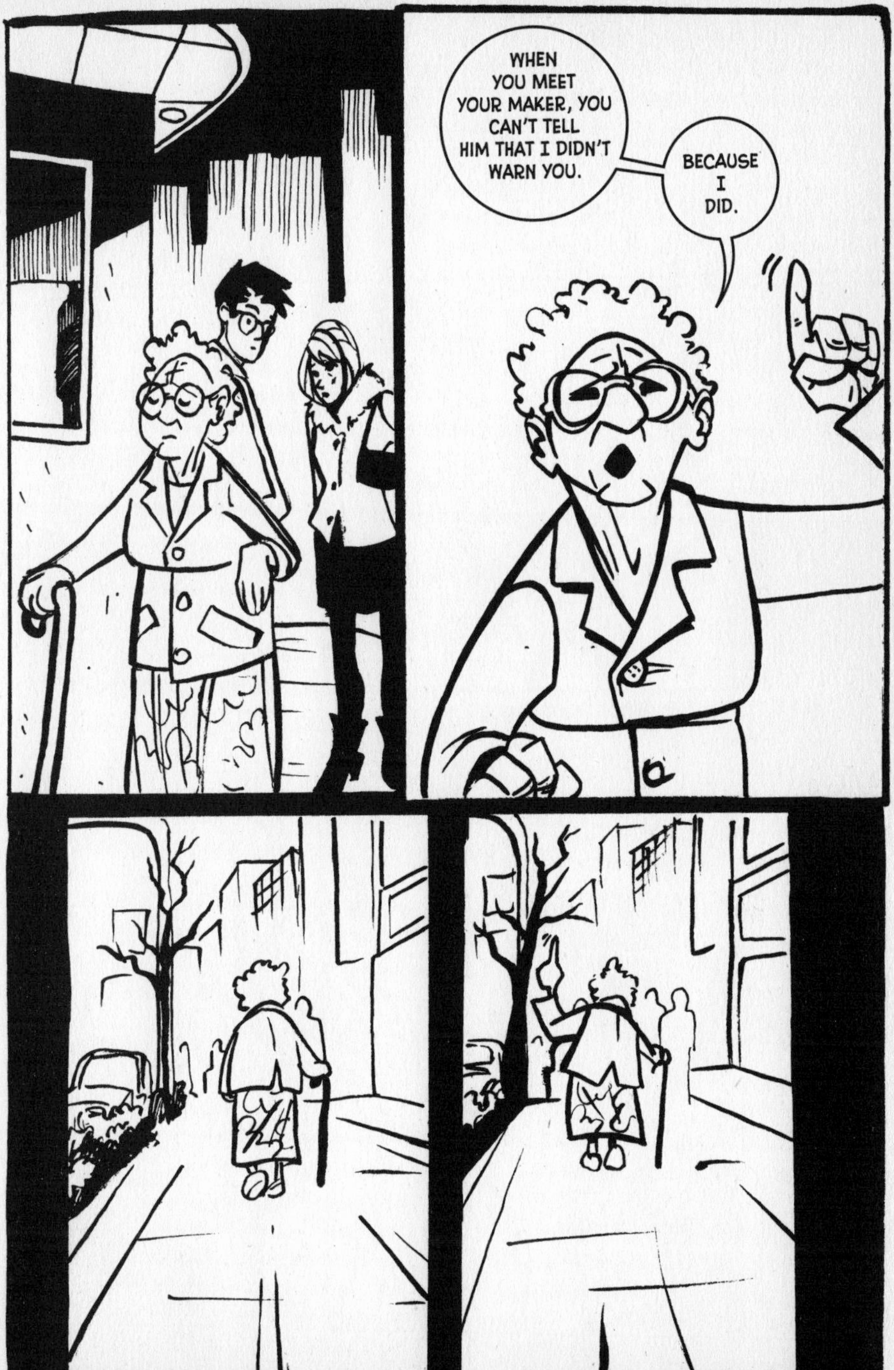
WHEN YOU MEET YOUR MAKER, YOU CAN'T TELL HIM THAT I DIDN'T WARN YOU.
BECAUSE I DID.

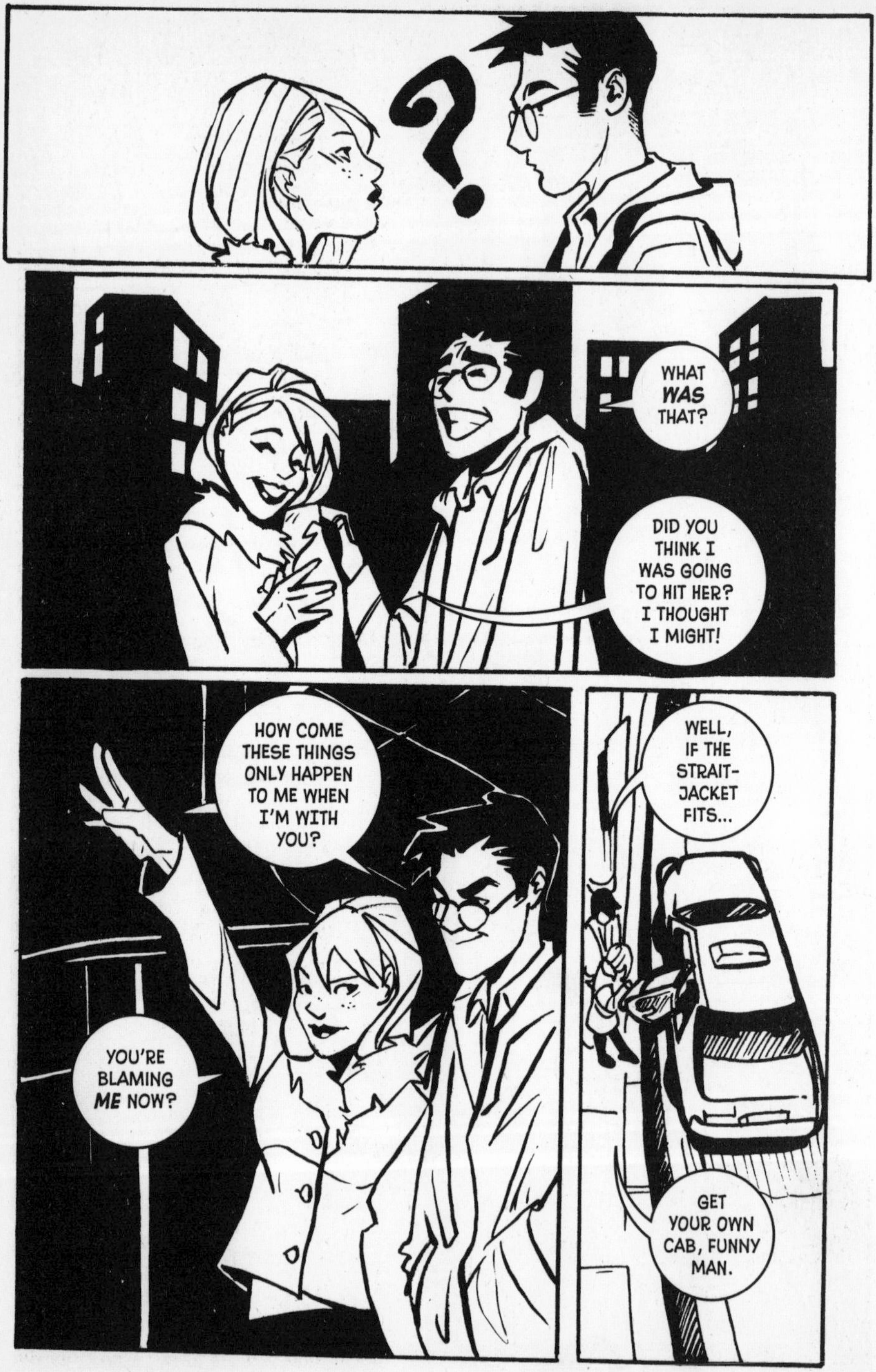
?
WHAT WAS THAT?
DID YOU THINK I WAS GOING TO HIT HER? I THOUGHT I MIGHT!
HOW COME THESE THINGS ONLY HAPPEN TO ME WHEN I'M WITH YOU?
YOU'RE BLAMING ME NOW?
WELL, IF THE STRAIT-JACKET FITS...
GET YOUR OWN CAB, FUNNY MAN.

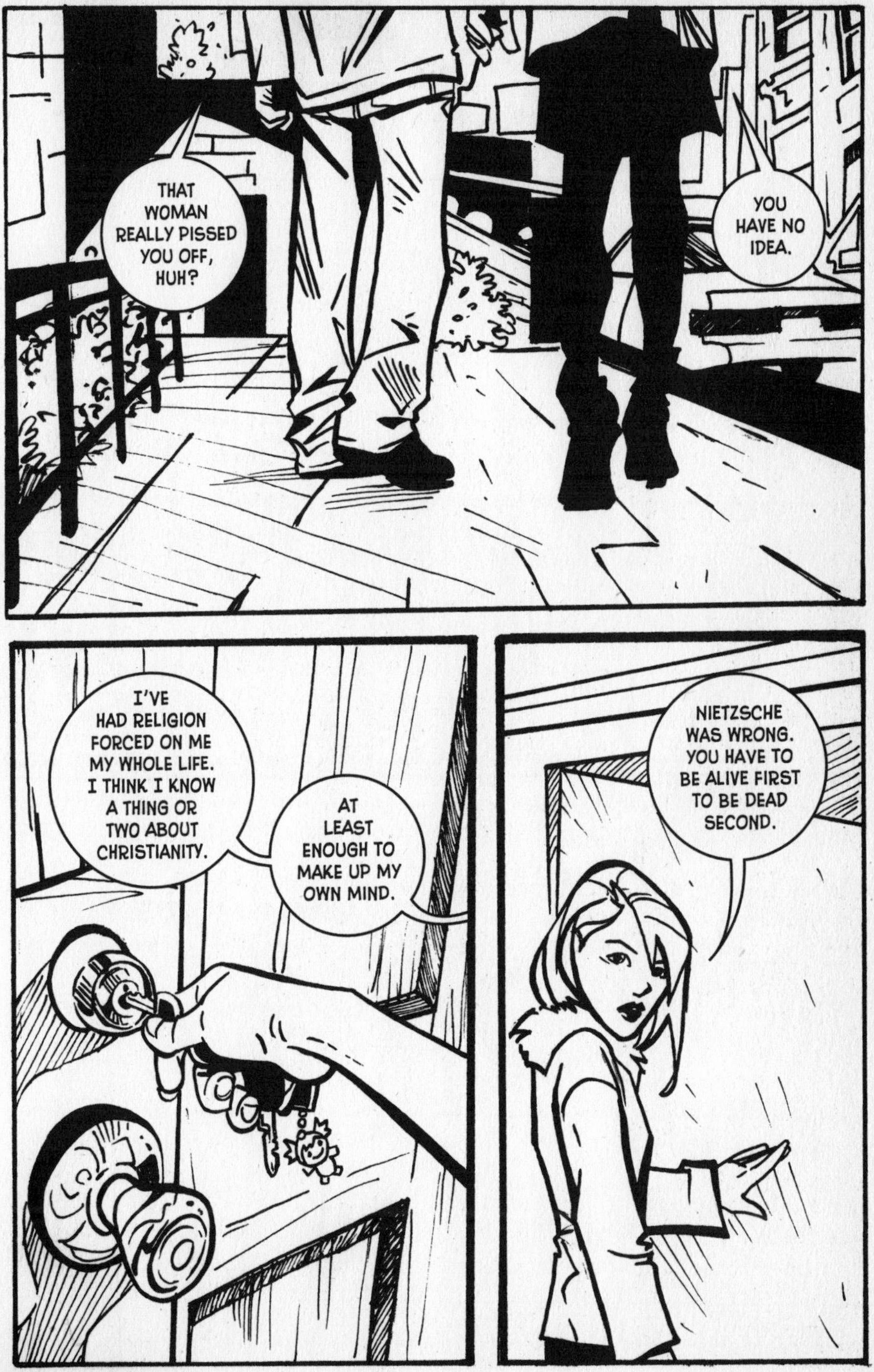
THAT WOMAN REALLY PISSED YOU OFF, HUH?
YOU HAVE NO IDEA.
I'VE HAD RELIGION FORCED ON ME MY WHOLE LIFE. I THINK I KNOW A THING OR TWO ABOUT CHRISTIANITY.
AT LEAST ENOUGH TO MAKE UP MY OWN MIND.
NIETZSCHE WAS WRONG. YOU HAVE TO BE ALIVE FIRST TO BE DEAD SECOND.

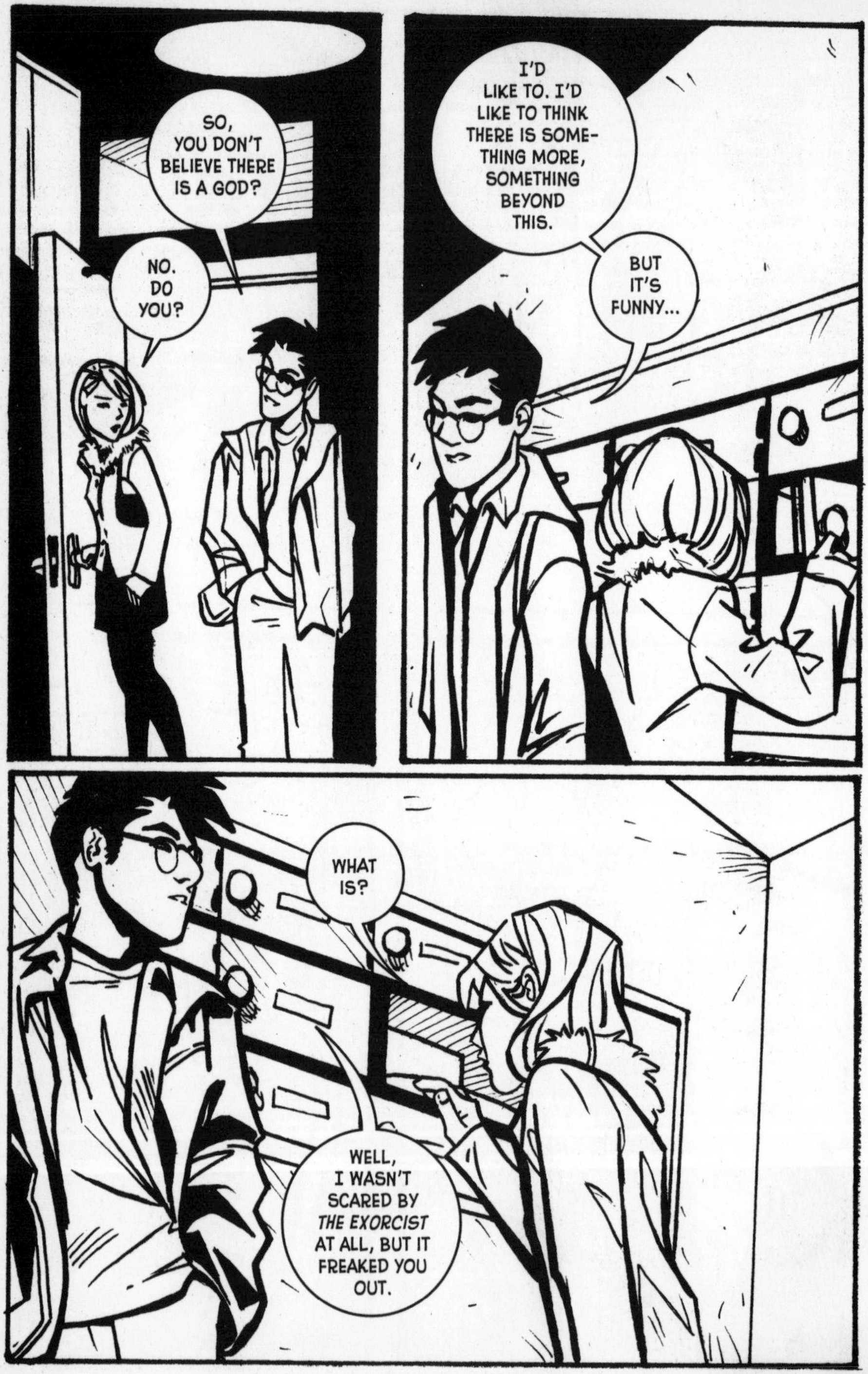
SO, YOU DON'T BELIEVE THERE IS A GOD?
NO. DO YOU?
I'D LIKE TO. I'D LIKE TO THINK THERE IS SOMETHING MORE, SOMETHING BEYOND THIS.
BUT IT'S FUNNY...
WHAT IS?
WELL, I WASN'T SCARED BY *THE EXORCIST* AT ALL, BUT IT FREAKED YOU OUT.

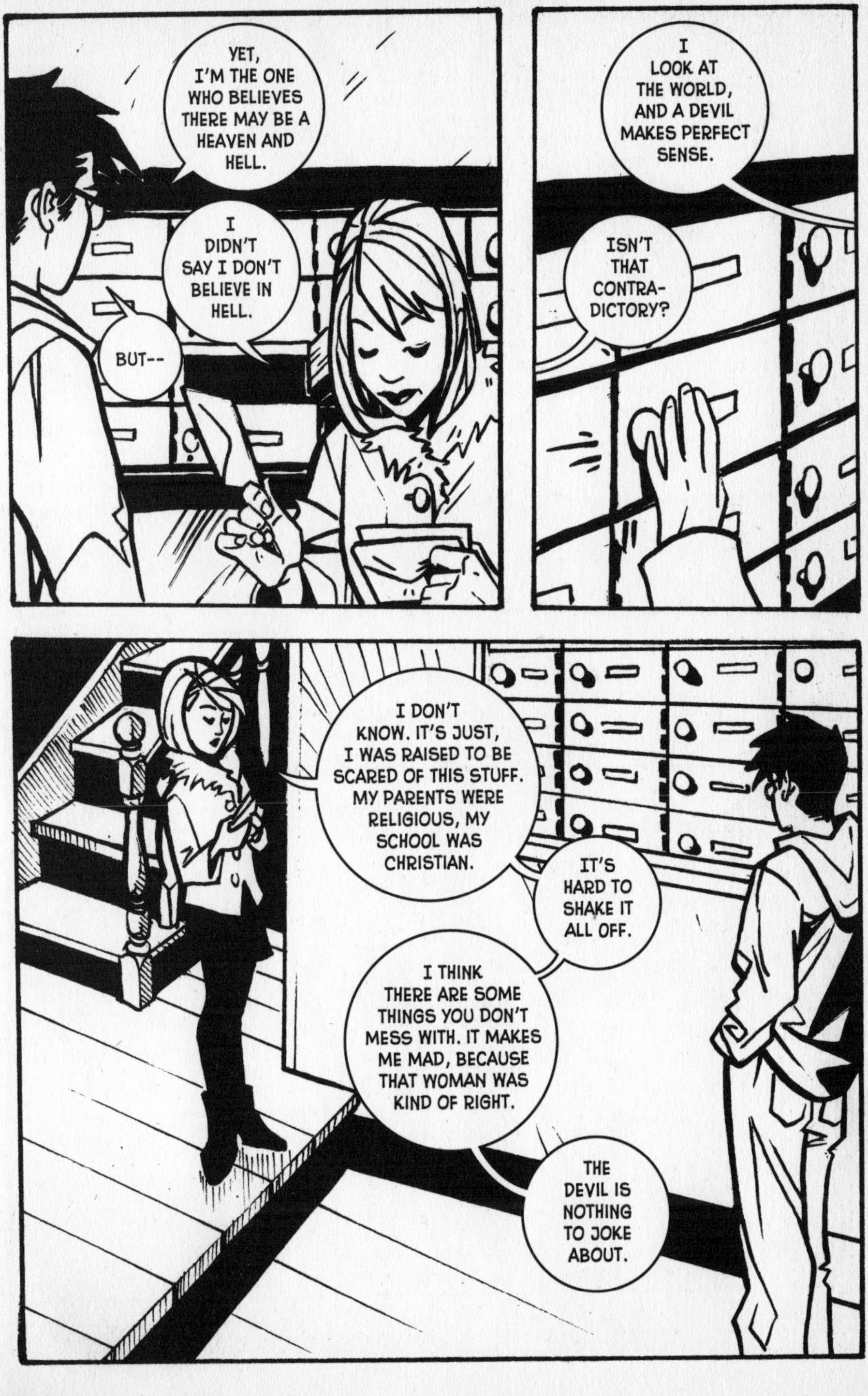
YET, I'M THE ONE WHO BELIEVES THERE MAY BE A HEAVEN AND HELL.
I DIDN'T SAY I DON'T BELIEVE IN HELL.
BUT--
I LOOK AT THE WORLD, AND A DEVIL MAKES PERFECT SENSE.
ISN'T THAT CONTRA-DICTORY?
I DON'T KNOW. IT'S JUST, I WAS RAISED TO BE SCARED OF THIS STUFF. MY PARENTS WERE RELIGIOUS, MY SCHOOL WAS CHRISTIAN.
IT'S HARD TO SHAKE IT ALL OFF.
I THINK THERE ARE SOME THINGS YOU DON'T MESS WITH. IT MAKES ME MAD, BECAUSE THAT WOMAN WAS KIND OF RIGHT.
THE DEVIL IS NOTHING TO JOKE ABOUT.

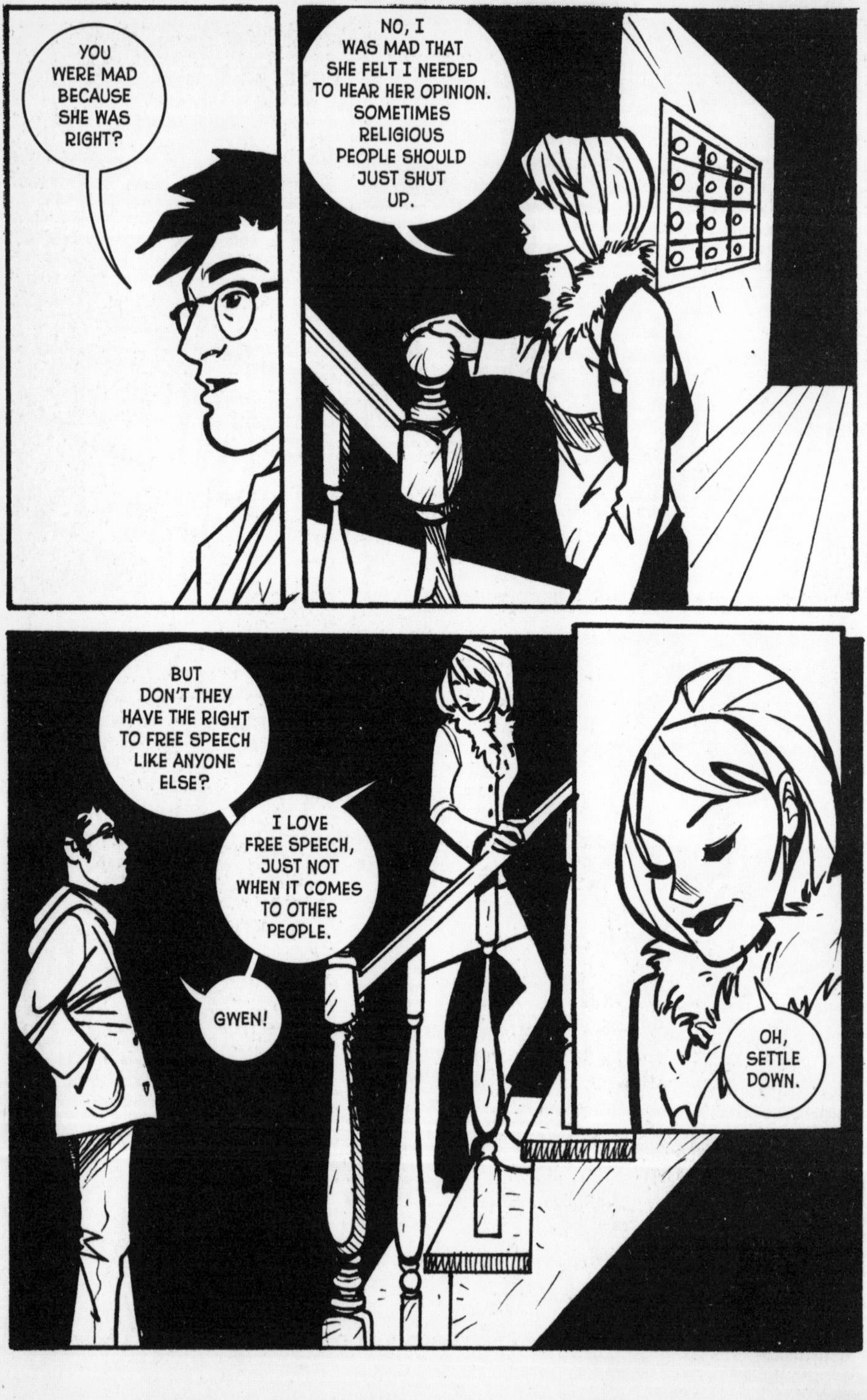
YOU WERE MAD BECAUSE SHE WAS RIGHT?
NO, I WAS MAD THAT SHE FELT I NEEDED TO HEAR HER OPINION. SOMETIMES RELIGIOUS PEOPLE SHOULD JUST SHUT UP.
BUT DON'T THEY HAVE THE RIGHT TO FREE SPEECH LIKE ANYONE ELSE?
I LOVE FREE SPEECH, JUST NOT WHEN IT COMES TO OTHER PEOPLE.
GWEN!
OH, SETTLE DOWN.

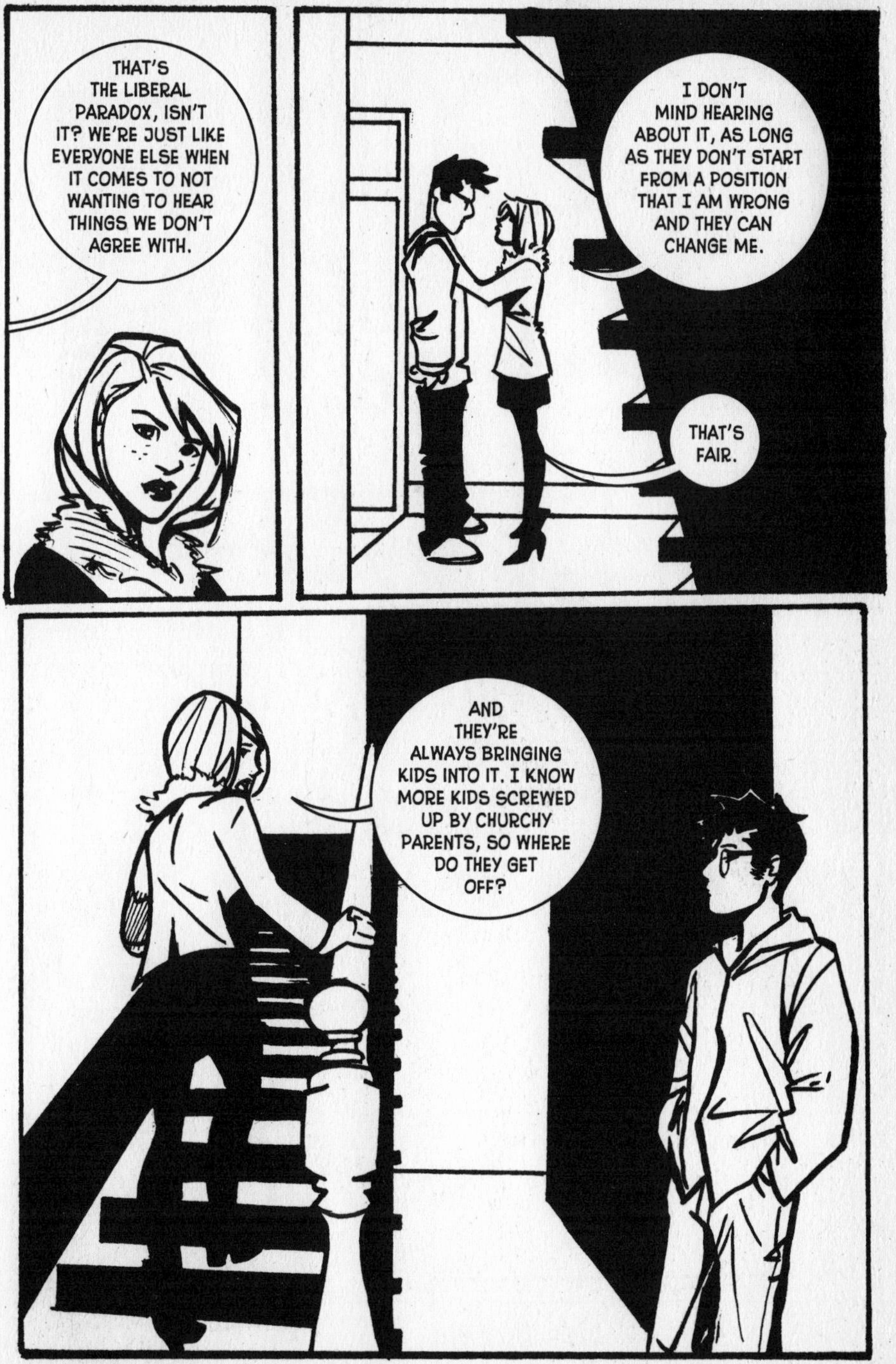
THAT'S THE LIBERAL PARADOX, ISN'T IT? WE'RE JUST LIKE EVERYONE ELSE WHEN IT COMES TO NOT WANTING TO HEAR THINGS WE DON'T AGREE WITH.
I DON'T MIND HEARING ABOUT IT, AS LONG AS THEY DON'T START FROM A POSITION THAT I AM WRONG AND THEY CAN CHANGE ME.
THAT'S FAIR.
AND THEY'RE ALWAYS BRINGING KIDS INTO IT. I KNOW MORE KIDS SCREWED UP BY CHURCHY PARENTS, SO WHERE DO THEY GET OFF?

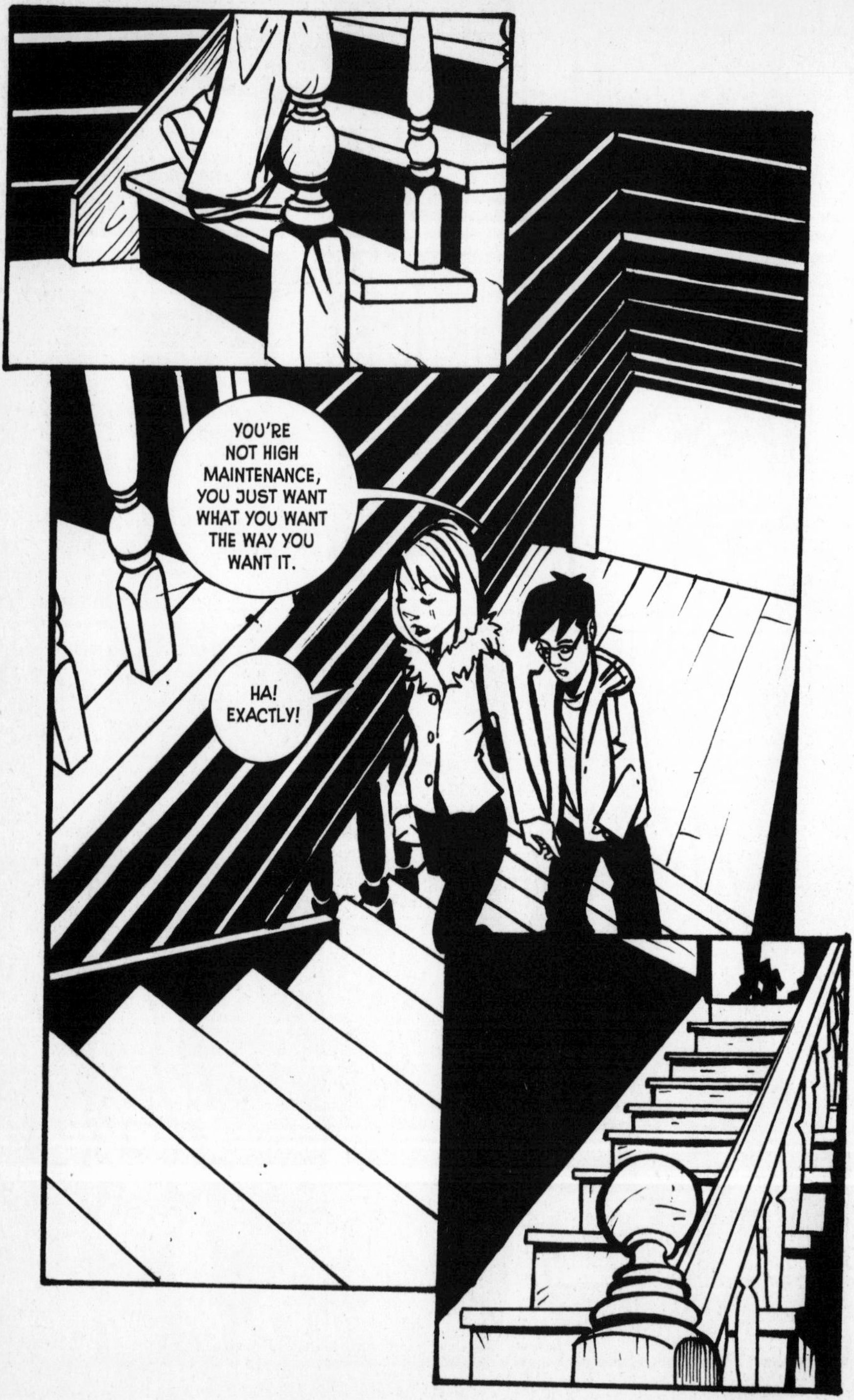
YOU'RE NOT HIGH MAINTENANCE, YOU JUST WANT WHAT YOU WANT THE WAY YOU WANT IT.
HA! EXACTLY!

Six

SONG

Menswear

"Can't Smile Without You"

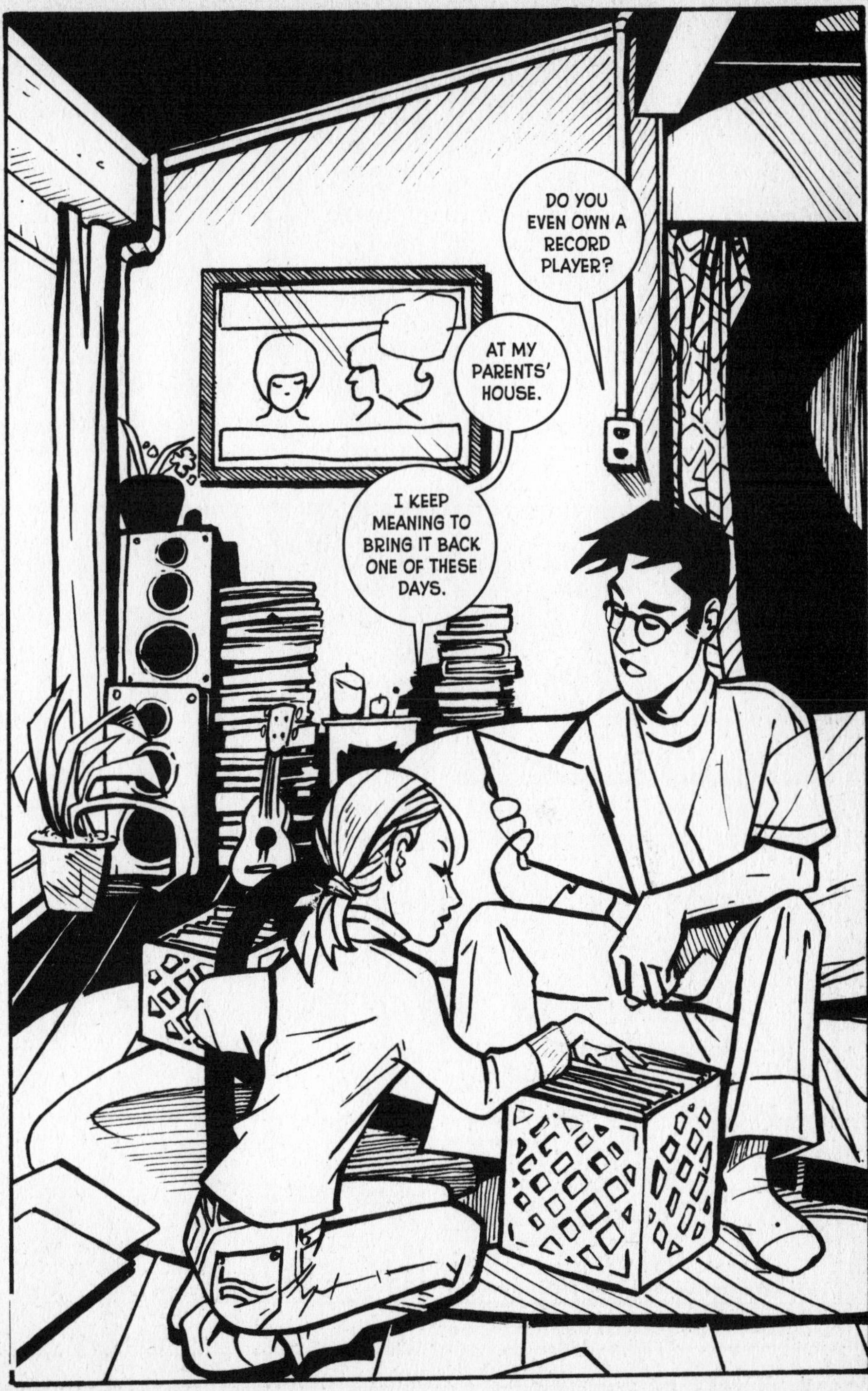
DO YOU EVEN OWN A RECORD PLAYER?
AT MY PARENTS' HOUSE.
I KEEP MEANING TO BRING IT BACK ONE OF THESE DAYS.

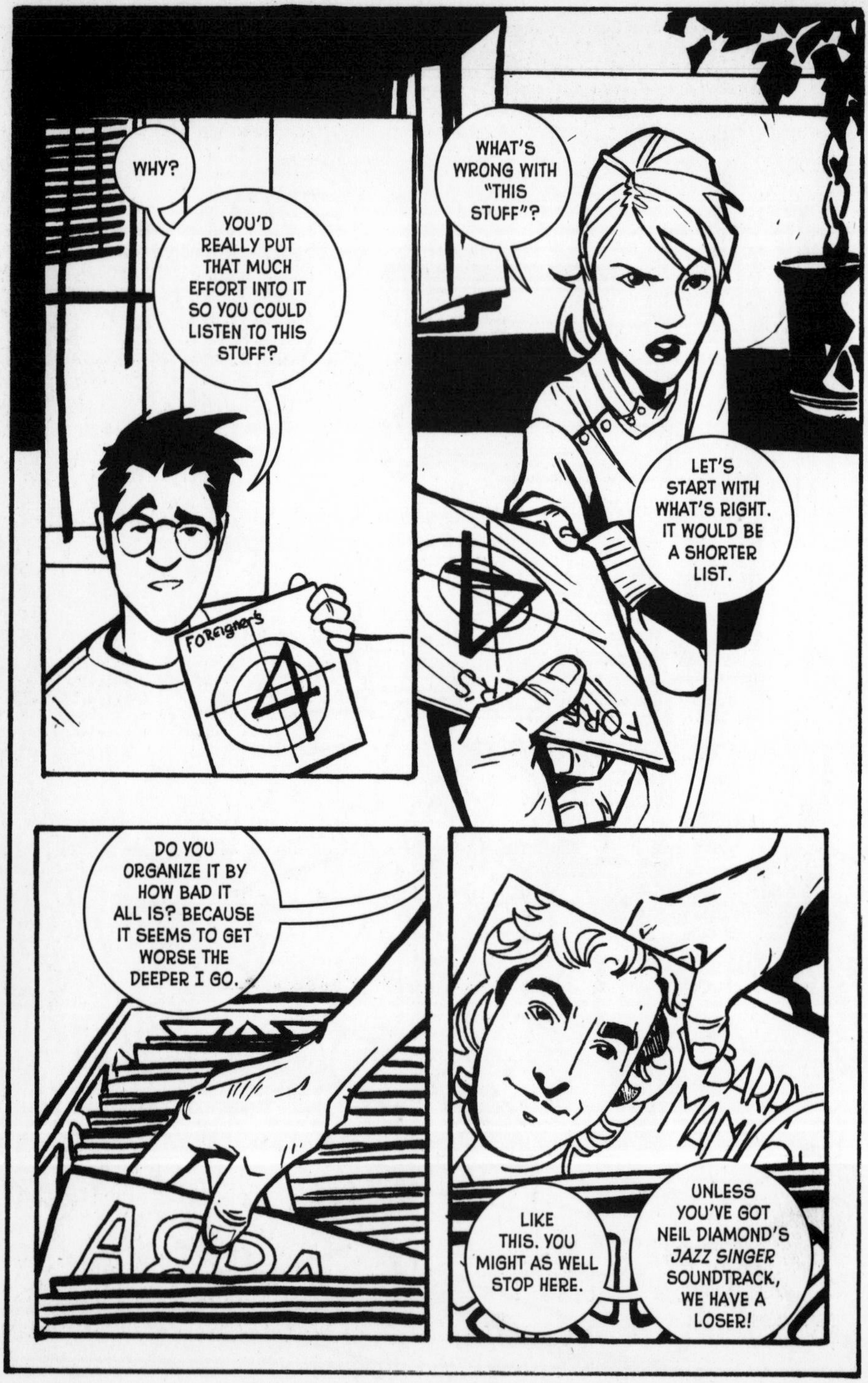
WHY?
YOU'D REALLY PUT THAT MUCH EFFORT INTO IT SO YOU COULD LISTEN TO THIS STUFF?
FOREIGNER'S 4
WHAT'S WRONG WITH "THIS STUFF"?
LET'S START WITH WHAT'S RIGHT. IT WOULD BE A SHORTER LIST.
DO YOU ORGANIZE IT BY HOW BAD IT ALL IS? BECAUSE IT SEEMS TO GET WORSE THE DEEPER I GO.
LIKE THIS. YOU MIGHT AS WELL STOP HERE.
UNLESS YOU'VE GOT NEIL DIAMOND'S *JAZZ SINGER* SOUNDTRACK, WE HAVE A LOSER!

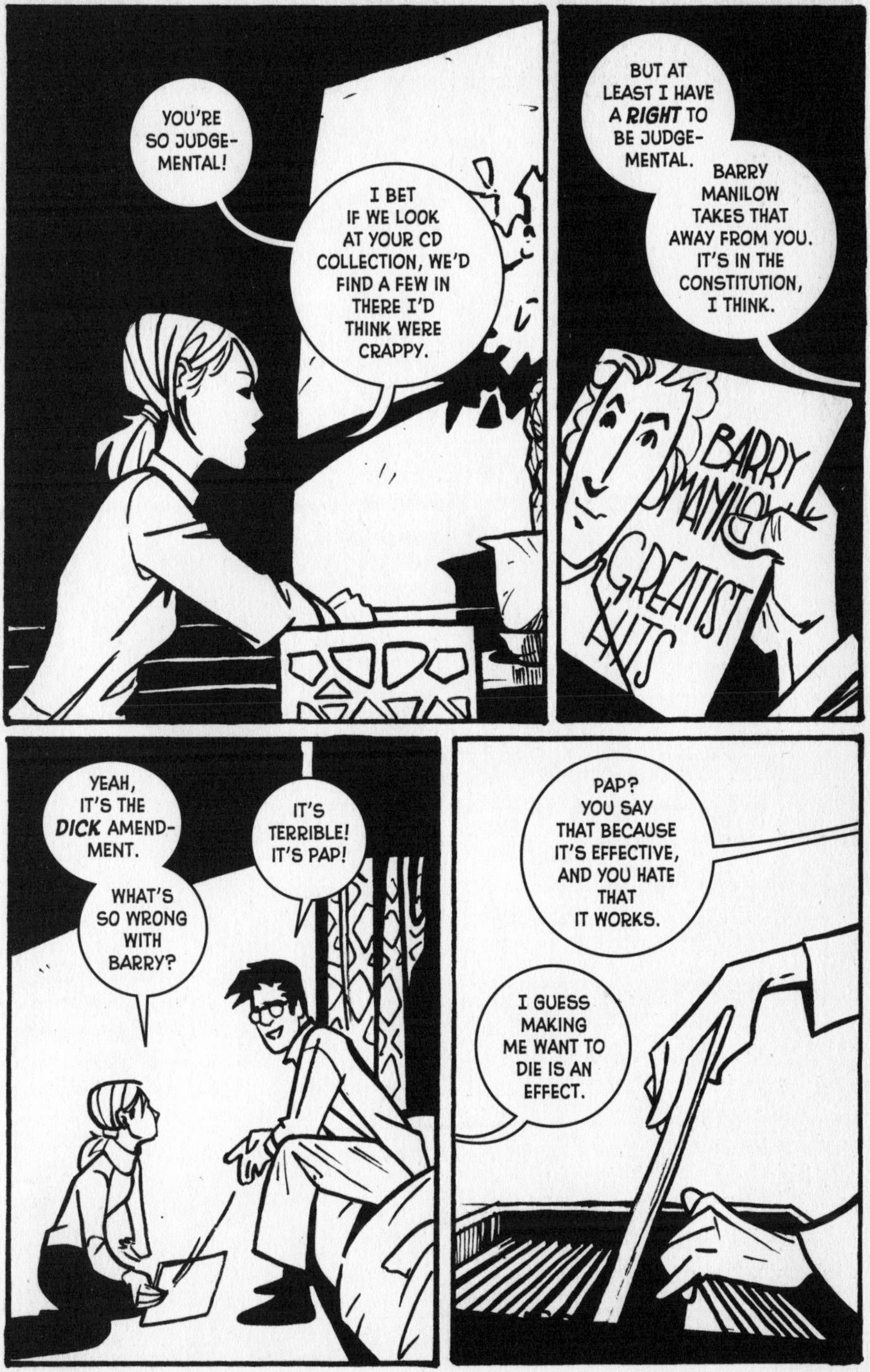
YOU'RE SO JUDGE-MENTAL!
I BET IF WE LOOK AT YOUR CD COLLECTION, WE'D FIND A FEW IN THERE I'D THINK WERE CRAPPY.
BUT AT LEAST I HAVE A *RIGHT* TO BE JUDGE-MENTAL.
BARRY MANILOW TAKES THAT AWAY FROM YOU. IT'S IN THE CONSTITUTION, I THINK.
BARRY MANILOW GREATIST HITS
YEAH, IT'S THE *DICK* AMEND-MENT.
WHAT'S SO WRONG WITH BARRY?
IT'S TERRIBLE! IT'S PAP!
PAP? YOU SAY THAT BECAUSE IT'S EFFECTIVE, AND YOU HATE THAT IT WORKS.
I GUESS MAKING ME WANT TO DIE IS AN EFFECT.

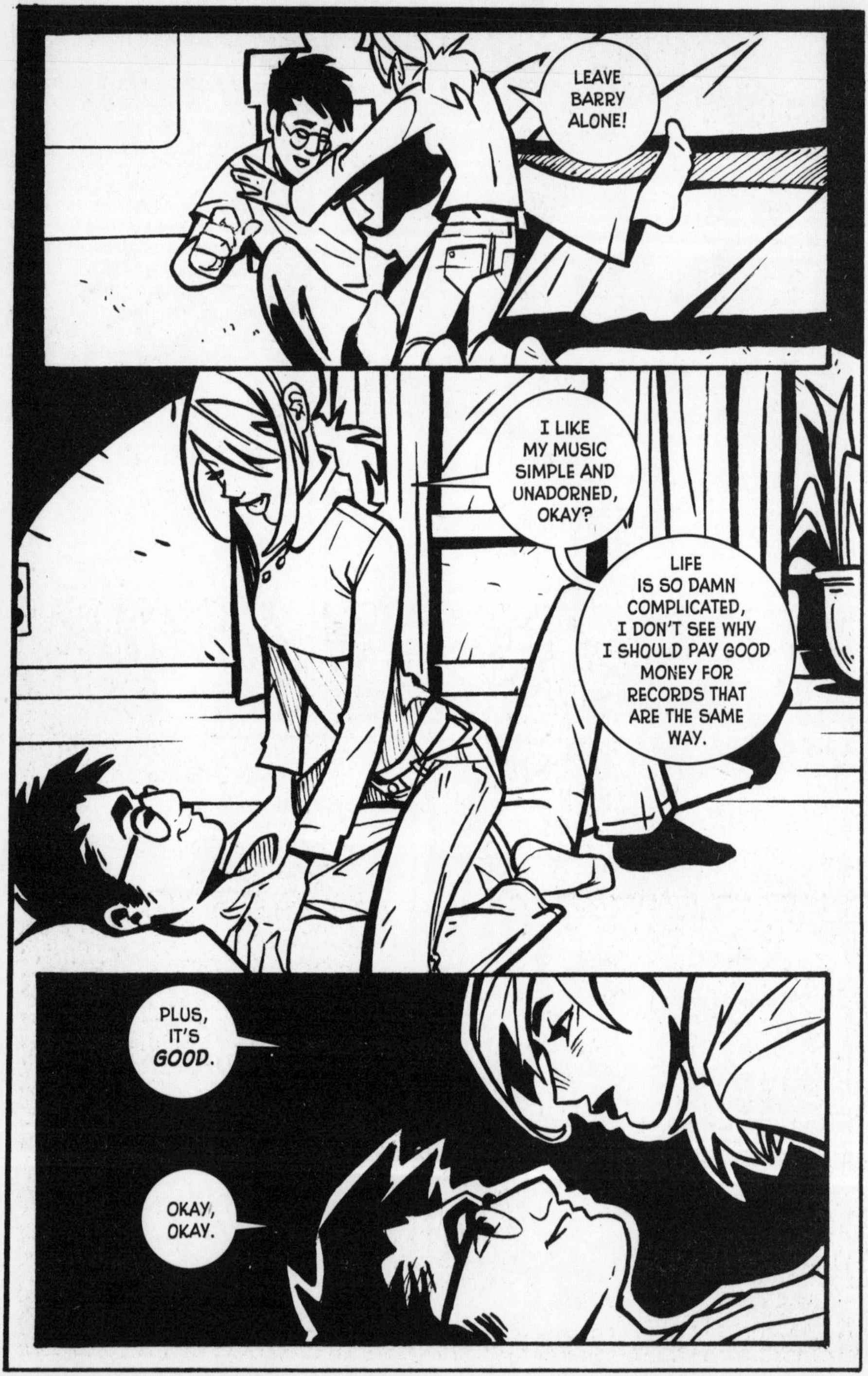
LEAVE BARRY ALONE!
I LIKE MY MUSIC SIMPLE AND UNADORNED, OKAY?
LIFE IS SO DAMN COMPLICATED, I DON'T SEE WHY I SHOULD PAY GOOD MONEY FOR RECORDS THAT ARE THE SAME WAY.
PLUS, IT'S *GOOD*.
OKAY, OKAY.

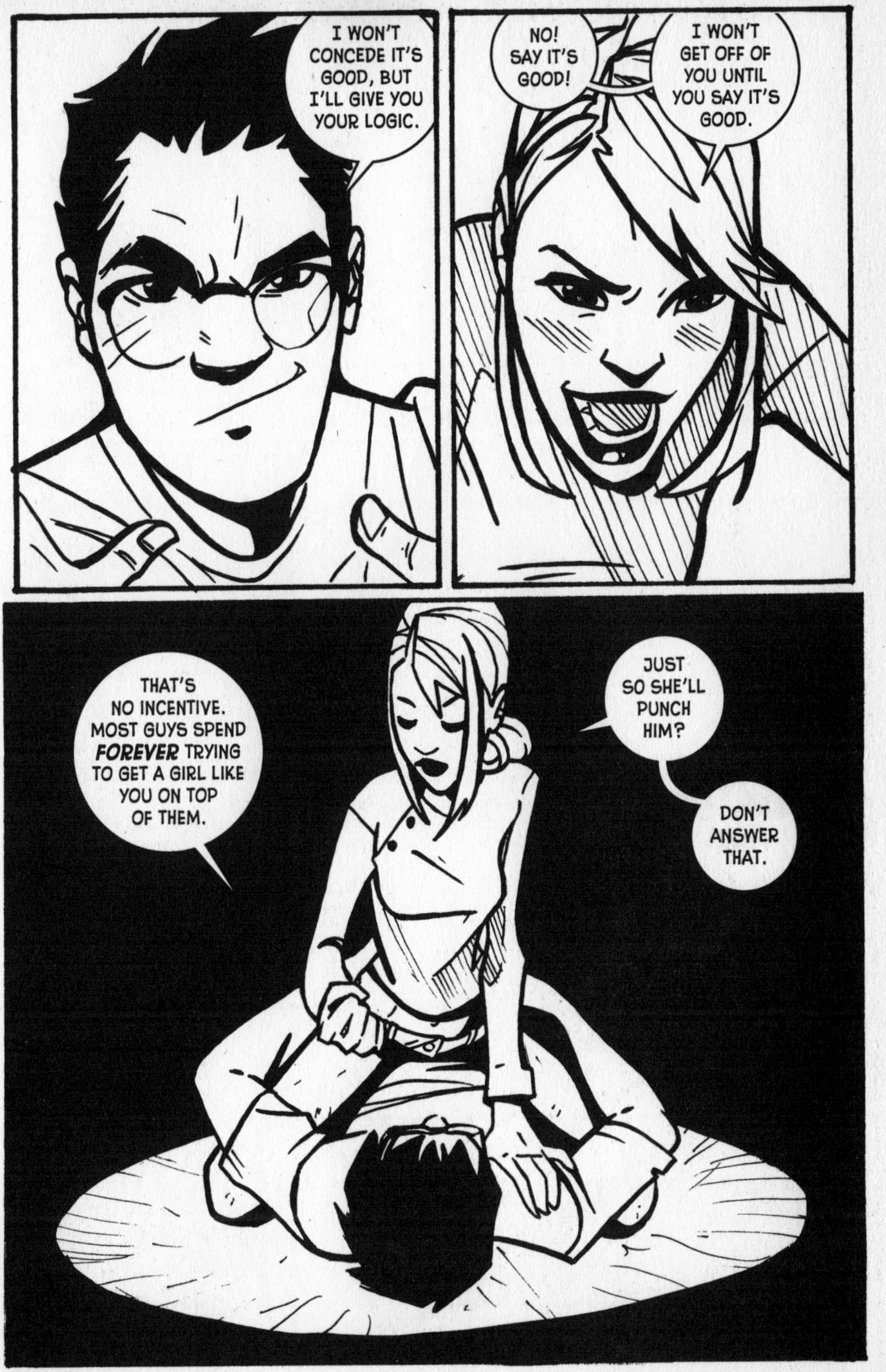
I WON'T CONCEDE IT'S GOOD, BUT I'LL GIVE YOU YOUR LOGIC.
NO! SAY IT'S GOOD!
I WON'T GET OFF OF YOU UNTIL YOU SAY IT'S GOOD.
THAT'S NO INCENTIVE. MOST GUYS SPEND **FOREVER** TRYING TO GET A GIRL LIKE YOU ON TOP OF THEM.
JUST SO SHE'LL PUNCH HIM?
DON'T ANSWER THAT.

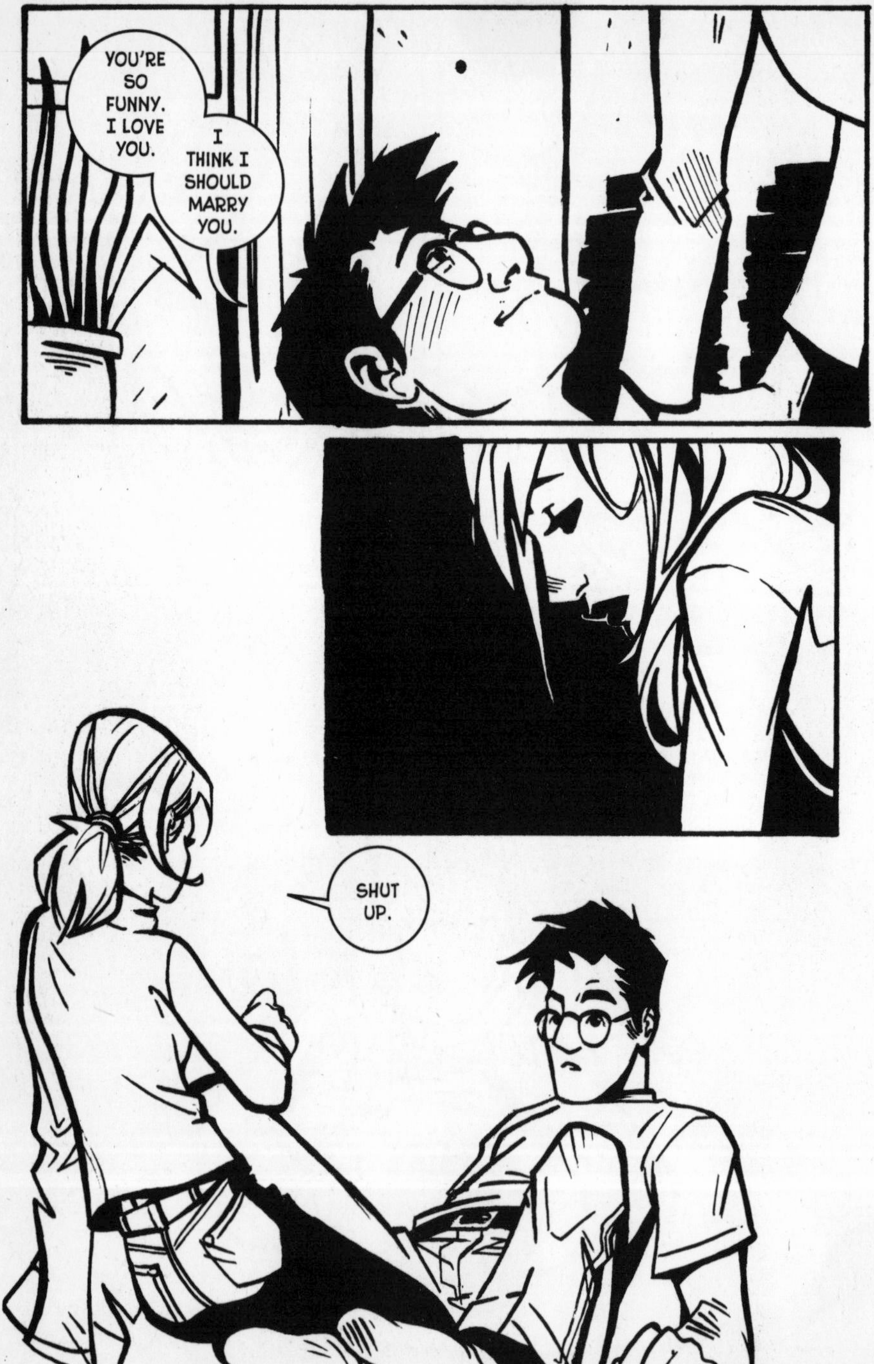
YOU'RE SO FUNNY. I LOVE YOU.
I THINK I SHOULD MARRY YOU.
SHUT UP.

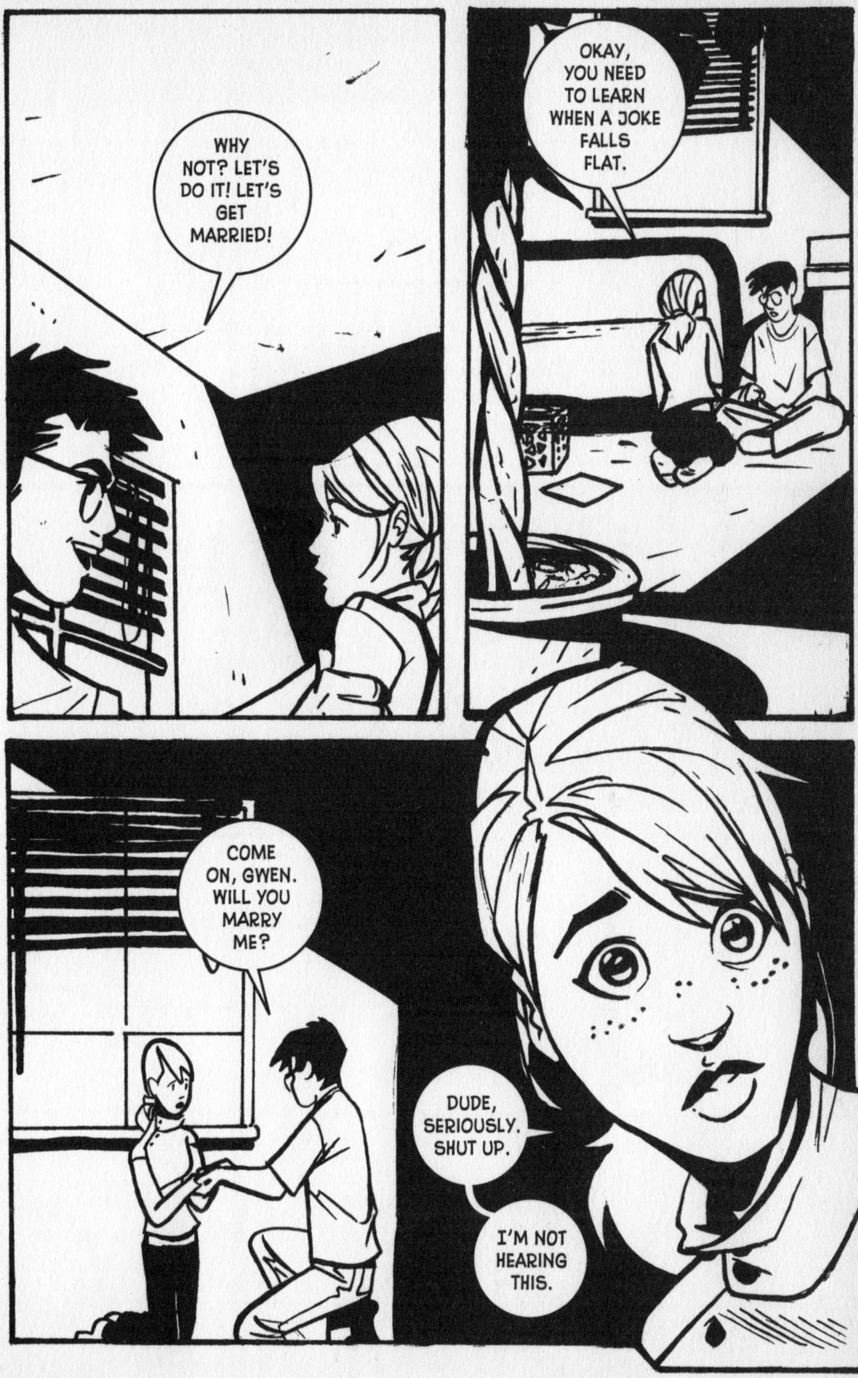
WHY NOT? LET'S DO IT! LET'S GET MARRIED!
OKAY, YOU NEED TO LEARN WHEN A JOKE FALLS FLAT.
COME ON, GWEN. WILL YOU MARRY ME?
DUDE, SERIOUSLY. SHUT UP.
I'M NOT HEARING THIS.

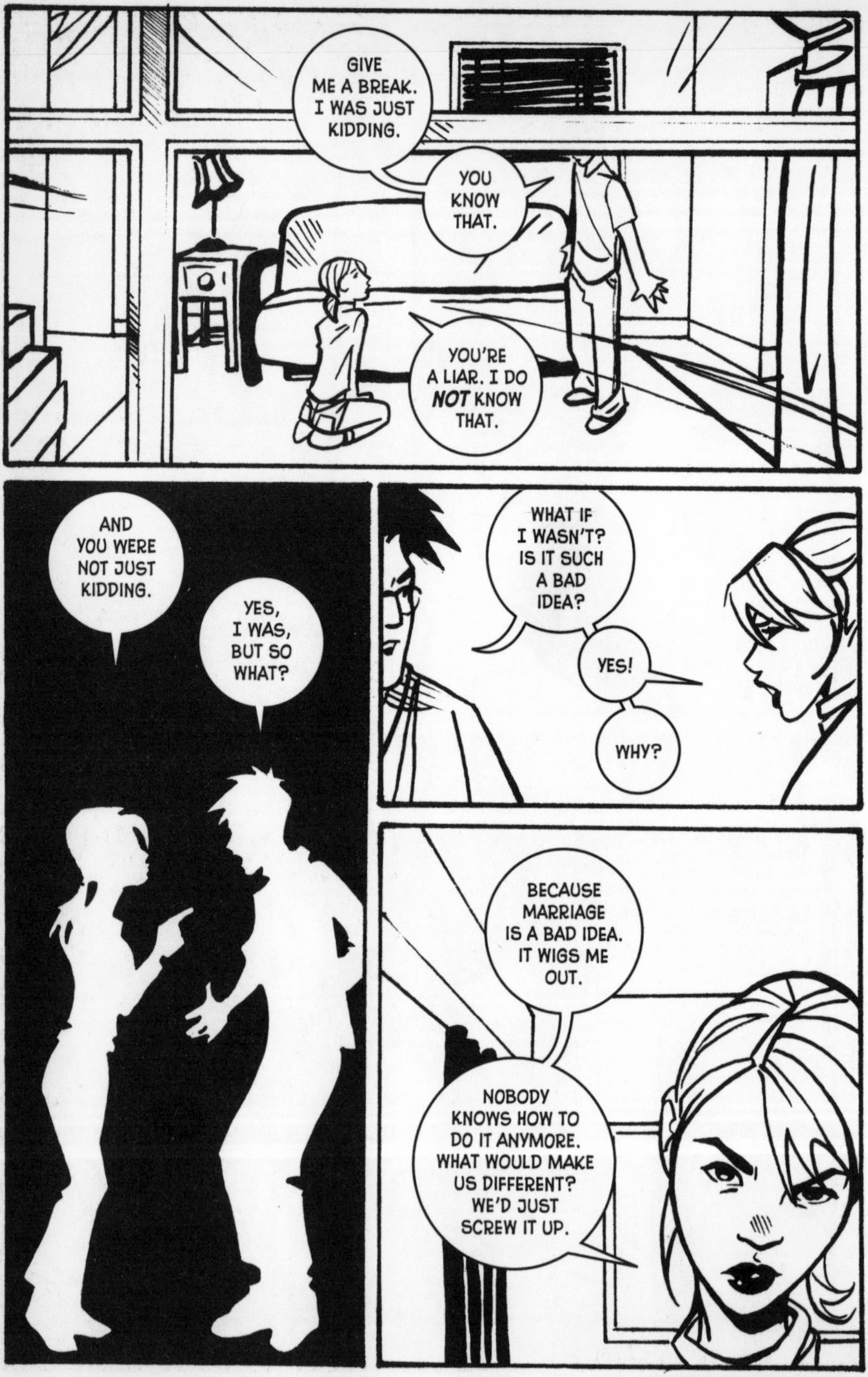
GIVE ME A BREAK. I WAS JUST KIDDING.
YOU KNOW THAT.
YOU'RE A LIAR. I DO NOT KNOW THAT.
AND YOU WERE NOT JUST KIDDING.
YES, I WAS, BUT SO WHAT?
WHAT IF I WASN'T? IS IT SUCH A BAD IDEA?
YES!
WHY?
BECAUSE MARRIAGE IS A BAD IDEA. IT WIGS ME OUT.
NOBODY KNOWS HOW TO DO IT ANYMORE. WHAT WOULD MAKE US DIFFERENT? WE'D JUST SCREW IT UP.

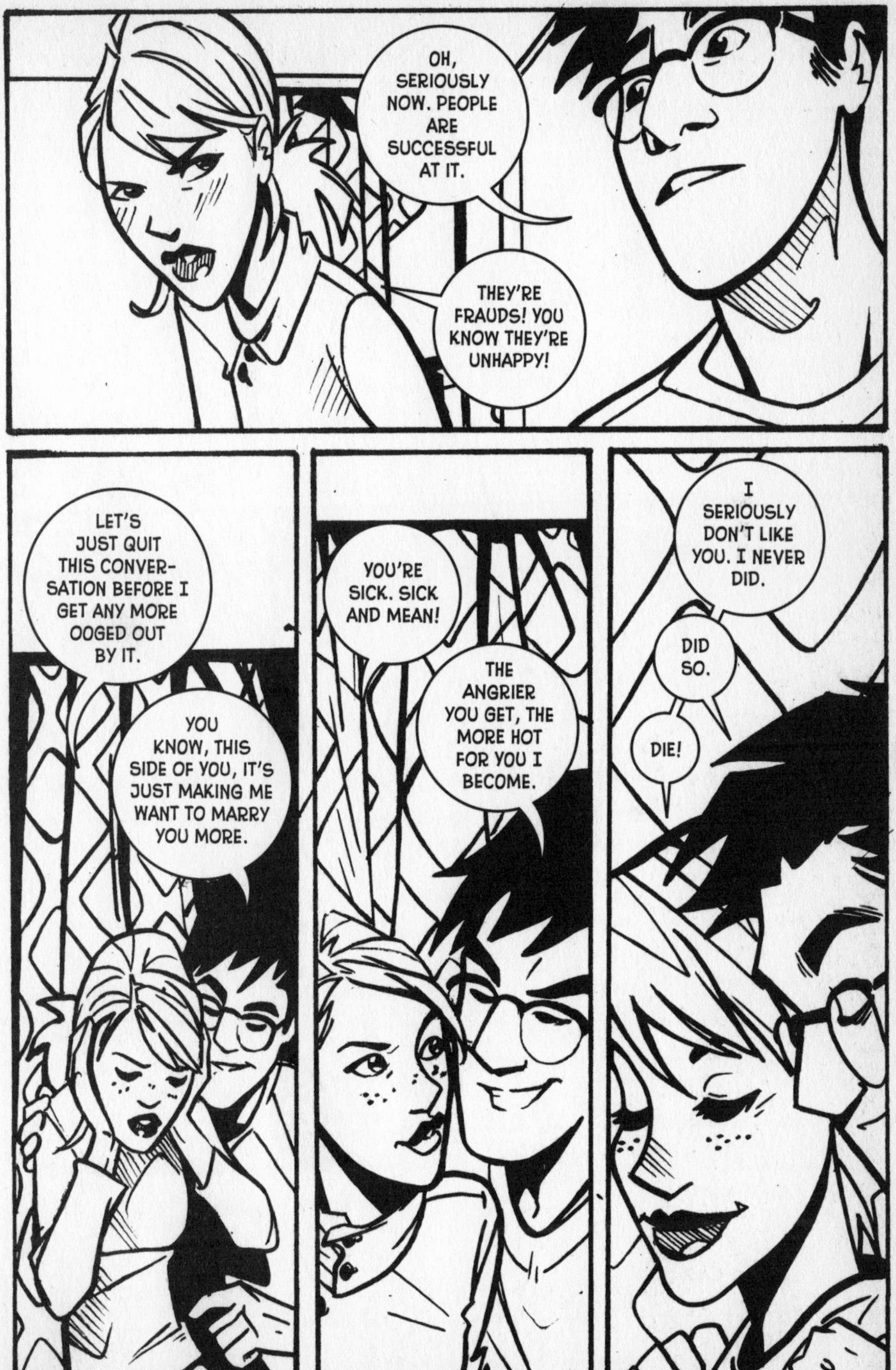
OH, SERIOUSLY NOW. PEOPLE ARE SUCCESSFUL AT IT.
THEY'RE FRAUDS! YOU KNOW THEY'RE UNHAPPY!
LET'S JUST QUIT THIS CONVER-SATION BEFORE I GET ANY MORE OOGED OUT BY IT.
YOU KNOW, THIS SIDE OF YOU, IT'S JUST MAKING ME WANT TO MARRY YOU MORE.
YOU'RE SICK. SICK AND MEAN!
THE ANGRIER YOU GET, THE MORE HOT FOR YOU I BECOME.
I SERIOUSLY DON'T LIKE YOU. I NEVER DID.
DID SO.
DIE!

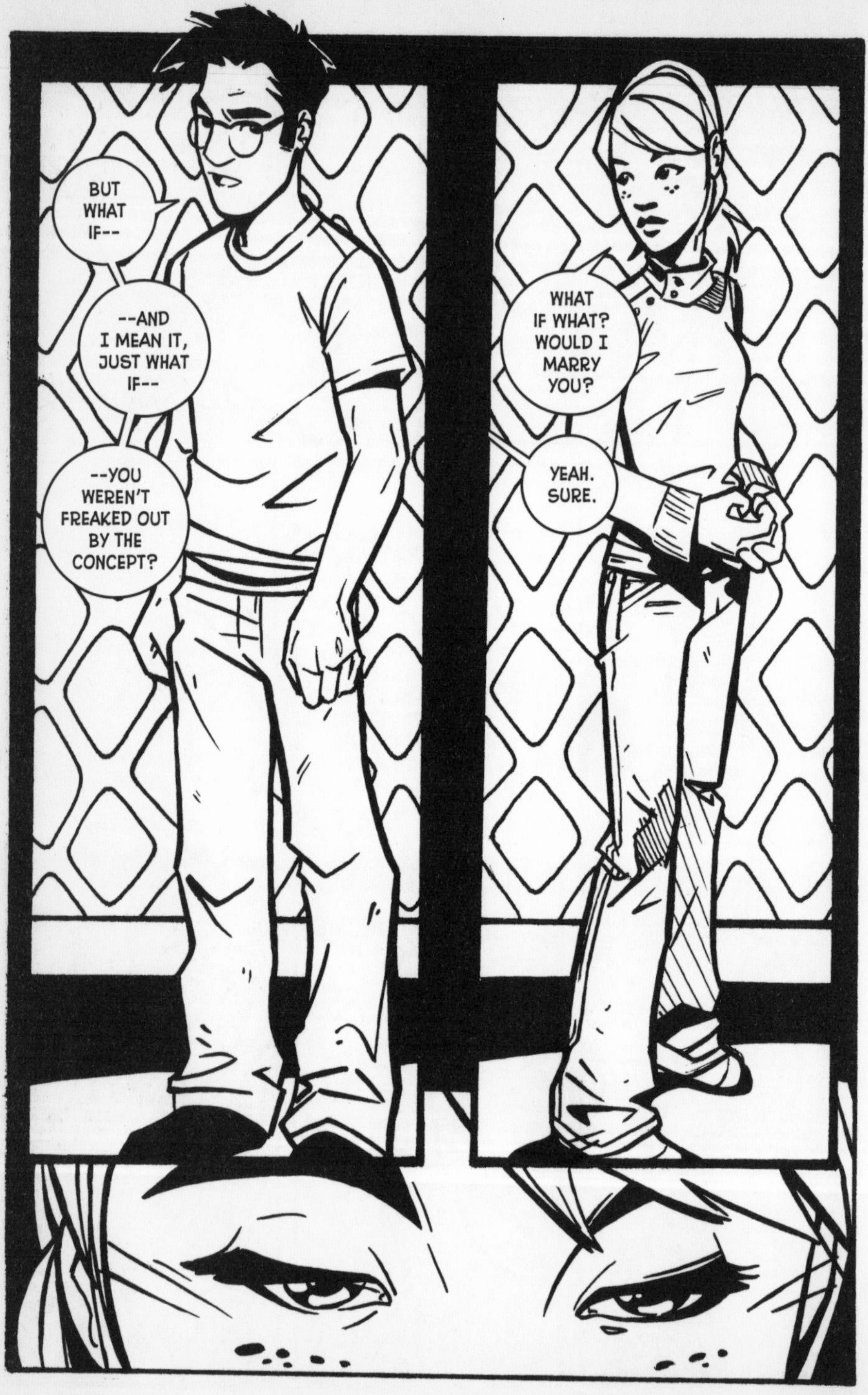
BUT WHAT IF--
--AND I MEAN IT, JUST WHAT IF--
--YOU WEREN'T FREAKED OUT BY THE CONCEPT?
WHAT IF WHAT? WOULD I MARRY YOU?
YEAH. SURE.

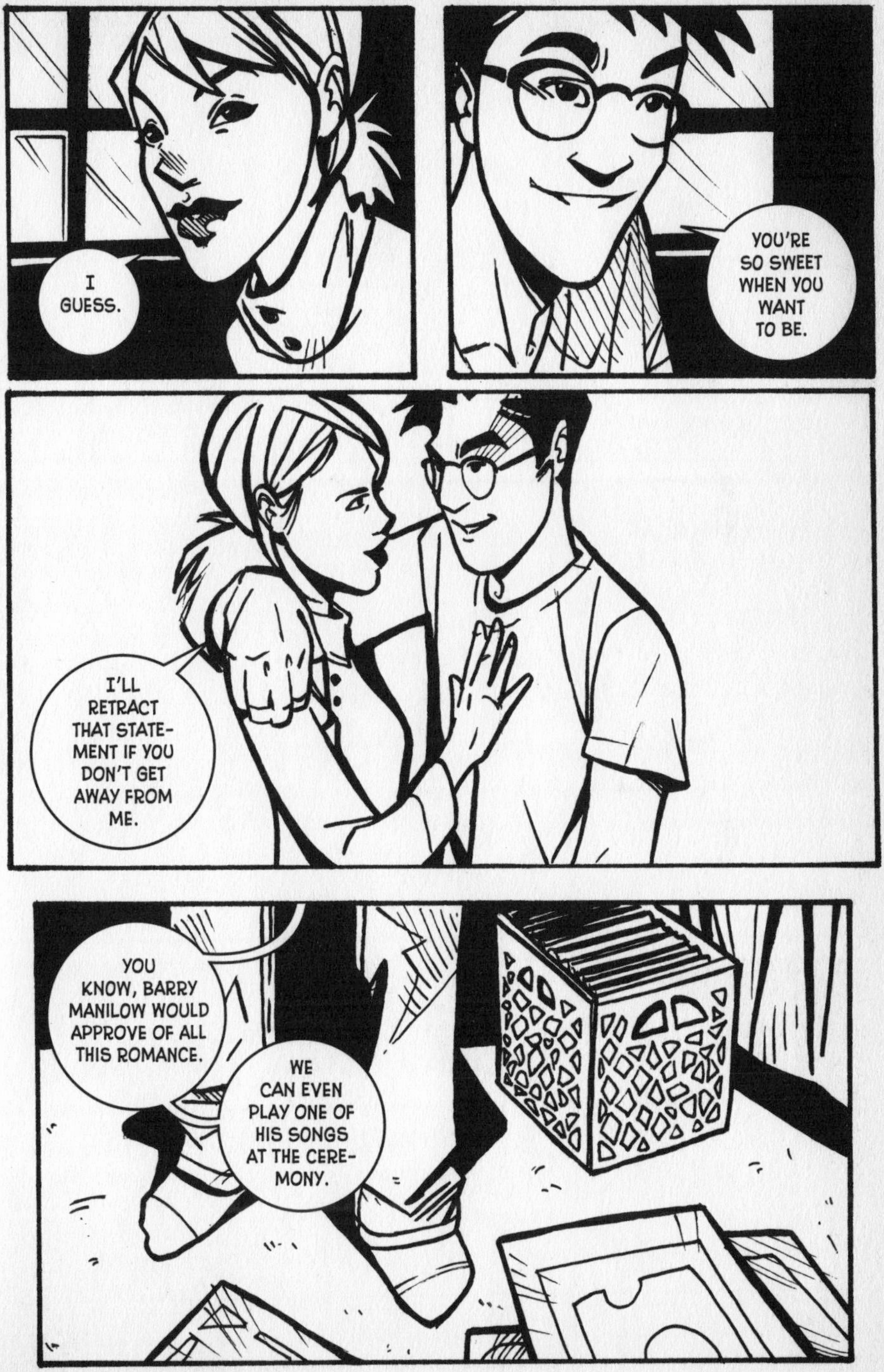
I GUESS.
YOU'RE SO SWEET WHEN YOU WANT TO BE.
I'LL RETRACT THAT STATE-MENT IF YOU DON'T GET AWAY FROM ME.
YOU KNOW, BARRY MANILOW WOULD APPROVE OF ALL THIS ROMANCE.
WE CAN EVEN PLAY ONE OF HIS SONGS AT THE CERE-MONY.

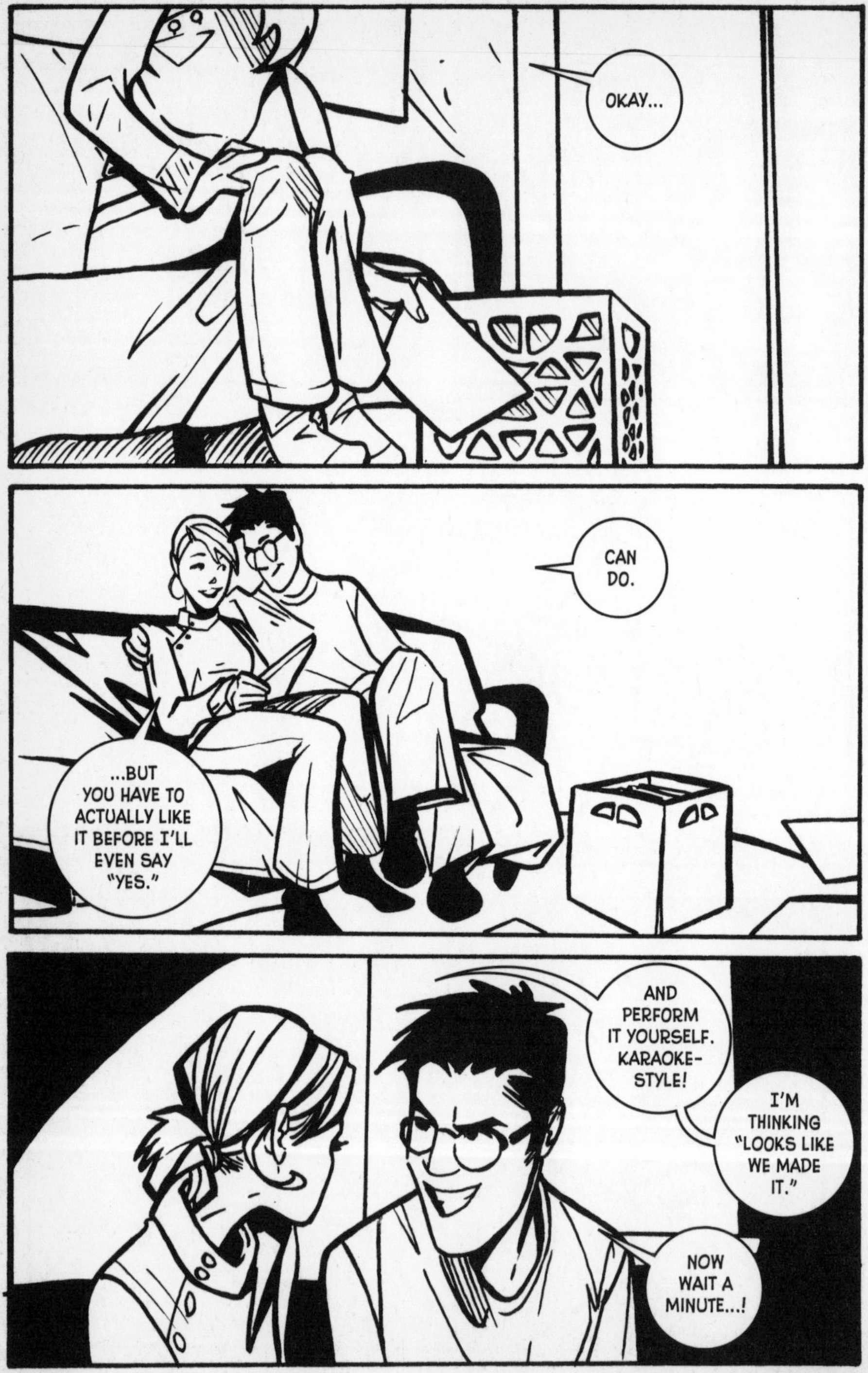
OKAY...
CAN DO.
...BUT YOU HAVE TO ACTUALLY LIKE IT BEFORE I'LL EVEN SAY "YES."
AND PERFORM IT YOURSELF. KARAOKE-STYLE!
I'M THINKING "LOOKS LIKE WE MADE IT."
NOW WAIT A MINUTE...!

Seven

SONG

Buffy Sainte-Marie
"Goodnight"

One night Gwen was making little noises in her sleep. I woke her and asked her what she was dreaming. "I wasn't," she said, and I insisted she mist have been, otherwise why was she making the noises

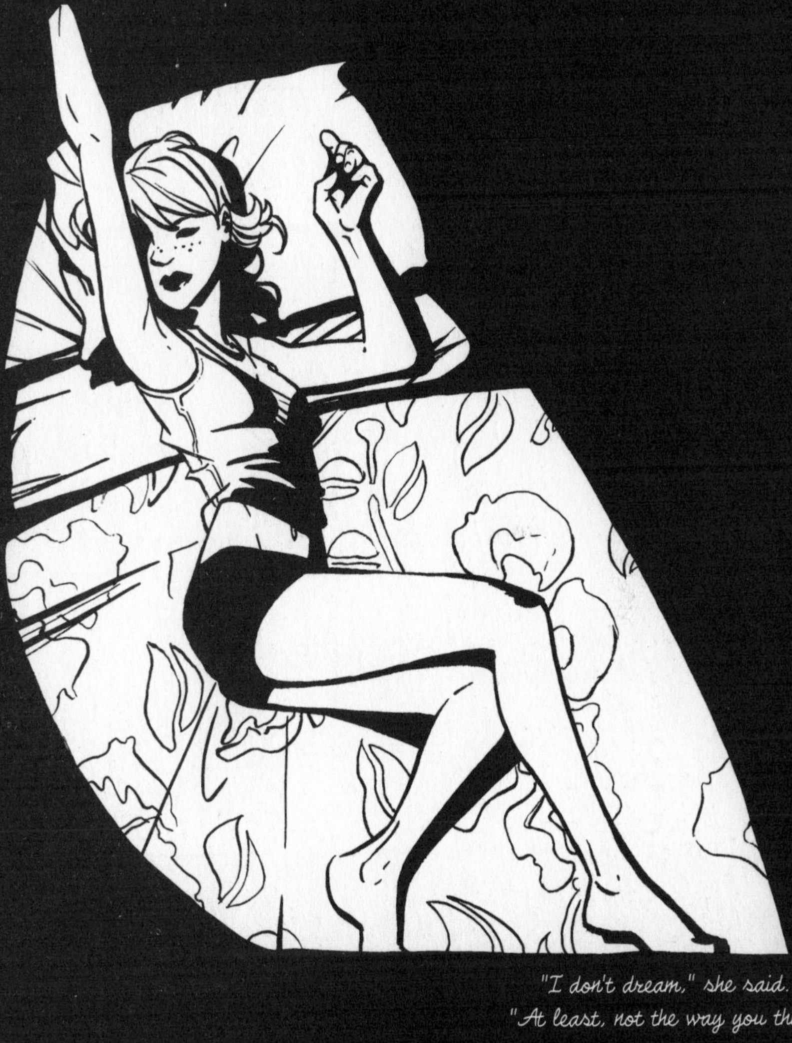

"I don't dream," she said. "At least, not the way you think."

She said she didn't like the sloppiness of real dreams, all the things that didn't make sense. Instead, she had all her dreams before she went to sleep. "As I'm drifting off, I think about all the good things I want. I create my own scenes in my head."

She says she dresses the world up as she would like to see it. Everyone is wearing classic Chinese dresses with high necks, like Maggie Cheung does in *In the Mood for Love*.

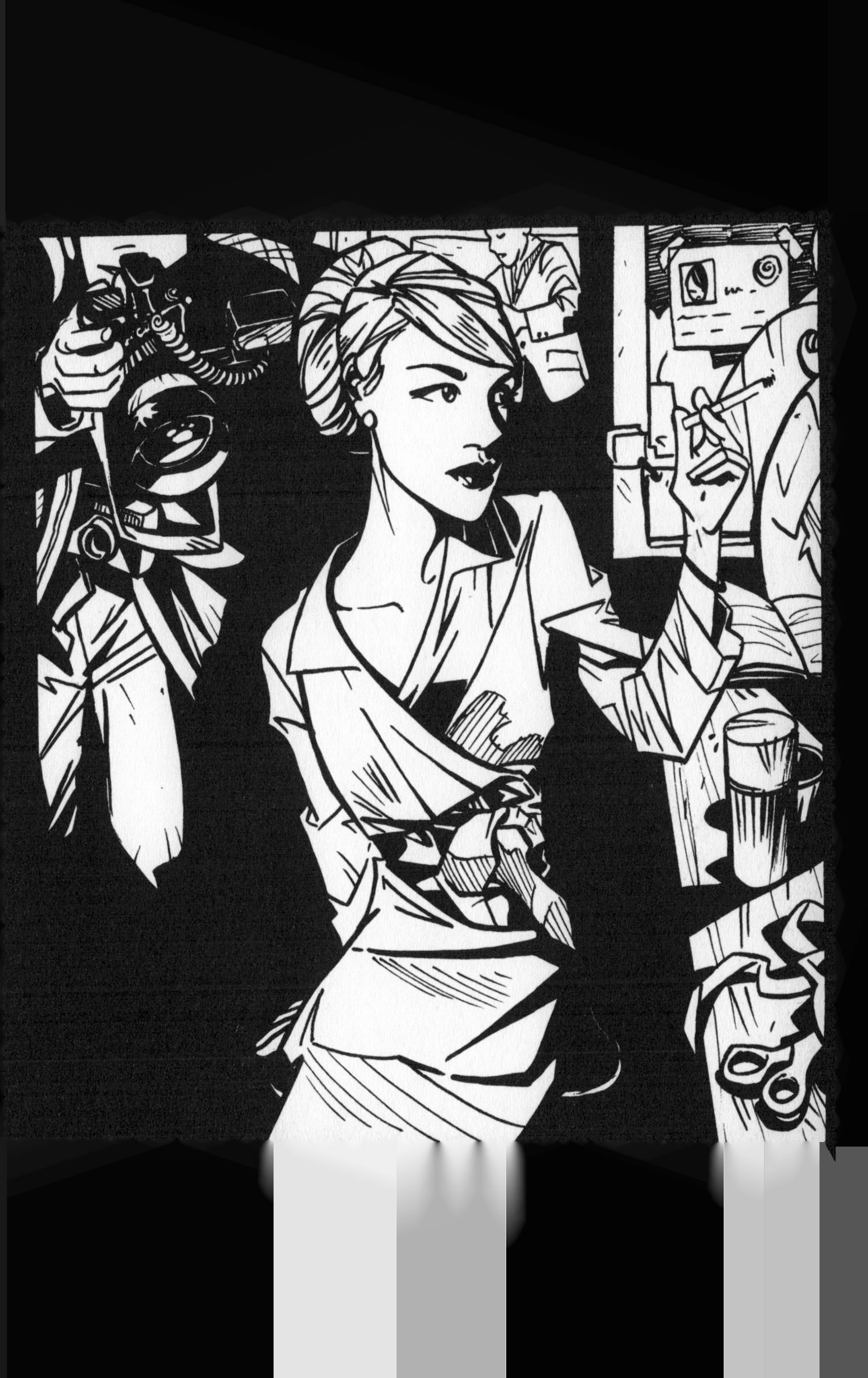

I asked her once if I was ever in this future, where I fit in the whole thing. She said I showed up occasionally. I was a professor at a prestigious college, where I wrote influential texts, inspired by her, on the reflection of fashion in literature. Like, the sparse text of Graham Greene matching the straight-forward, functional clothes of the '50s.

All the female students would be in love with me, and I would enjoy their attention.

Of course, I only have eyes for one girl.

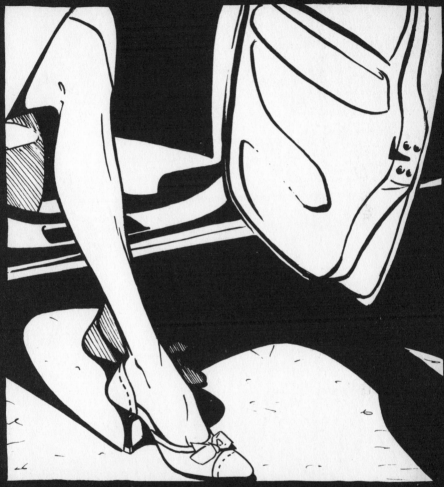

(Though it surprises me a little that she imagines a future with me
in it. It's flattering, and confirms my hopes and suspicions
about how she really sees having a life together.
Not so jaded after all, is she?)

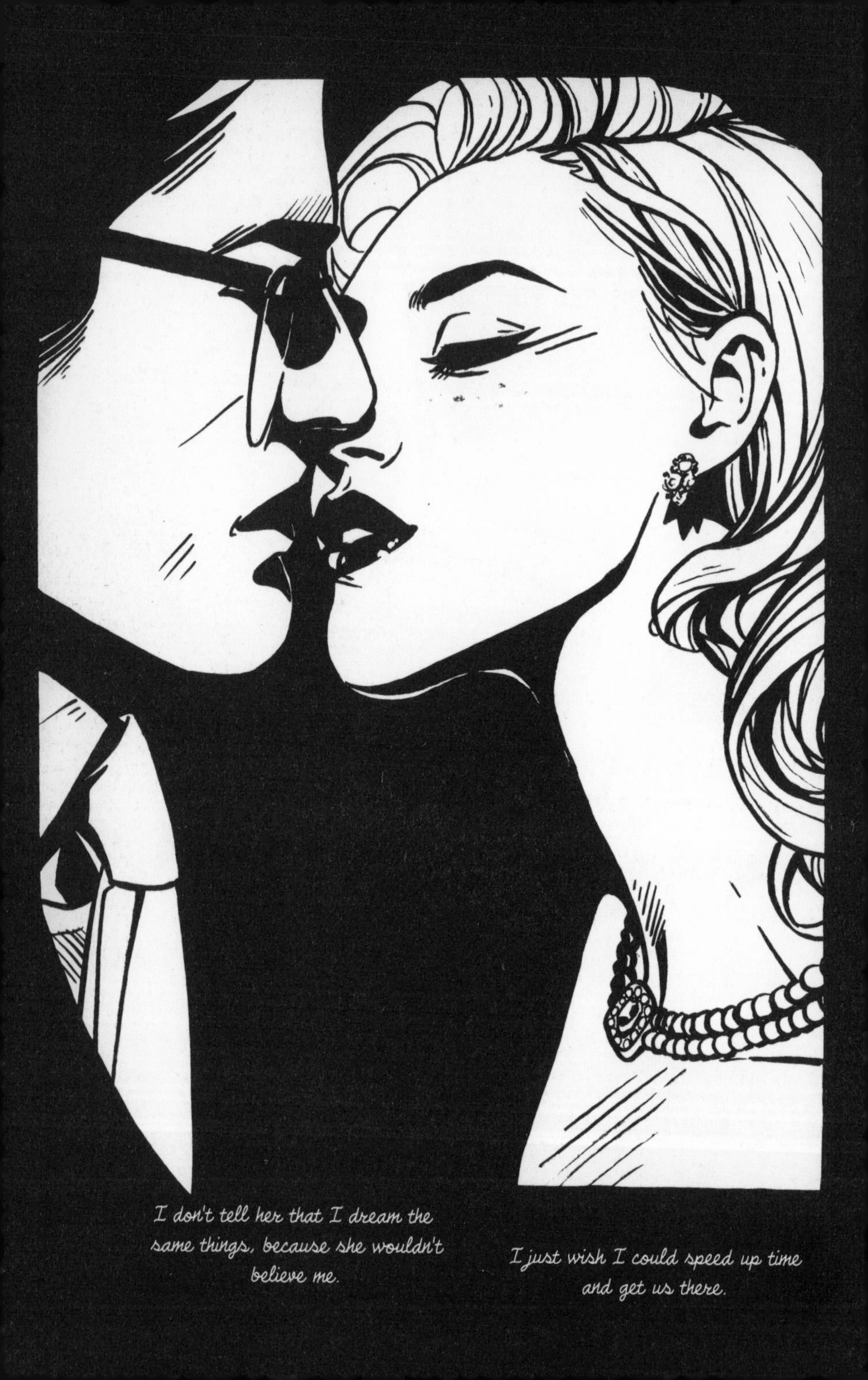
I don't tell her that I dream the same things, because she wouldn't believe me.
I just wish I could speed up time and get us there.

Eight

SONG

Travis

"We Are Monkeys"

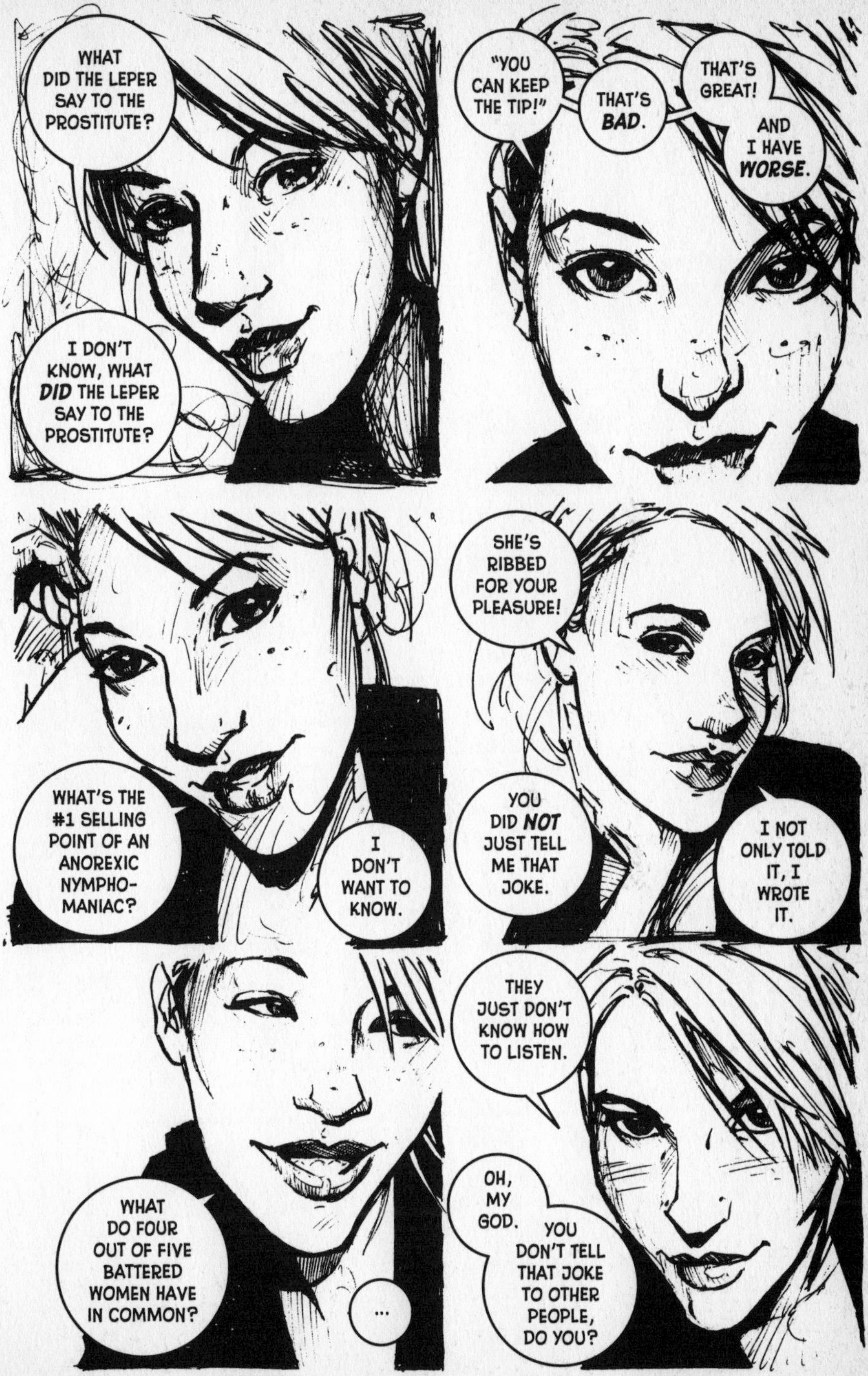
WHAT DID THE LEPER SAY TO THE PROSTITUTE?
I DON'T KNOW, WHAT DID THE LEPER SAY TO THE PROSTITUTE?
"YOU CAN KEEP THE TIP!"
THAT'S BAD.
THAT'S GREAT!
AND I HAVE WORSE.
WHAT'S THE #1 SELLING POINT OF AN ANOREXIC NYMPHO-MANIAC?
I DON'T WANT TO KNOW.
SHE'S RIBBED FOR YOUR PLEASURE!
YOU DID NOT JUST TELL ME THAT JOKE.
I NOT ONLY TOLD IT, I WROTE IT.
WHAT DO FOUR OUT OF FIVE BATTERED WOMEN HAVE IN COMMON?
...
THEY JUST DON'T KNOW HOW TO LISTEN.
OH, MY GOD.
YOU DON'T TELL THAT JOKE TO OTHER PEOPLE, DO YOU?

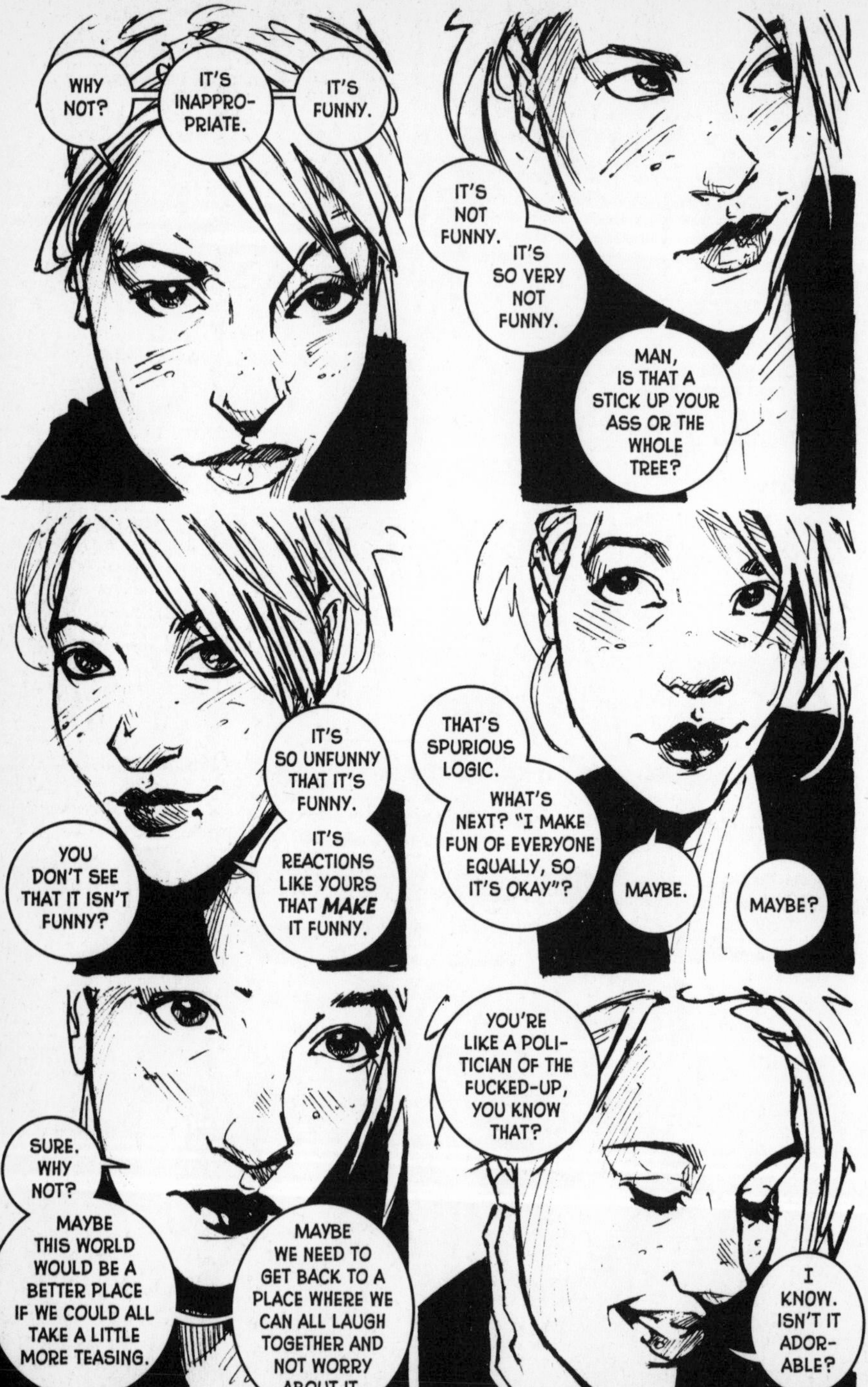
WHY NOT?
IT'S INAPPRO-PRIATE.
IT'S FUNNY.
IT'S NOT FUNNY.
IT'S SO VERY NOT FUNNY.
MAN, IS THAT A STICK UP YOUR ASS OR THE WHOLE TREE?
IT'S SO UNFUNNY THAT IT'S FUNNY.
YOU DON'T SEE THAT IT ISN'T FUNNY?
IT'S REACTIONS LIKE YOURS THAT *MAKE* IT FUNNY.
THAT'S SPURIOUS LOGIC.
WHAT'S NEXT? "I MAKE FUN OF EVERYONE EQUALLY, SO IT'S OKAY"?
MAYBE.
MAYBE?
SURE. WHY NOT?
MAYBE THIS WORLD WOULD BE A BETTER PLACE IF WE COULD ALL TAKE A LITTLE MORE TEASING.
MAYBE WE NEED TO GET BACK TO A PLACE WHERE WE CAN ALL LAUGH TOGETHER AND NOT WORRY ABOUT IT.
YOU'RE LIKE A POLI-TICIAN OF THE FUCKED-UP, YOU KNOW THAT?
I KNOW. ISN'T IT ADOR-ABLE?

Nine

SONG

Astrud Gilberto
"A Certain Sadness"

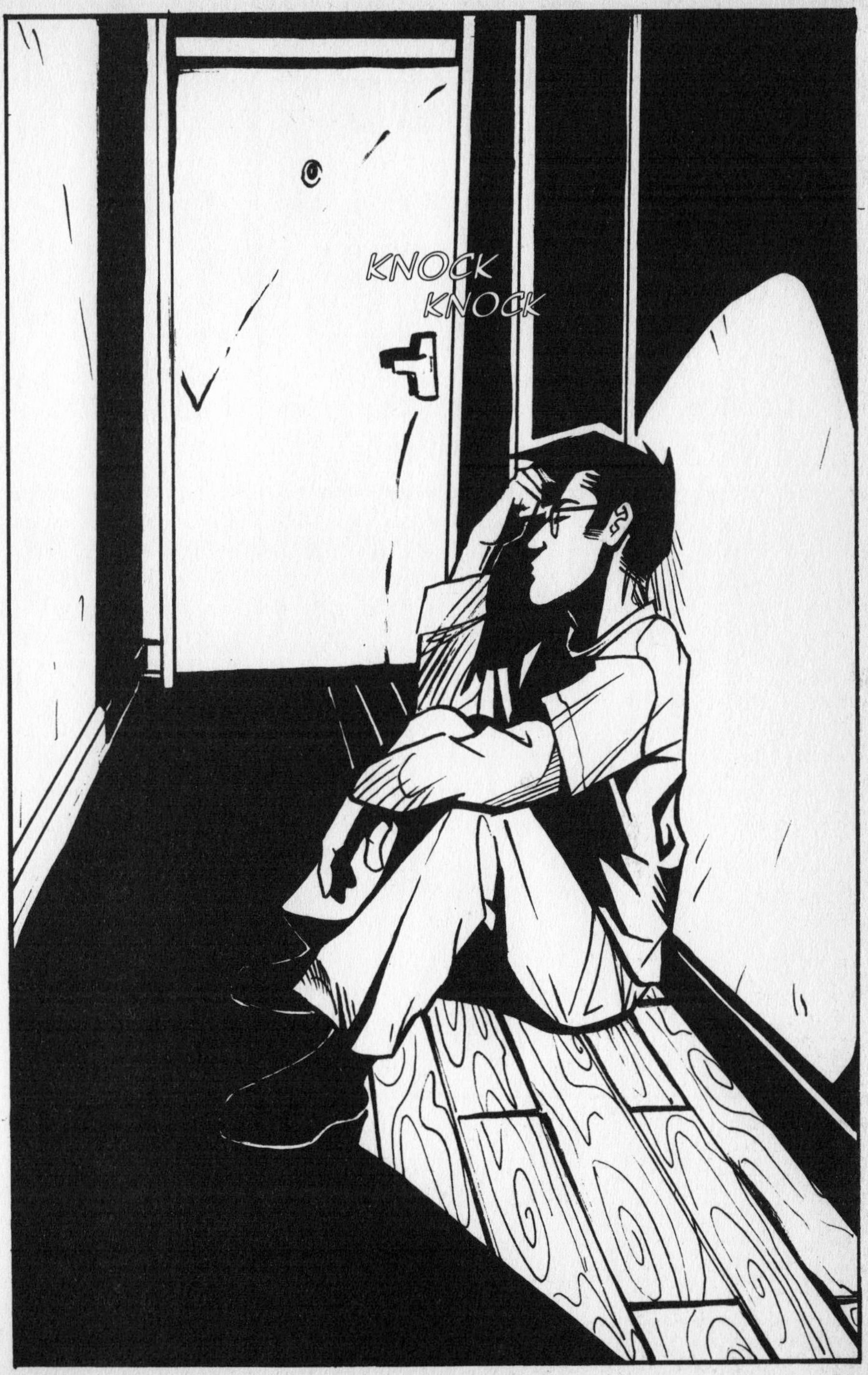
KNOCK
KNOCK

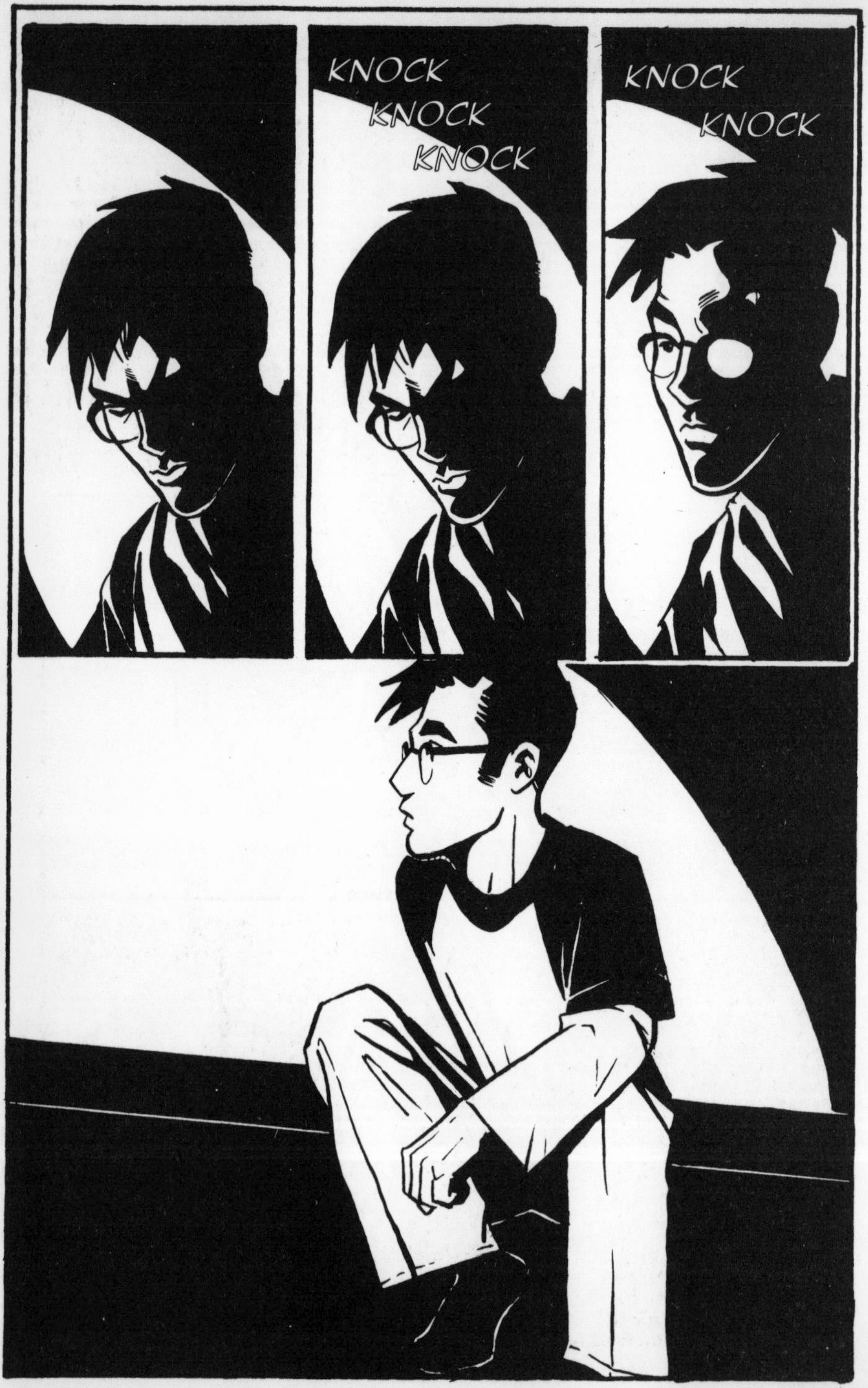
KNOCK
KNOCK
KNOCK
KNOCK
KNOCK

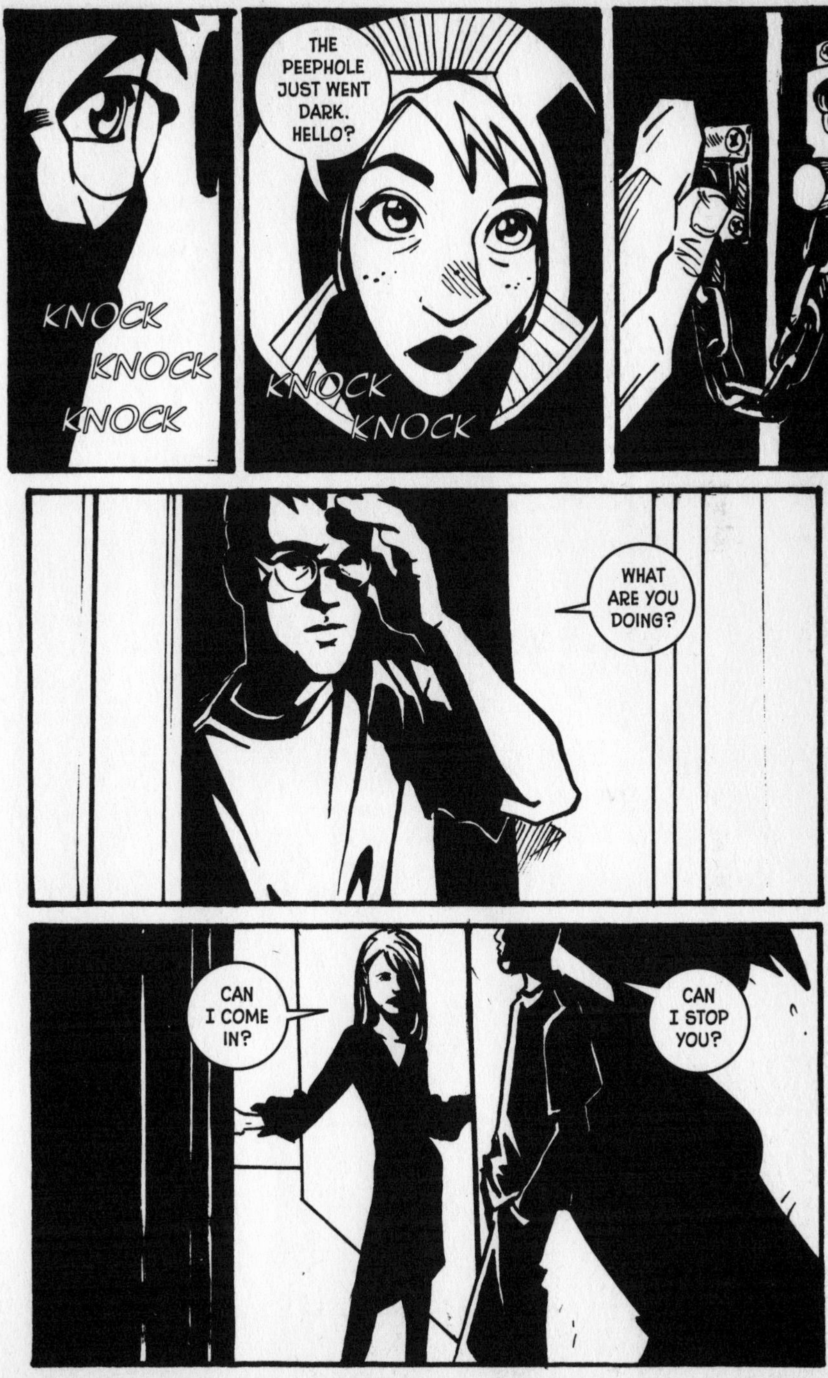
KNOCK
KNOCK
KNOCK
THE PEEPHOLE JUST WENT DARK. HELLO?
KNOCK
KNOCK
WHAT ARE YOU DOING?
CAN I COME IN?
CAN I STOP YOU?

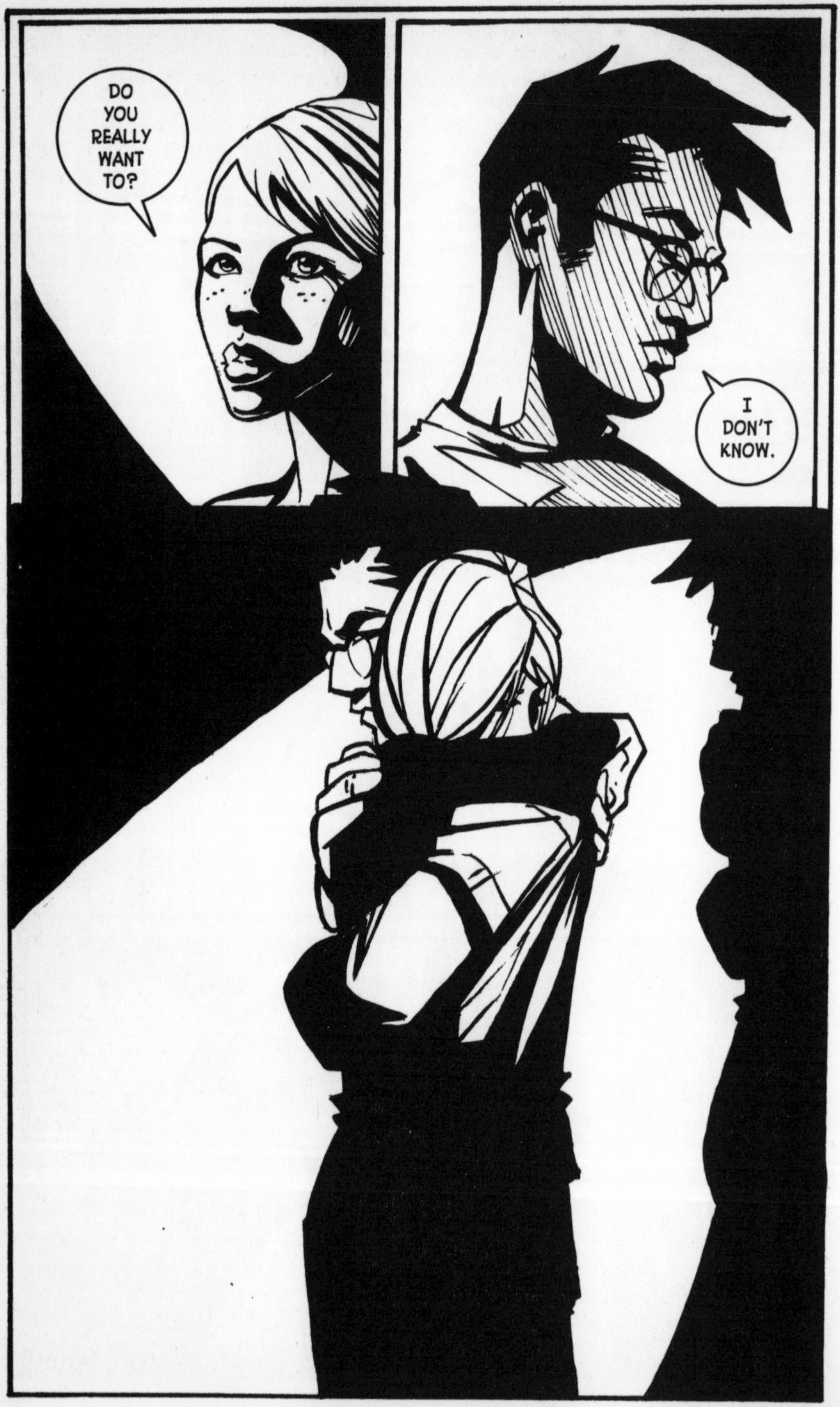
DO YOU REALLY WANT TO?
I DON'T KNOW.

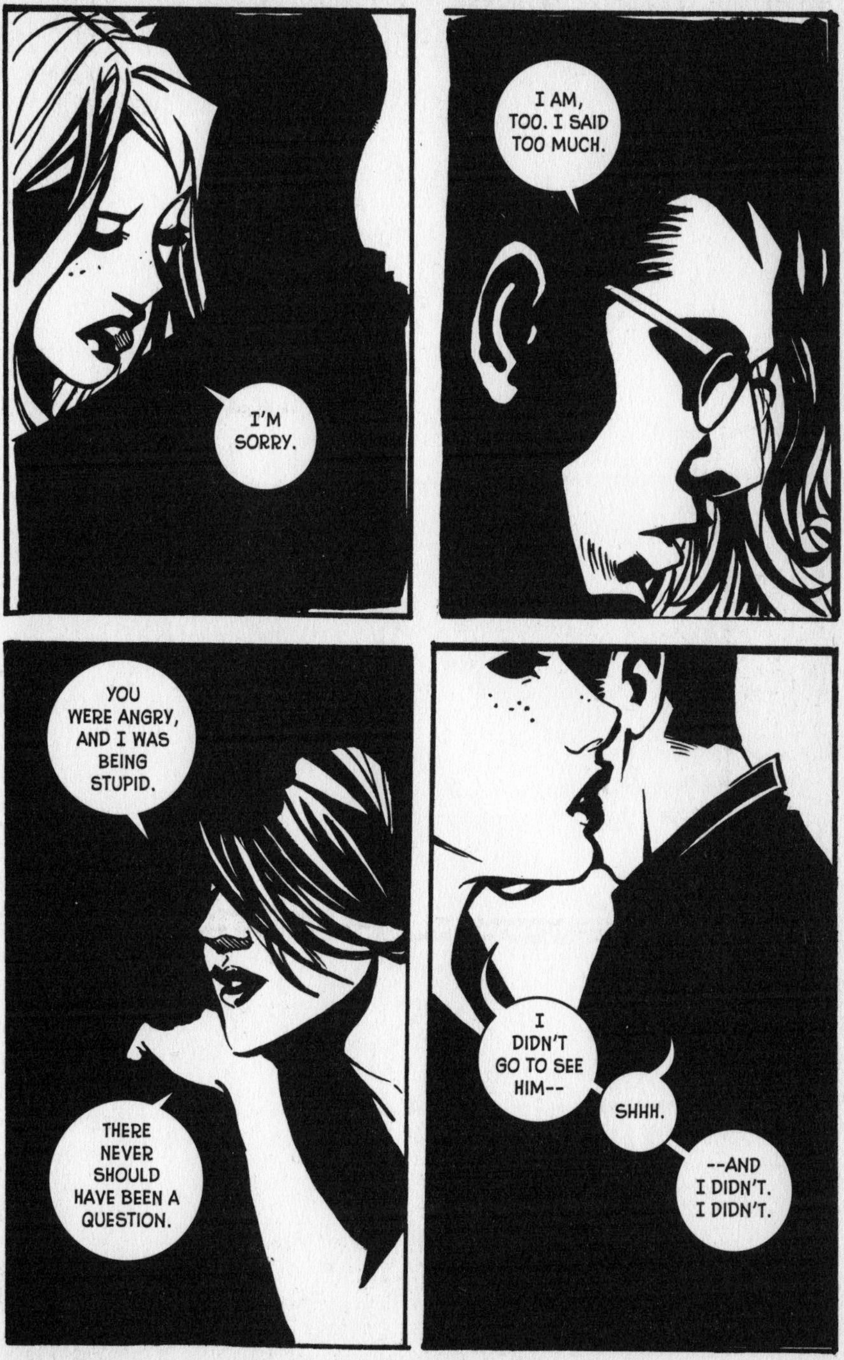
I'M SORRY.
I AM, TOO. I SAID TOO MUCH.
YOU WERE ANGRY, AND I WAS BEING STUPID.
THERE NEVER SHOULD HAVE BEEN A QUESTION.
I DIDN'T GO TO SEE HIM--
SHHH.
--AND I DIDN'T. I DIDN'T.

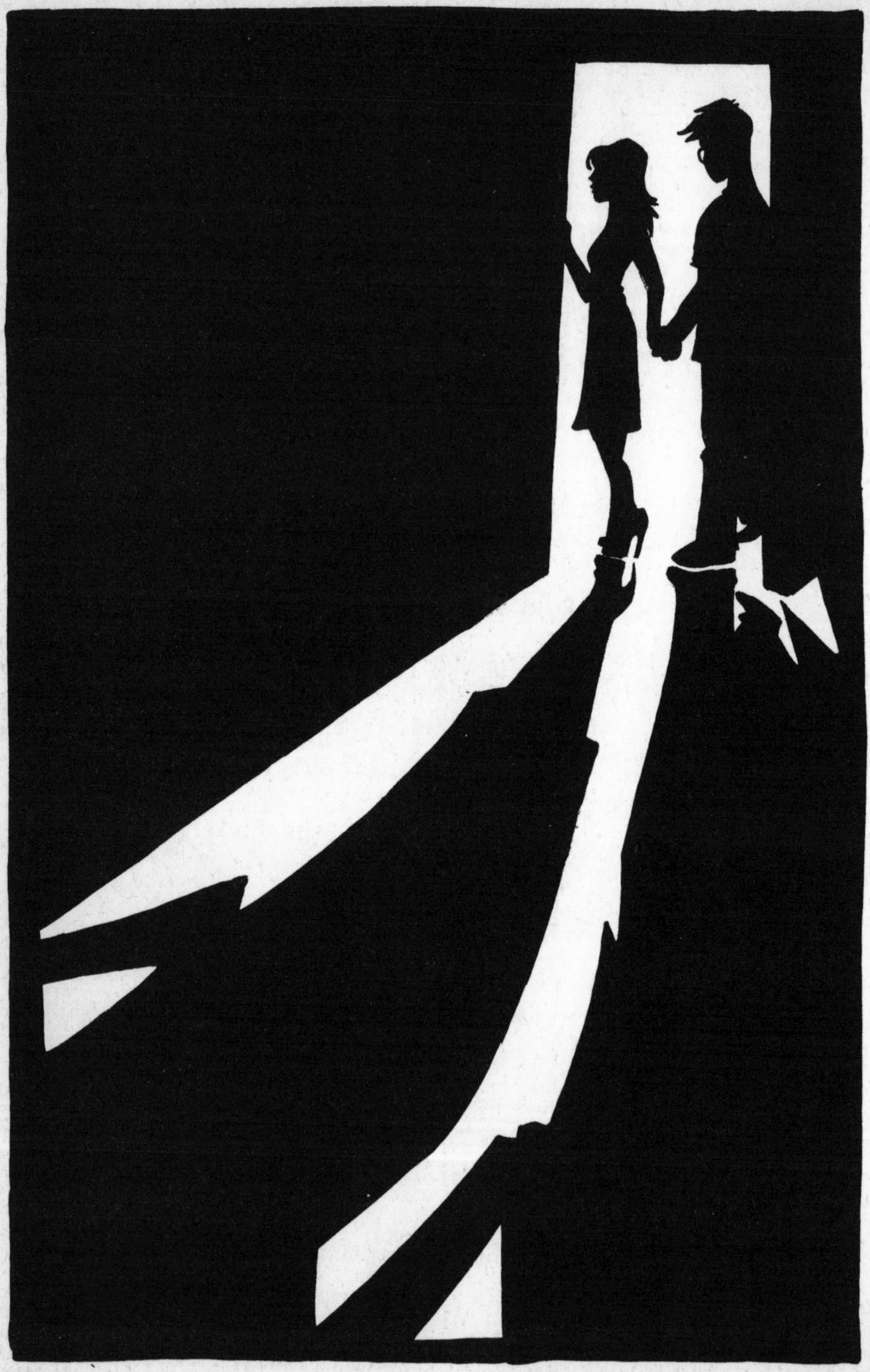

Ten

SONG

Belly

"Spaceman"

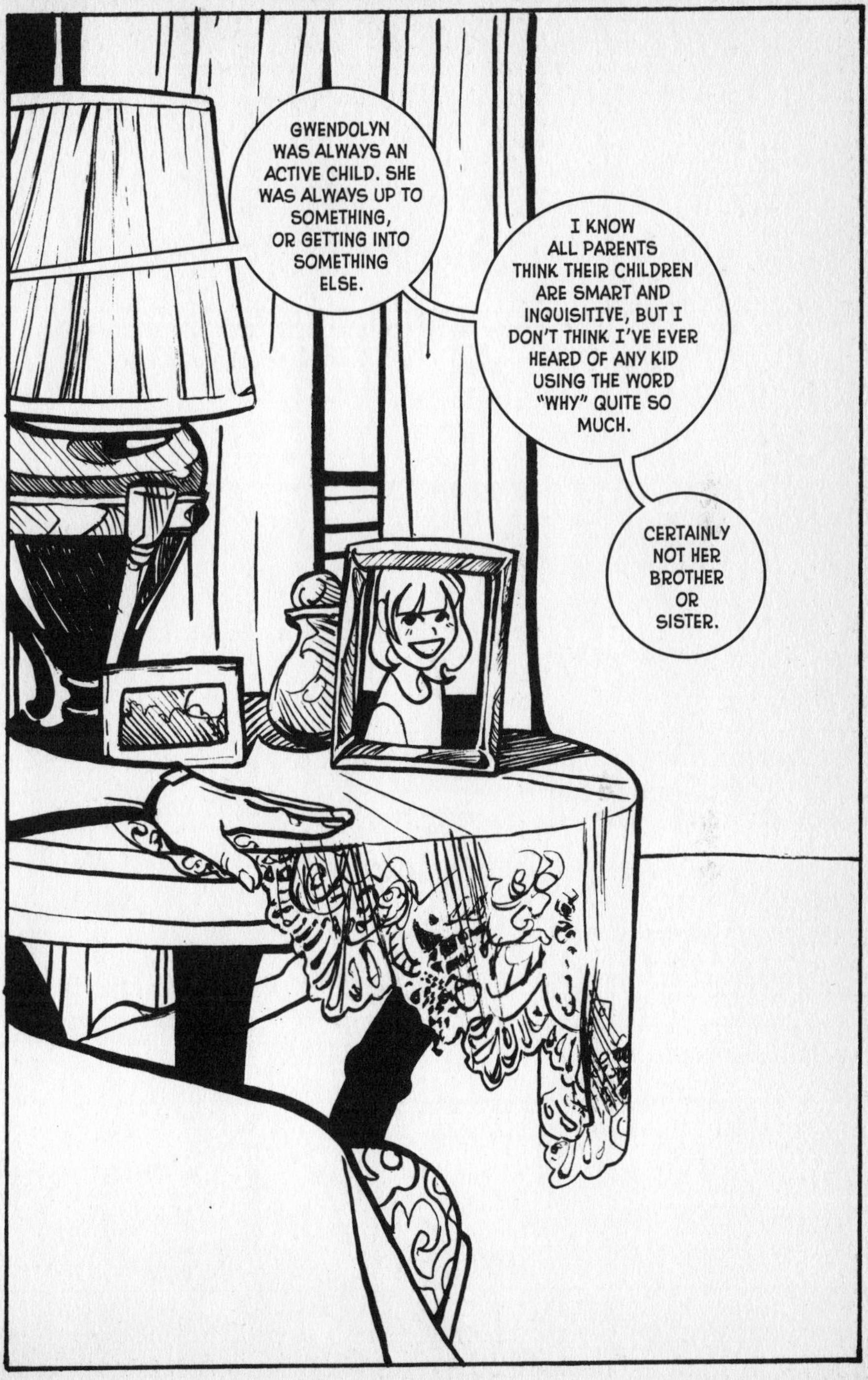
GWENDOLYN WAS ALWAYS AN ACTIVE CHILD. SHE WAS ALWAYS UP TO SOMETHING, OR GETTING INTO SOMETHING ELSE.
I KNOW ALL PARENTS THINK THEIR CHILDREN ARE SMART AND INQUISITIVE, BUT I DON'T THINK I'VE EVER HEARD OF ANY KID USING THE WORD "WHY" QUITE SO MUCH.
CERTAINLY NOT HER BROTHER OR SISTER.

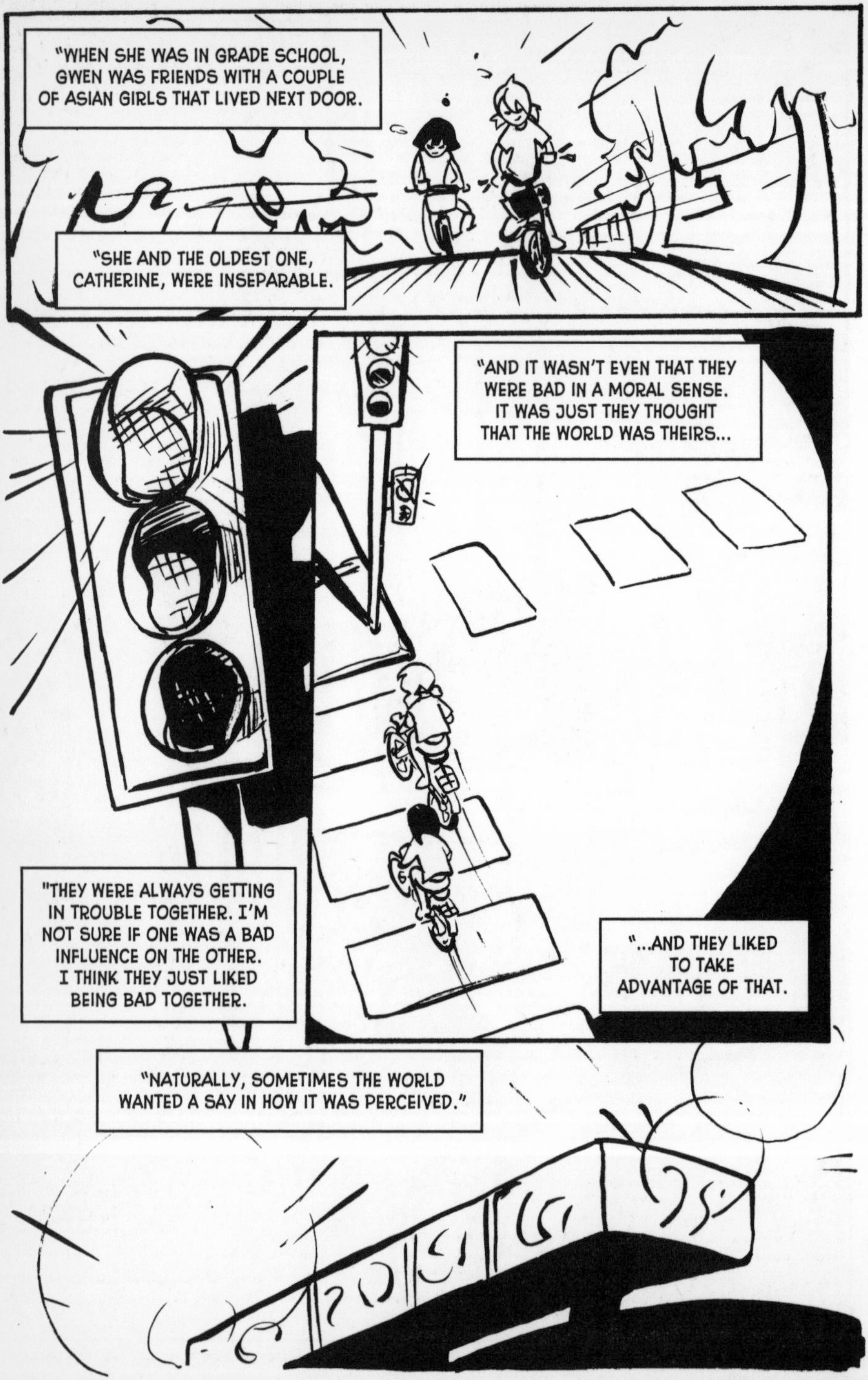
"WHEN SHE WAS IN GRADE SCHOOL, GWEN WAS FRIENDS WITH A COUPLE OF ASIAN GIRLS THAT LIVED NEXT DOOR.
"SHE AND THE OLDEST ONE, CATHERINE, WERE INSEPARABLE.
"THEY WERE ALWAYS GETTING IN TROUBLE TOGETHER. I'M NOT SURE IF ONE WAS A BAD INFLUENCE ON THE OTHER. I THINK THEY JUST LIKED BEING BAD TOGETHER.
"AND IT WASN'T EVEN THAT THEY WERE BAD IN A MORAL SENSE. IT WAS JUST THEY THOUGHT THAT THE WORLD WAS THEIRS...
"...AND THEY LIKED TO TAKE ADVANTAGE OF THAT.
"NATURALLY, SOMETIMES THE WORLD WANTED A SAY IN HOW IT WAS PERCEIVED."

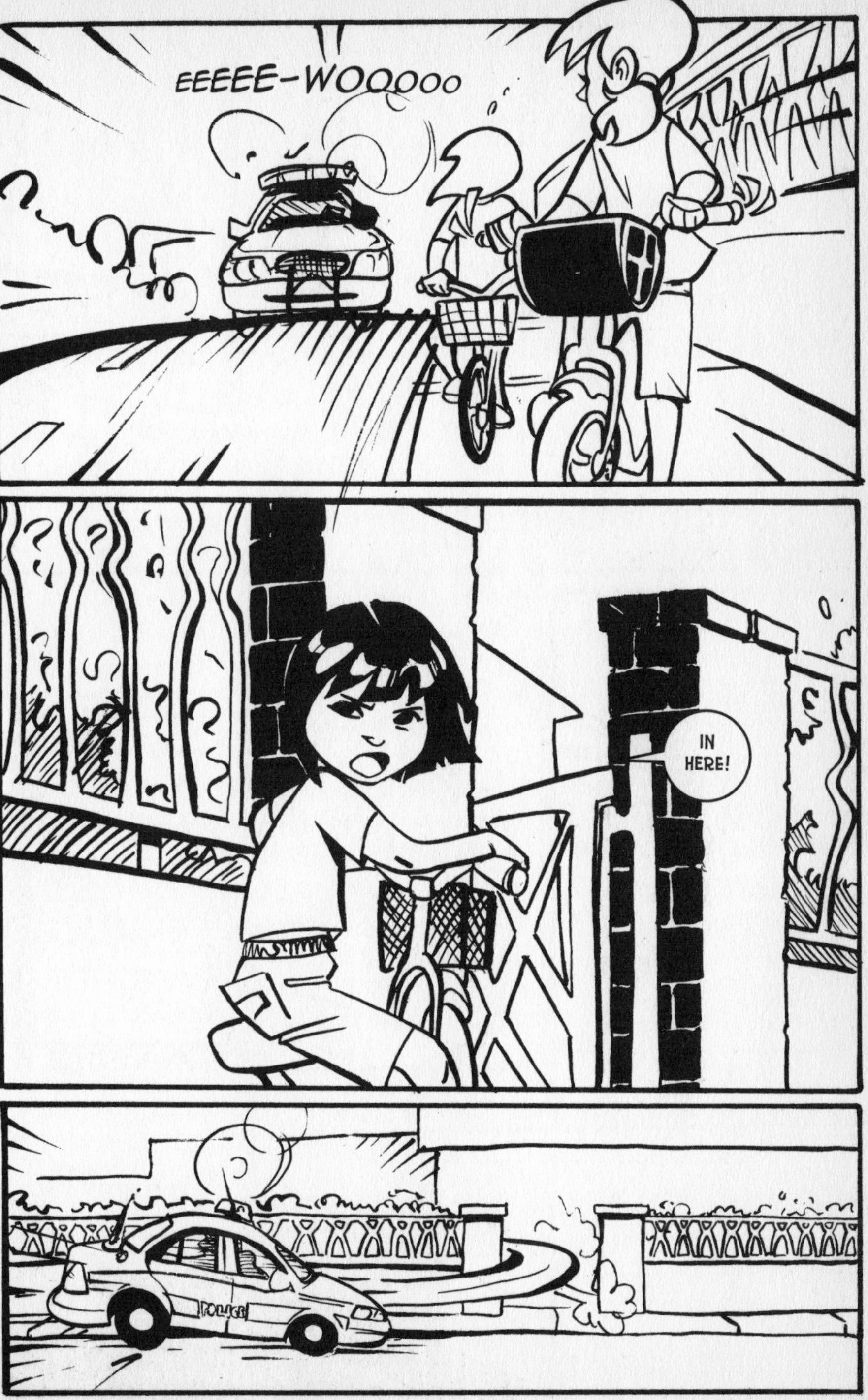
EEEEE-WOOOoo
IN HERE!
POLICE

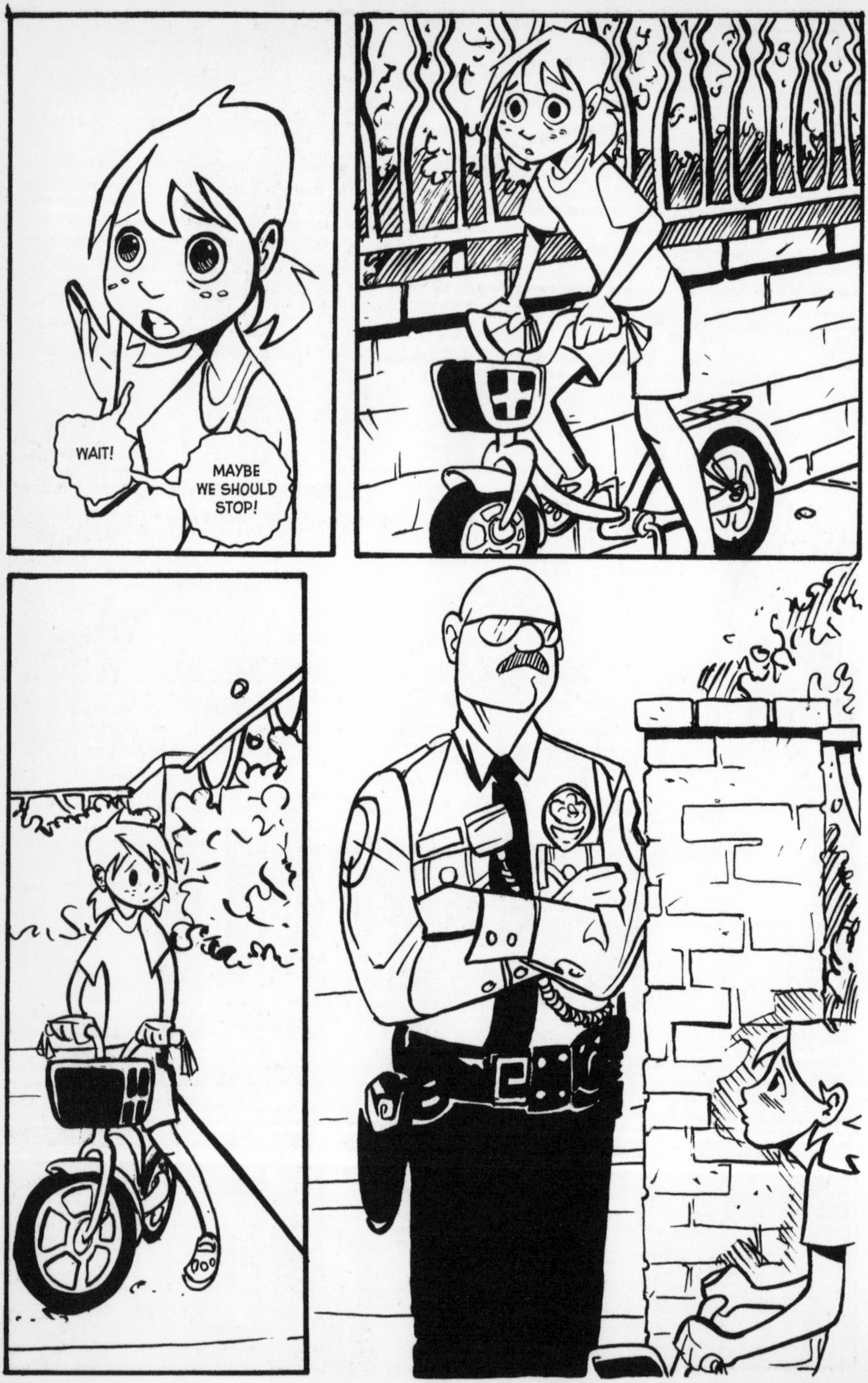
WAIT!
MAYBE WE SHOULD STOP!

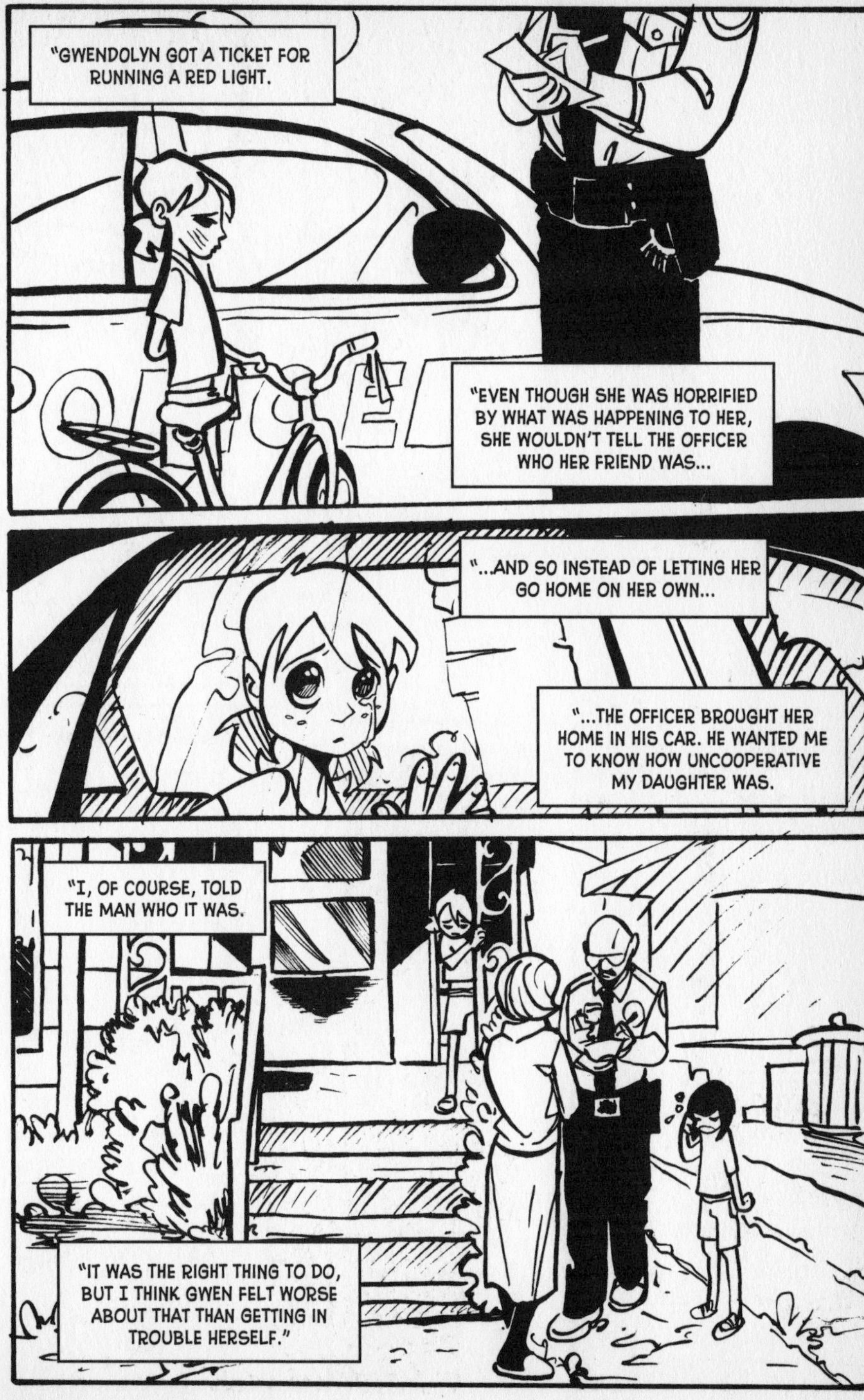
"GWENDOLYN GOT A TICKET FOR RUNNING A RED LIGHT.
"EVEN THOUGH SHE WAS HORRIFIED BY WHAT WAS HAPPENING TO HER, SHE WOULDN'T TELL THE OFFICER WHO HER FRIEND WAS...
"...AND SO INSTEAD OF LETTING HER GO HOME ON HER OWN...
"...THE OFFICER BROUGHT HER HOME IN HIS CAR. HE WANTED ME TO KNOW HOW UNCOOPERATIVE MY DAUGHTER WAS.
"I, OF COURSE, TOLD THE MAN WHO IT WAS.
"IT WAS THE RIGHT THING TO DO, BUT I THINK GWEN FELT WORSE ABOUT THAT THAN GETTING IN TROUBLE HERSELF."

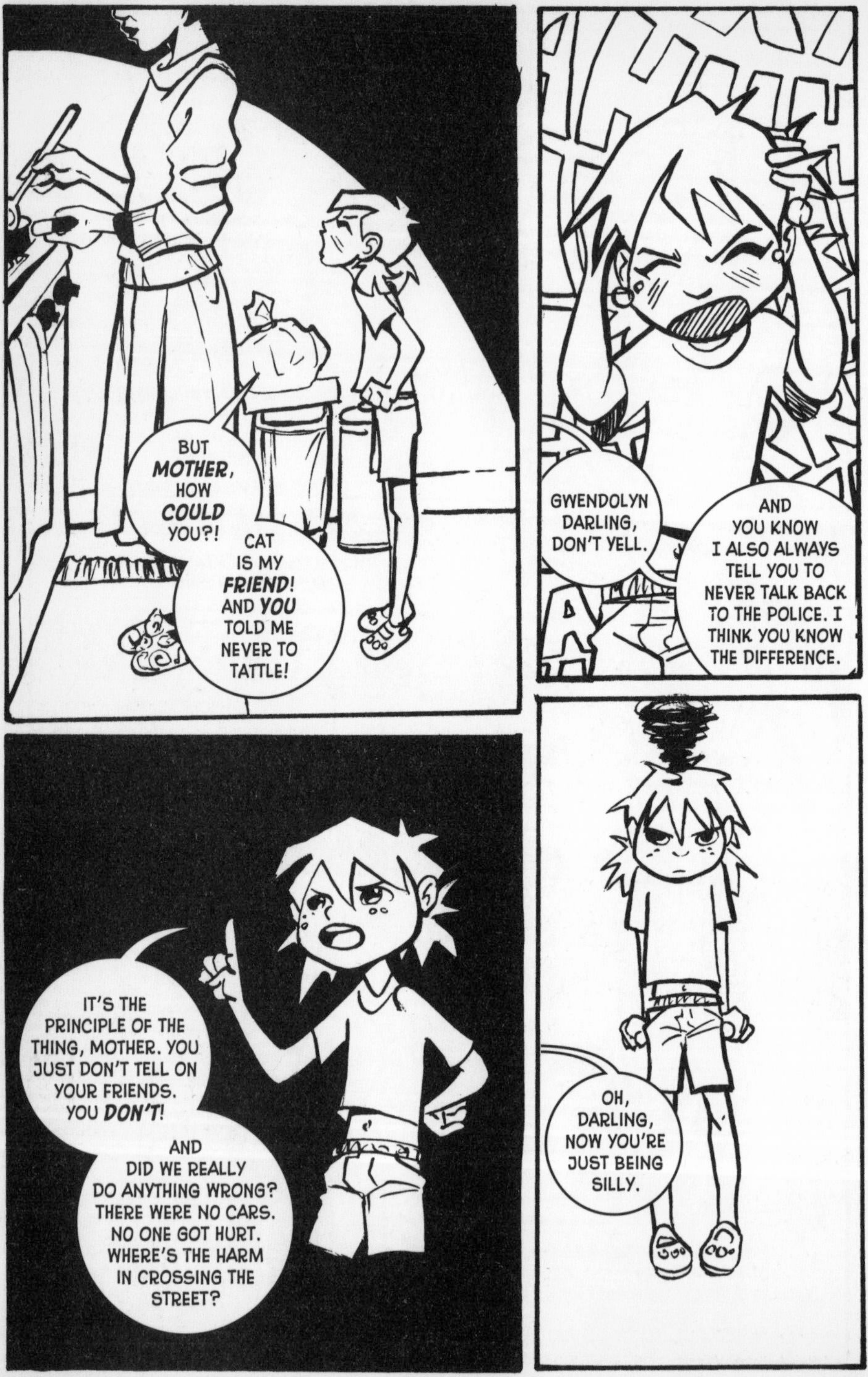

BUT **MOTHER**, HOW **COULD** YOU?!
CAT IS MY **FRIEND**! AND **YOU** TOLD ME NEVER TO TATTLE!
GWENDOLYN DARLING, DON'T YELL.
AND YOU KNOW I ALSO ALWAYS TELL YOU TO NEVER TALK BACK TO THE POLICE. I THINK YOU KNOW THE DIFFERENCE.
IT'S THE PRINCIPLE OF THE THING, MOTHER. YOU JUST DON'T TELL ON YOUR FRIENDS. YOU **DON'T**!
AND DID WE REALLY DO ANYTHING WRONG? THERE WERE NO CARS. NO ONE GOT HURT. WHERE'S THE HARM IN CROSSING THE STREET?
OH, DARLING, NOW YOU'RE JUST BEING SILLY.

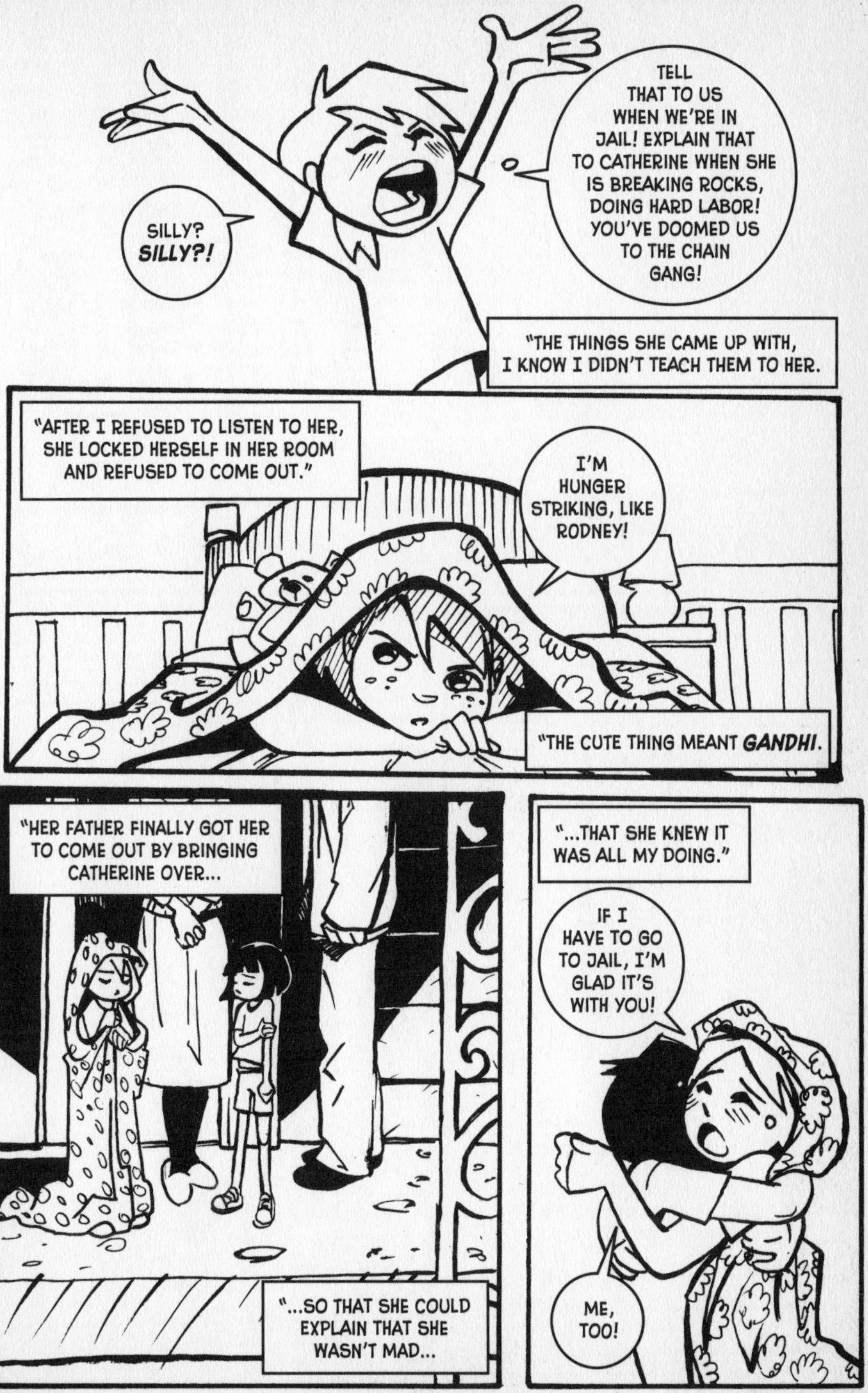

SILLY? *SILLY?!*
TELL THAT TO US WHEN WE'RE IN JAIL! EXPLAIN THAT TO CATHERINE WHEN SHE IS BREAKING ROCKS, DOING HARD LABOR! YOU'VE DOOMED US TO THE CHAIN GANG!
"THE THINGS SHE CAME UP WITH, I KNOW I DIDN'T TEACH THEM TO HER.
"AFTER I REFUSED TO LISTEN TO HER, SHE LOCKED HERSELF IN HER ROOM AND REFUSED TO COME OUT."
I'M HUNGER STRIKING, LIKE RODNEY!
"THE CUTE THING MEANT *GANDHI*.
"HER FATHER FINALLY GOT HER TO COME OUT BY BRINGING CATHERINE OVER...
"...SO THAT SHE COULD EXPLAIN THAT SHE WASN'T MAD...
"...THAT SHE KNEW IT WAS ALL MY DOING."
IF I HAVE TO GO TO JAIL, I'M GLAD IT'S WITH YOU!
ME, TOO!

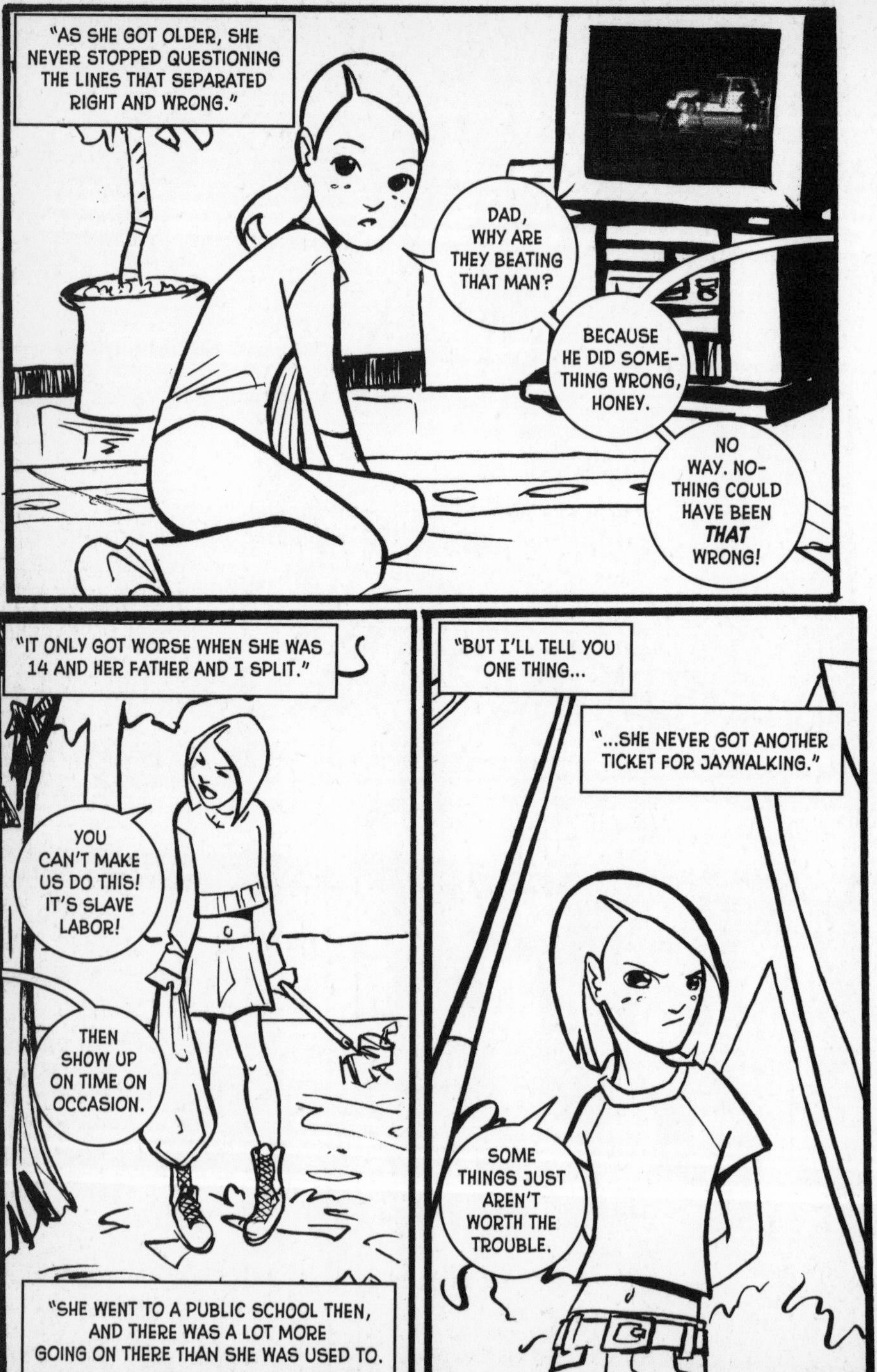
"AS SHE GOT OLDER, SHE NEVER STOPPED QUESTIONING THE LINES THAT SEPARATED RIGHT AND WRONG."
DAD, WHY ARE THEY BEATING THAT MAN?
BECAUSE HE DID SOME-THING WRONG, HONEY.
NO WAY. NO-THING COULD HAVE BEEN *THAT* WRONG!
"IT ONLY GOT WORSE WHEN SHE WAS 14 AND HER FATHER AND I SPLIT."
YOU CAN'T MAKE US DO THIS! IT'S SLAVE LABOR!
THEN SHOW UP ON TIME ON OCCASION.
"SHE WENT TO A PUBLIC SCHOOL THEN, AND THERE WAS A LOT MORE GOING ON THERE THAN SHE WAS USED TO.
"BUT I'LL TELL YOU ONE THING...
"...SHE NEVER GOT ANOTHER TICKET FOR JAYWALKING."
SOME THINGS JUST AREN'T WORTH THE TROUBLE.

Eleven

SONG

A Perfect Circle

"When the Levee Breaks"

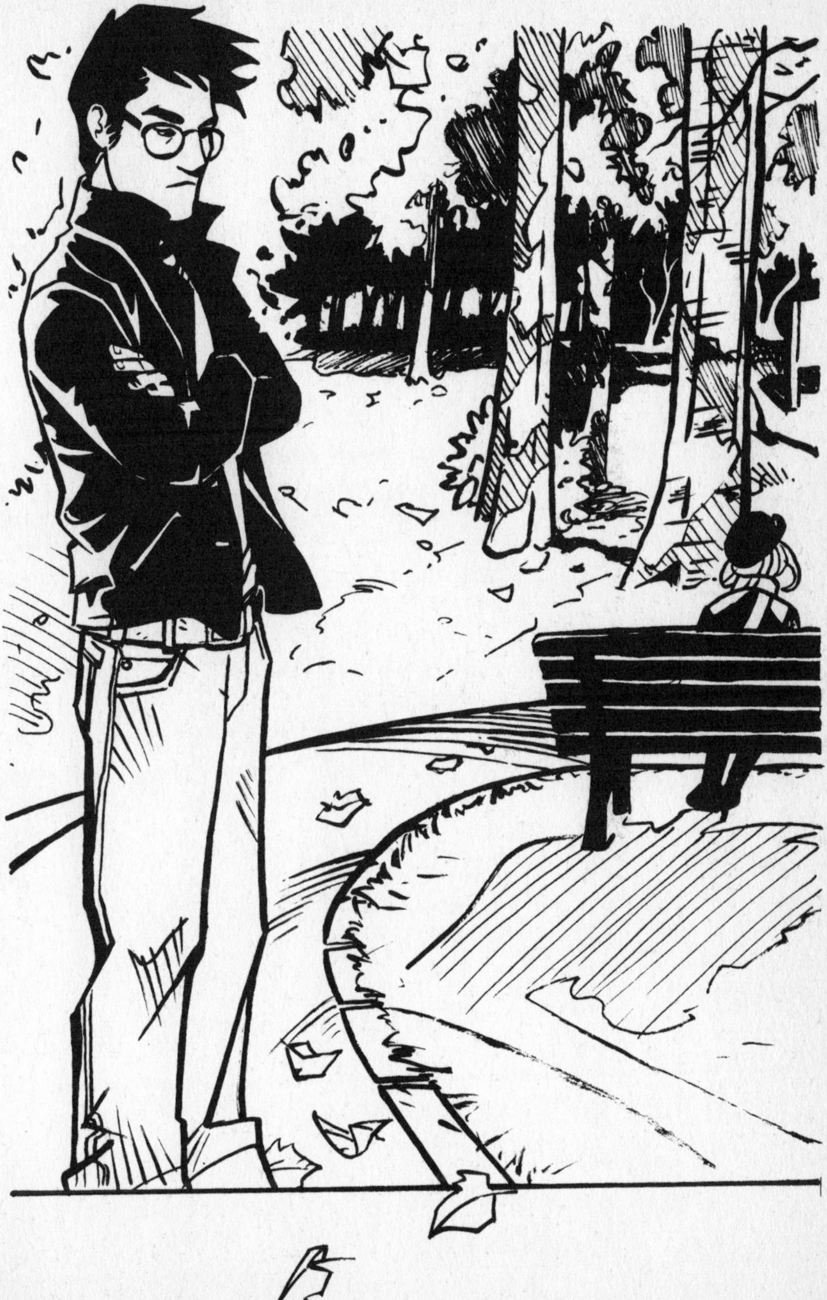

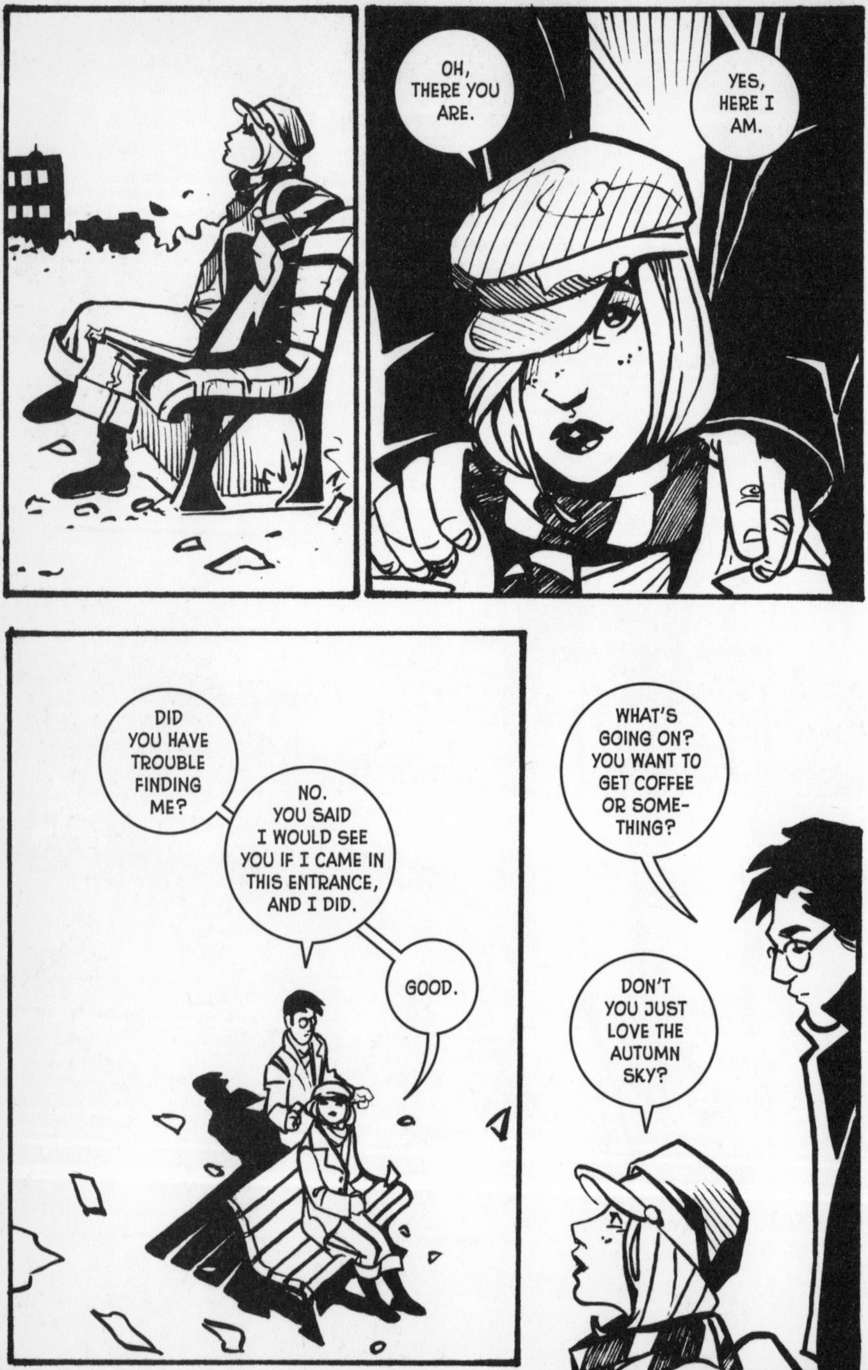
OH, THERE YOU ARE.
YES, HERE I AM.
DID YOU HAVE TROUBLE FINDING ME?
NO. YOU SAID I WOULD SEE YOU IF I CAME IN THIS ENTRANCE, AND I DID.
GOOD.
WHAT'S GOING ON? YOU WANT TO GET COFFEE OR SOME-THING?
DON'T YOU JUST LOVE THE AUTUMN SKY?

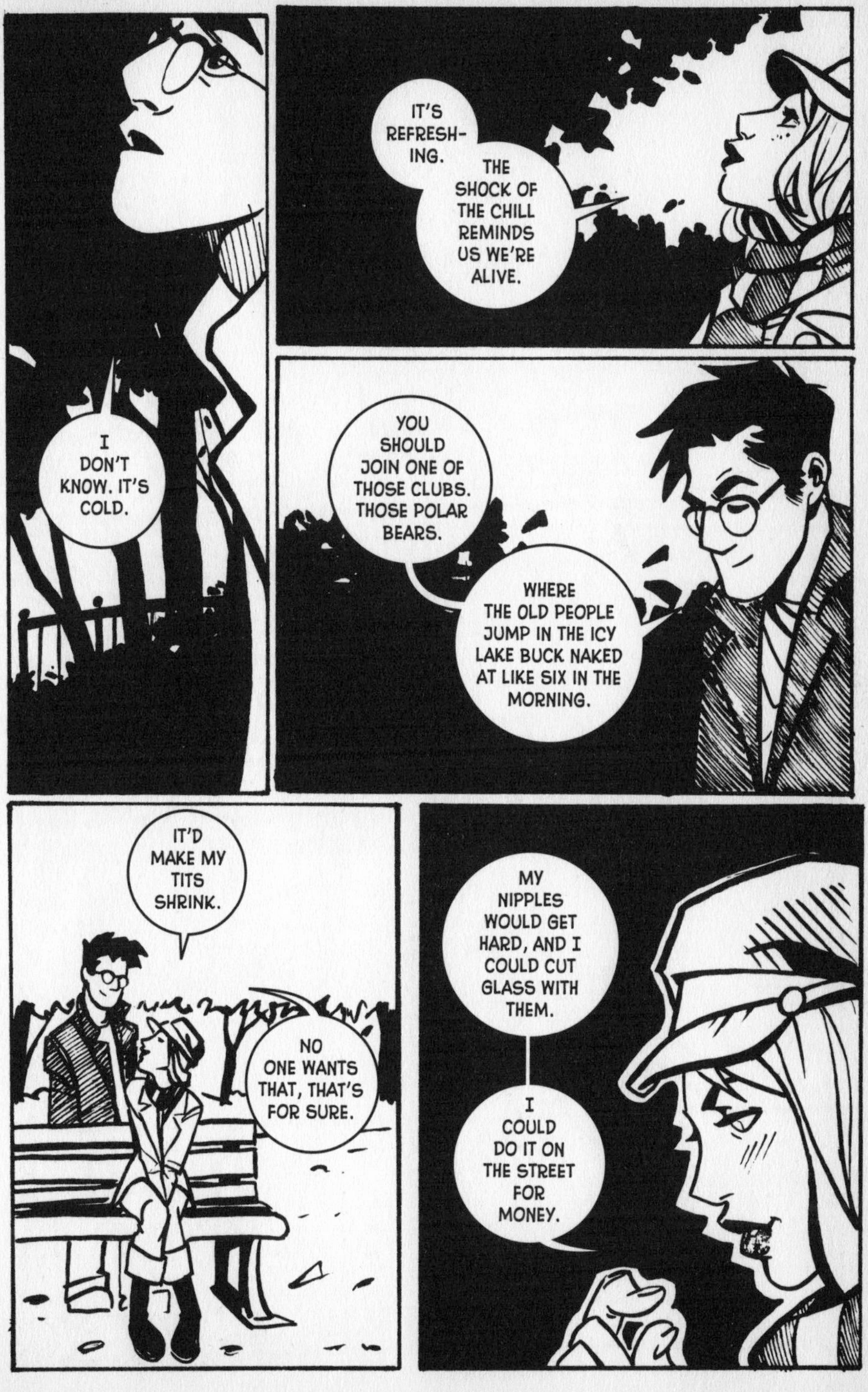
I DON'T KNOW. IT'S COLD.
IT'S REFRESHING.
THE SHOCK OF THE CHILL REMINDS US WE'RE ALIVE.
YOU SHOULD JOIN ONE OF THOSE CLUBS. THOSE POLAR BEARS.
WHERE THE OLD PEOPLE JUMP IN THE ICY LAKE BUCK NAKED AT LIKE SIX IN THE MORNING.
IT'D MAKE MY TITS SHRINK.
NO ONE WANTS THAT, THAT'S FOR SURE.
MY NIPPLES WOULD GET HARD, AND I COULD CUT GLASS WITH THEM.
I COULD DO IT ON THE STREET FOR MONEY.

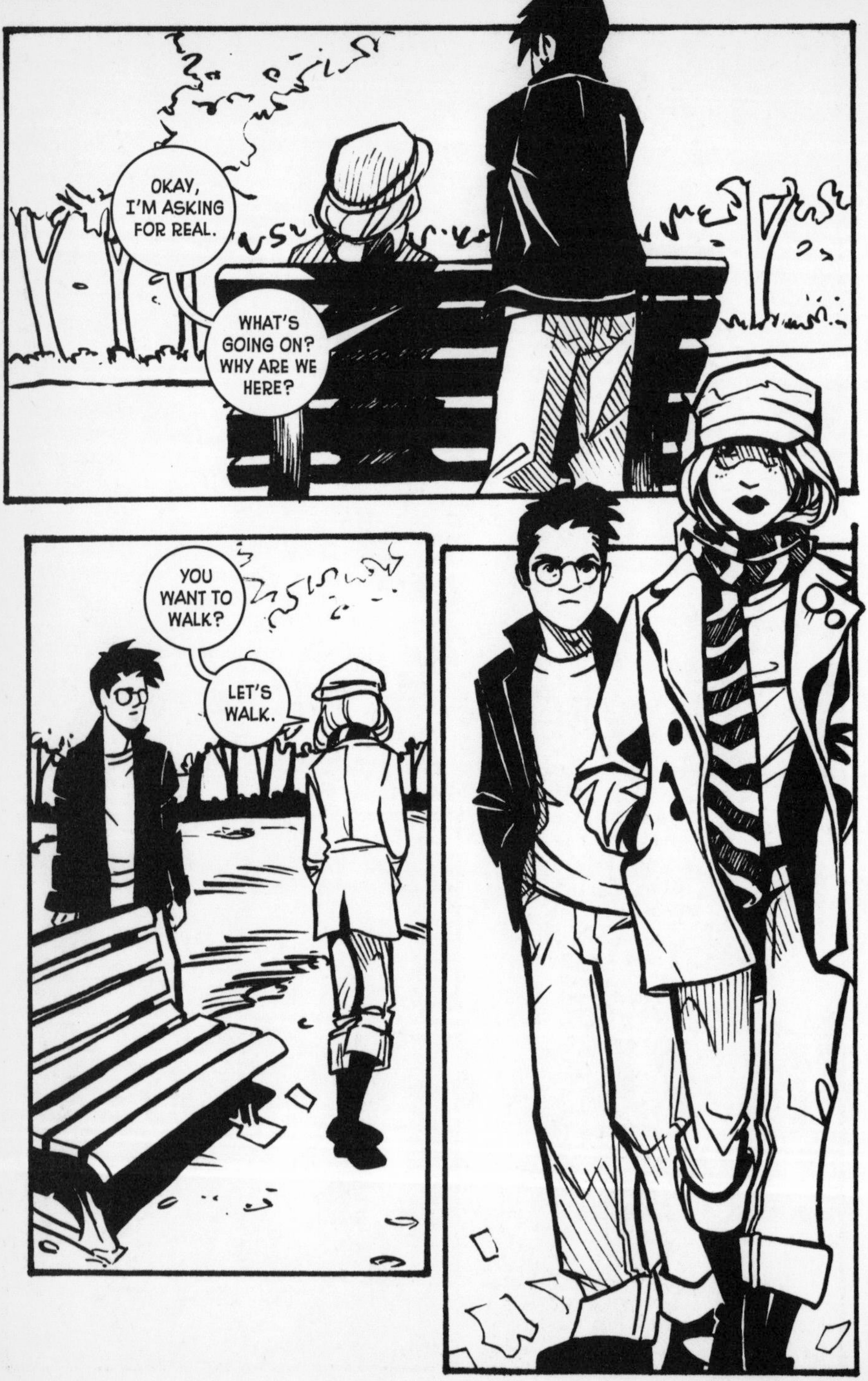
OKAY, I'M ASKING FOR REAL.
WHAT'S GOING ON? WHY ARE WE HERE?
YOU WANT TO WALK?
LET'S WALK.

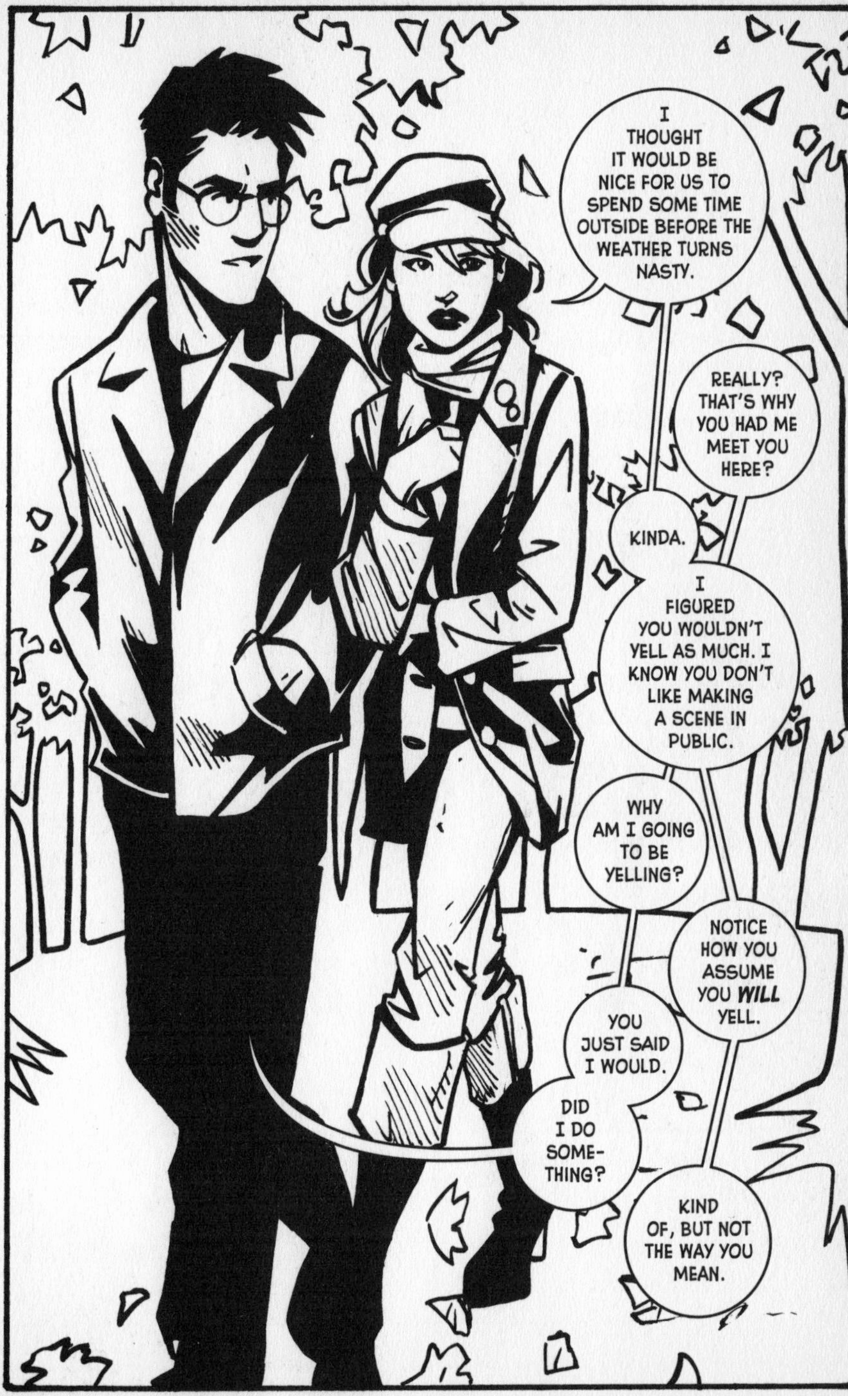
I THOUGHT IT WOULD BE NICE FOR US TO SPEND SOME TIME OUTSIDE BEFORE THE WEATHER TURNS NASTY.
REALLY? THAT'S WHY YOU HAD ME MEET YOU HERE?
KINDA.
I FIGURED YOU WOULDN'T YELL AS MUCH. I KNOW YOU DON'T LIKE MAKING A SCENE IN PUBLIC.
WHY AM I GOING TO BE YELLING?
NOTICE HOW YOU ASSUME YOU *WILL* YELL.
YOU JUST SAID I WOULD.
DID I DO SOME-THING?
KIND OF, BUT NOT THE WAY YOU MEAN.

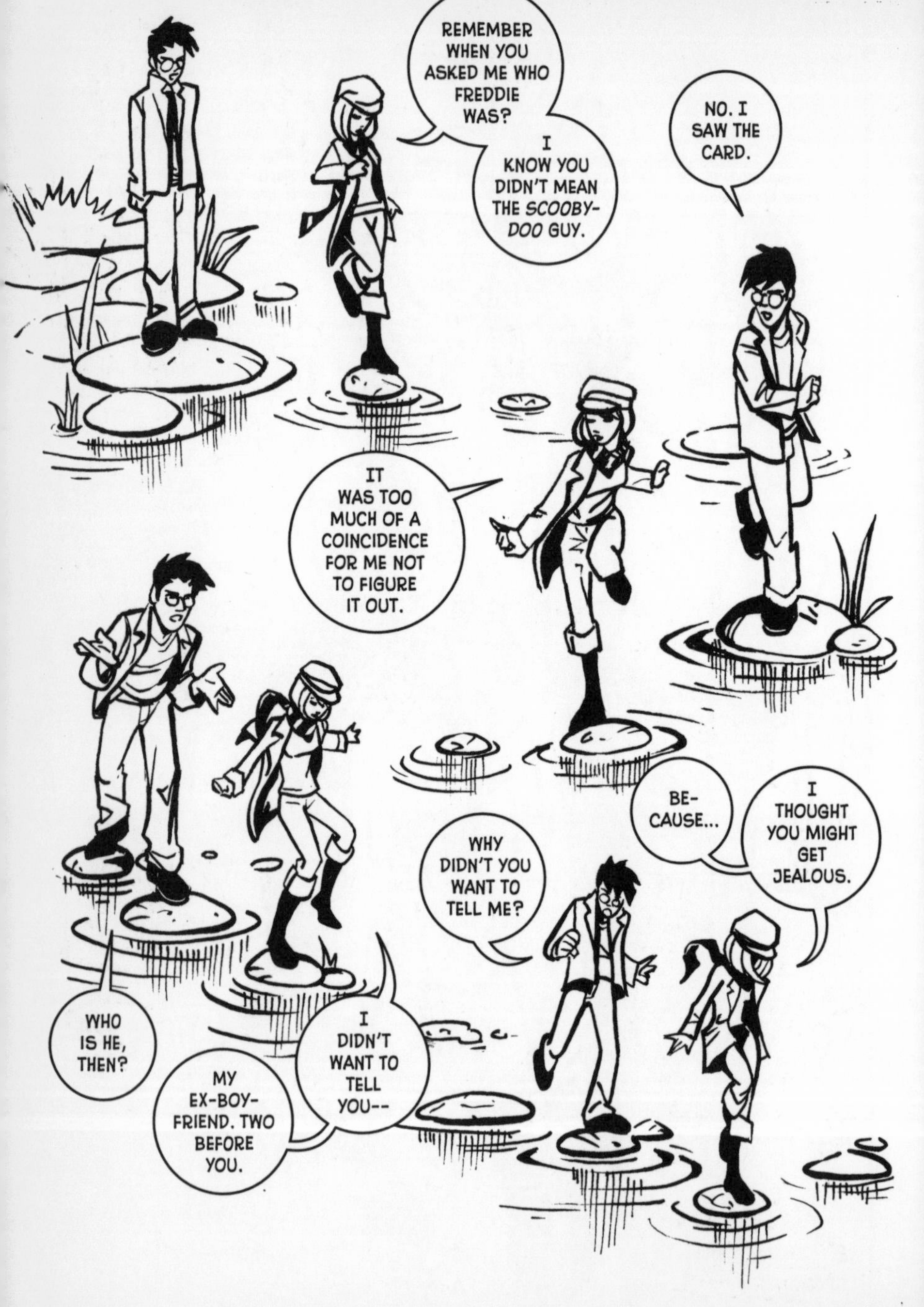
REMEMBER WHEN YOU ASKED ME WHO FREDDIE WAS?
I KNOW YOU DIDN'T MEAN THE *SCOOBY-DOO* GUY.
NO. I SAW THE CARD.
IT WAS TOO MUCH OF A COINCIDENCE FOR ME NOT TO FIGURE IT OUT.
WHO IS HE, THEN?
MY EX-BOY-FRIEND. TWO BEFORE YOU.
I DIDN'T WANT TO TELL YOU--
WHY DIDN'T YOU WANT TO TELL ME?
BE-CAUSE...
I THOUGHT YOU MIGHT GET JEALOUS.

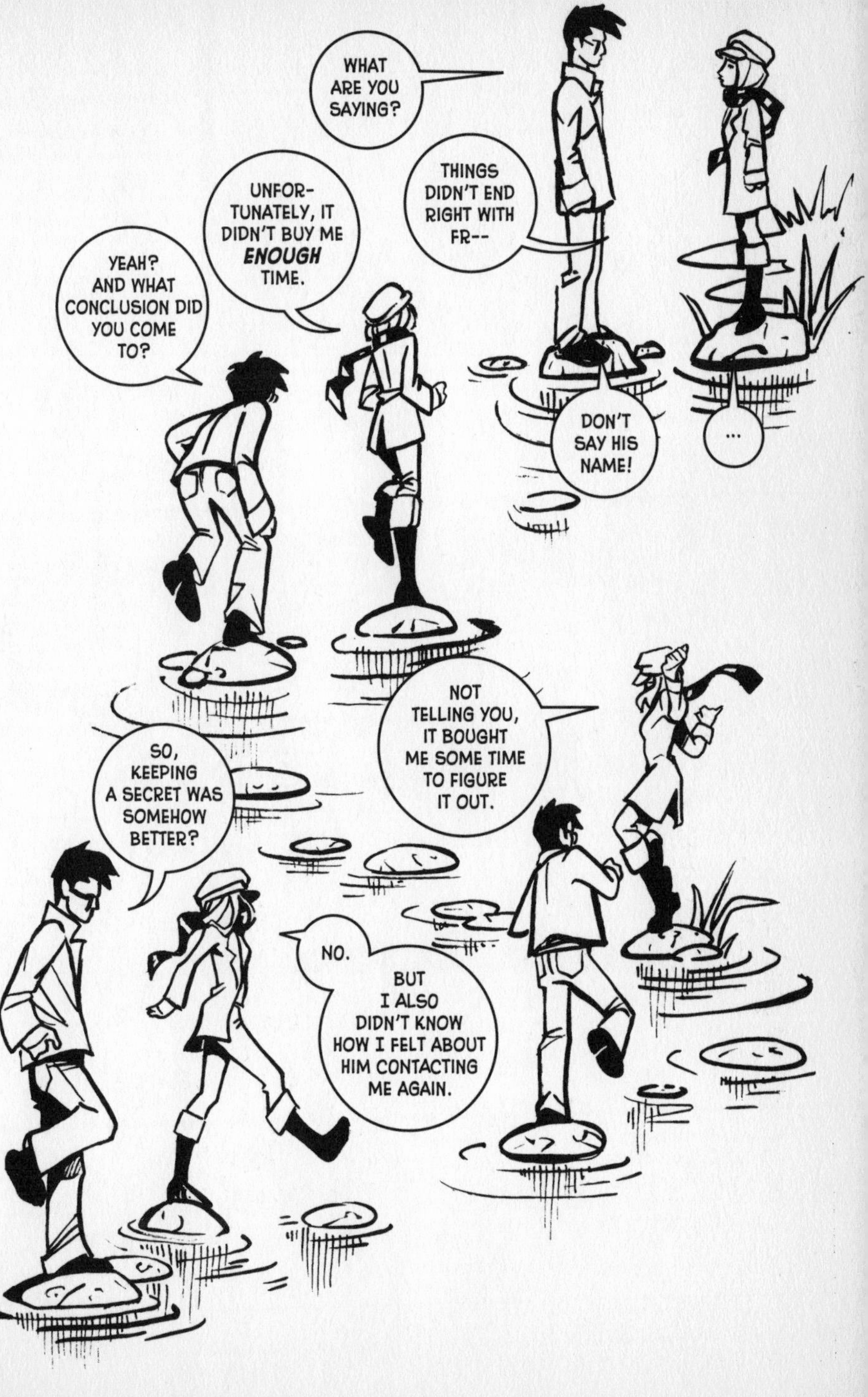
WHAT ARE YOU SAYING?
THINGS DIDN'T END RIGHT WITH FR--
DON'T SAY HIS NAME!
...
UNFOR-TUNATELY, IT DIDN'T BUY ME ***ENOUGH*** TIME.
YEAH? AND WHAT CONCLUSION DID YOU COME TO?
NOT TELLING YOU, IT BOUGHT ME SOME TIME TO FIGURE IT OUT.
SO, KEEPING A SECRET WAS SOMEHOW BETTER?
NO.
BUT I ALSO DIDN'T KNOW HOW I FELT ABOUT HIM CONTACTING ME AGAIN.

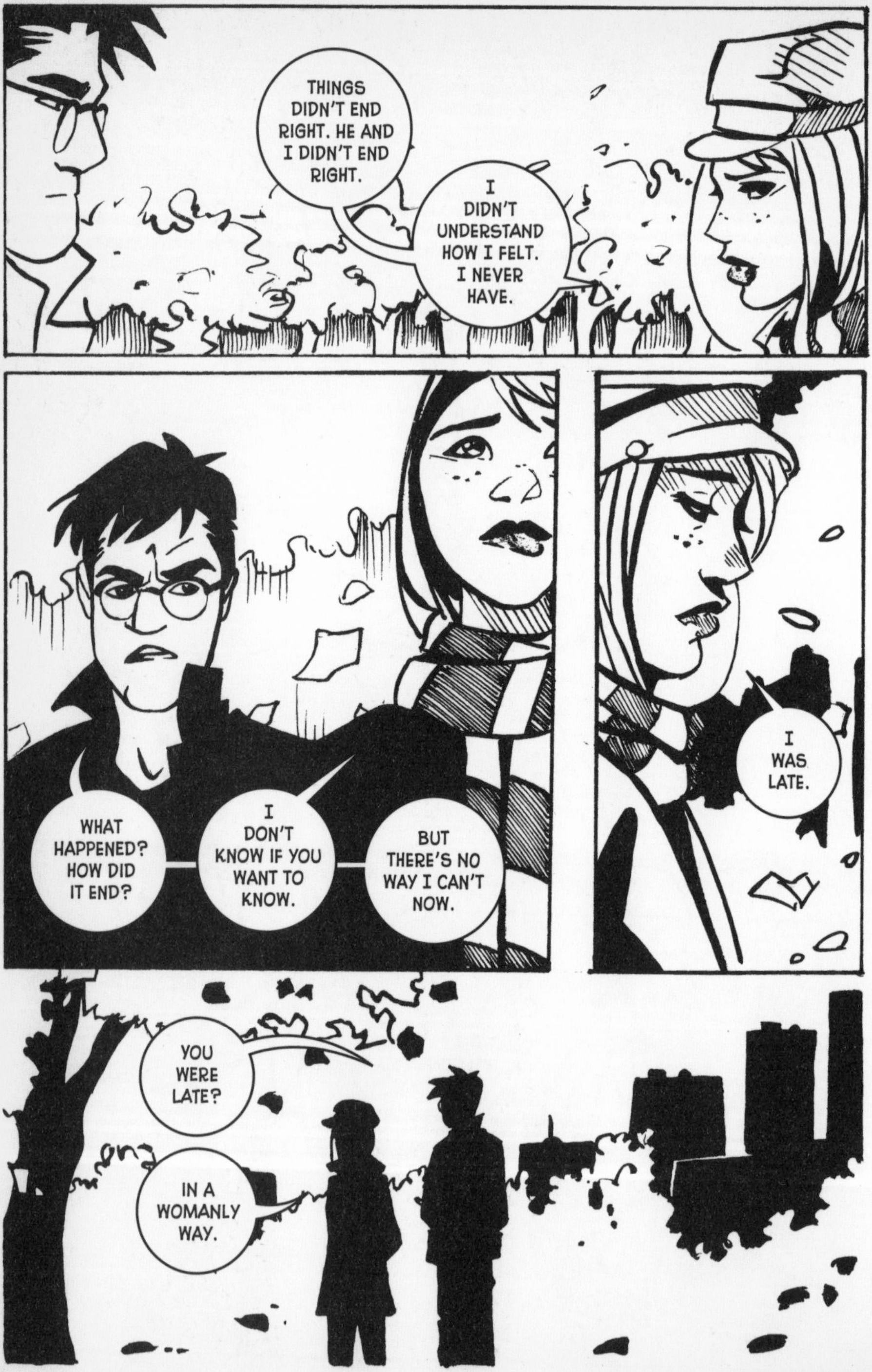
THINGS DIDN'T END RIGHT. HE AND I DIDN'T END RIGHT.
I DIDN'T UNDERSTAND HOW I FELT. I NEVER HAVE.
WHAT HAPPENED? HOW DID IT END?
I DON'T KNOW IF YOU WANT TO KNOW.
BUT THERE'S NO WAY I CAN'T NOW.
I WAS LATE.
YOU WERE LATE?
IN A WOMANLY WAY.

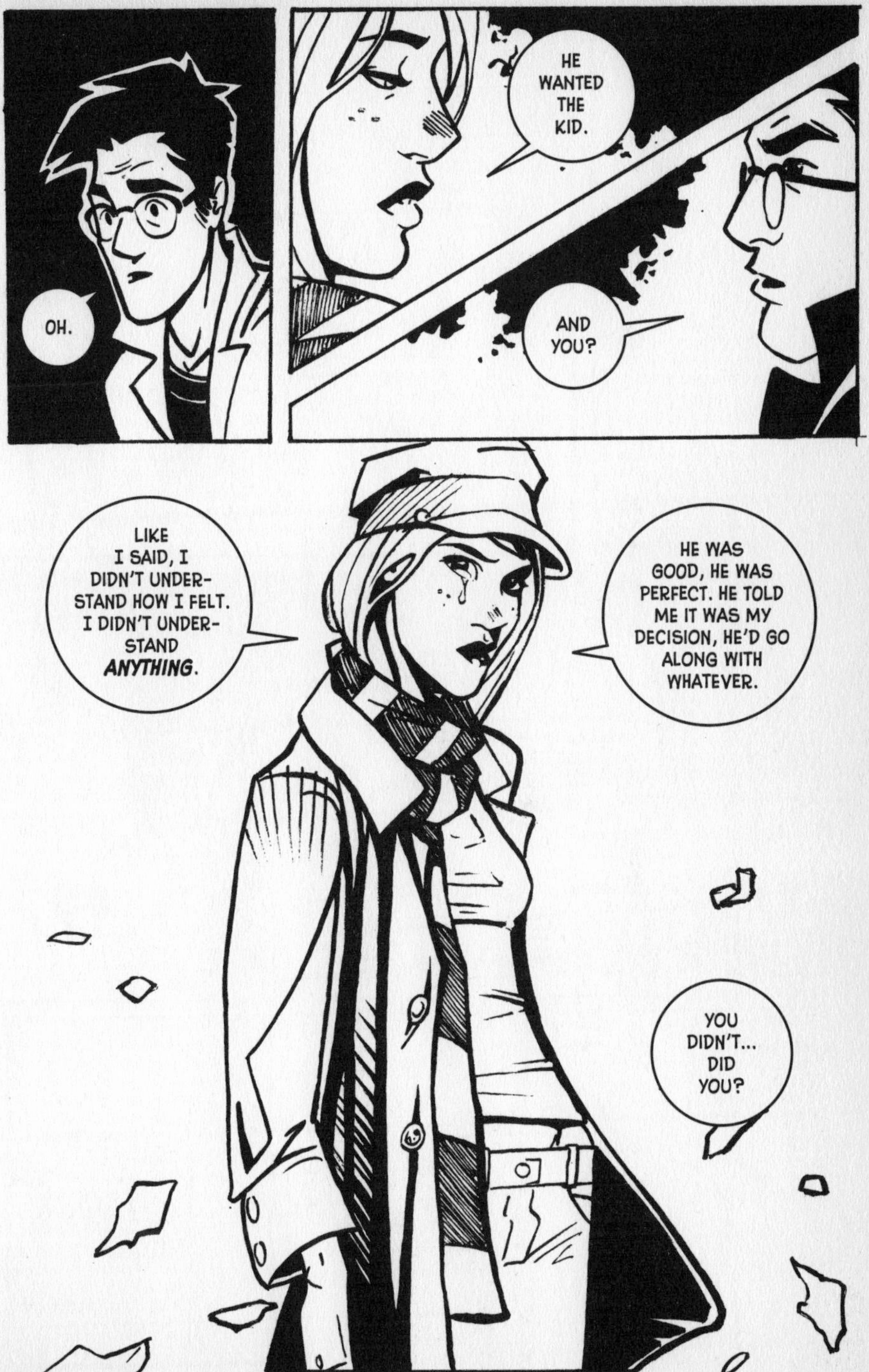
OH.
HE WANTED THE KID.
AND YOU?
LIKE I SAID, I DIDN'T UNDER-STAND HOW I FELT. I DIDN'T UNDER-STAND *ANYTHING*.
HE WAS GOOD, HE WAS PERFECT. HE TOLD ME IT WAS MY DECISION, HE'D GO ALONG WITH WHATEVER.
YOU DIDN'T... DID YOU?

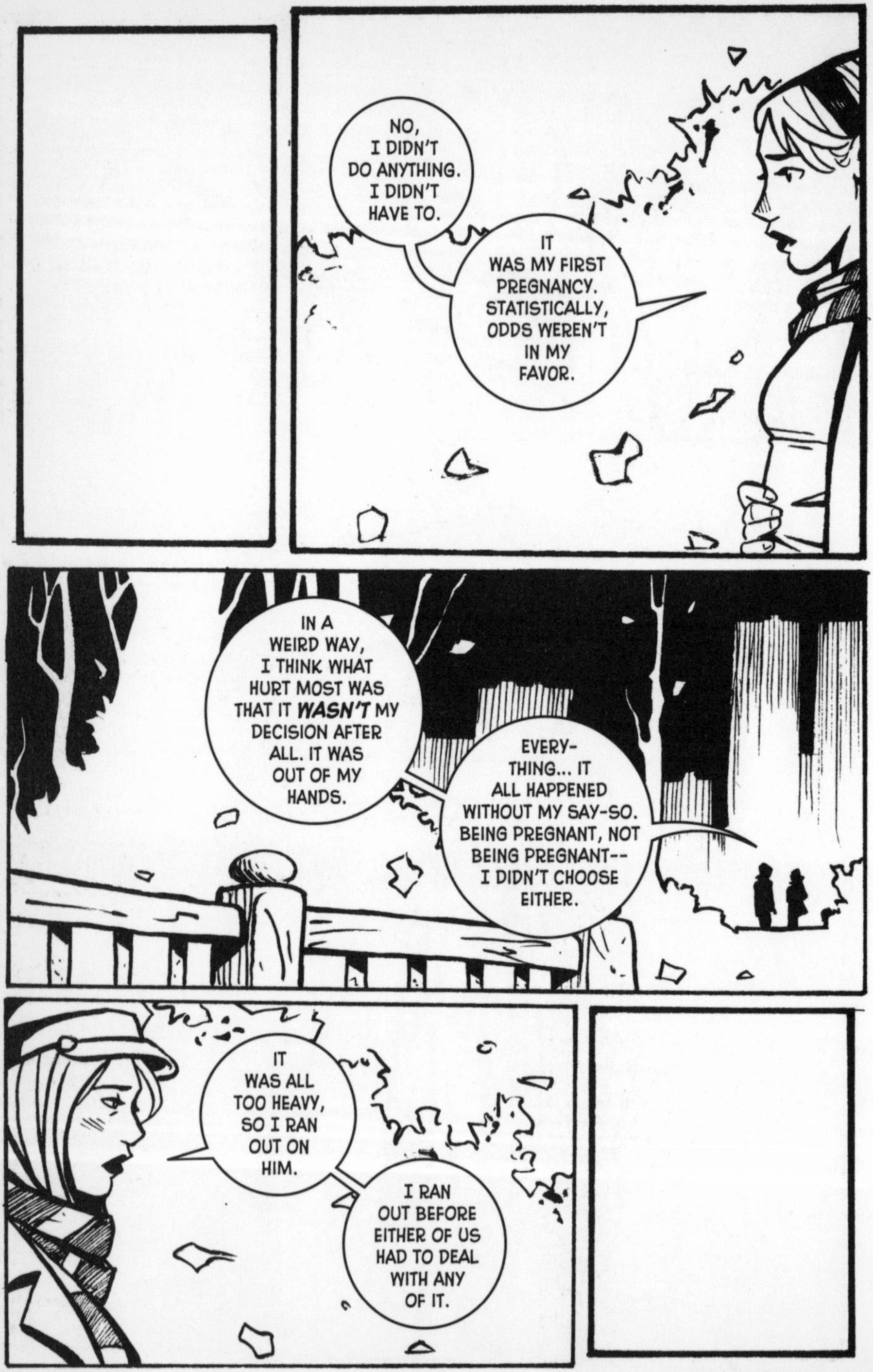
NO, I DIDN'T DO ANYTHING. I DIDN'T HAVE TO.
IT WAS MY FIRST PREGNANCY. STATISTICALLY, ODDS WEREN'T IN MY FAVOR.
IN A WEIRD WAY, I THINK WHAT HURT MOST WAS THAT IT WASN'T MY DECISION AFTER ALL. IT WAS OUT OF MY HANDS.
EVERY-THING... IT ALL HAPPENED WITHOUT MY SAY-SO. BEING PREGNANT, NOT BEING PREGNANT-- I DIDN'T CHOOSE EITHER.
IT WAS ALL TOO HEAVY, SO I RAN OUT ON HIM.
I RAN OUT BEFORE EITHER OF US HAD TO DEAL WITH ANY OF IT.

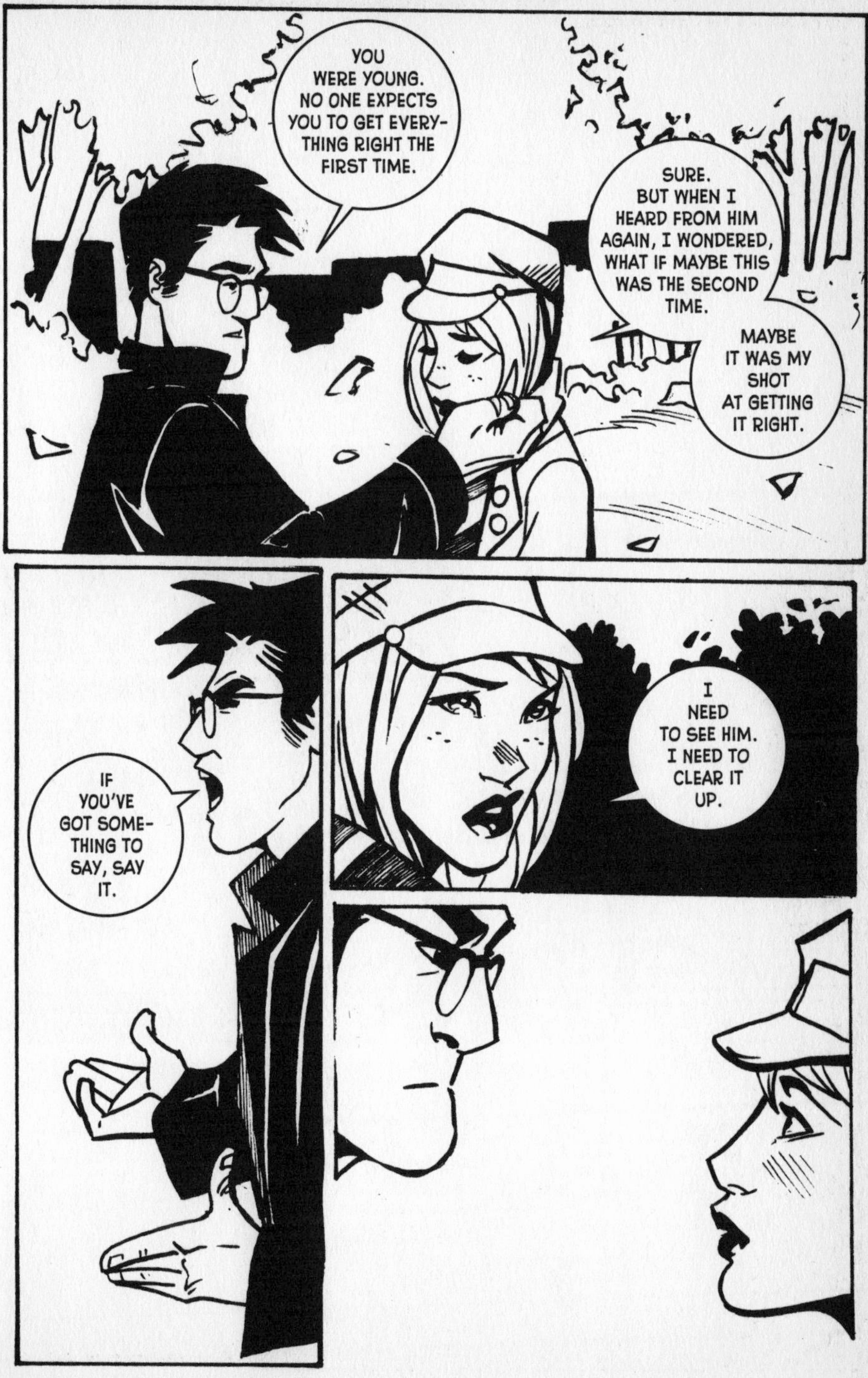
YOU WERE YOUNG. NO ONE EXPECTS YOU TO GET EVERY-THING RIGHT THE FIRST TIME.
SURE. BUT WHEN I HEARD FROM HIM AGAIN, I WONDERED, WHAT IF MAYBE THIS WAS THE SECOND TIME.
MAYBE IT WAS MY SHOT AT GETTING IT RIGHT.
I NEED TO SEE HIM. I NEED TO CLEAR IT UP.
IF YOU'VE GOT SOME-THING TO SAY, SAY IT.

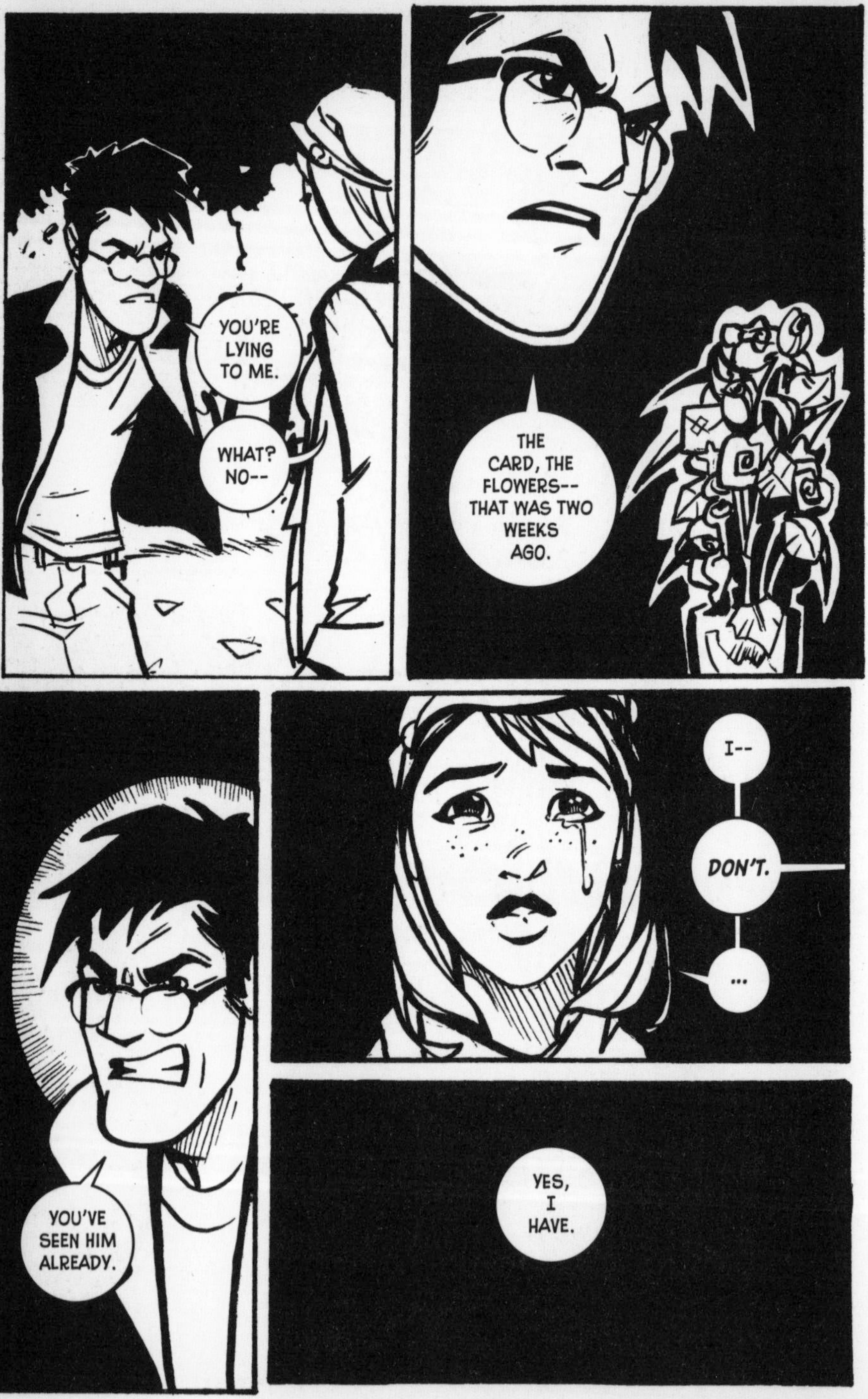
YOU'RE LYING TO ME.
WHAT? NO--
THE CARD, THE FLOWERS-- THAT WAS TWO WEEKS AGO.
YOU'VE SEEN HIM ALREADY.
I--
DON'T.
...
YES, I HAVE.

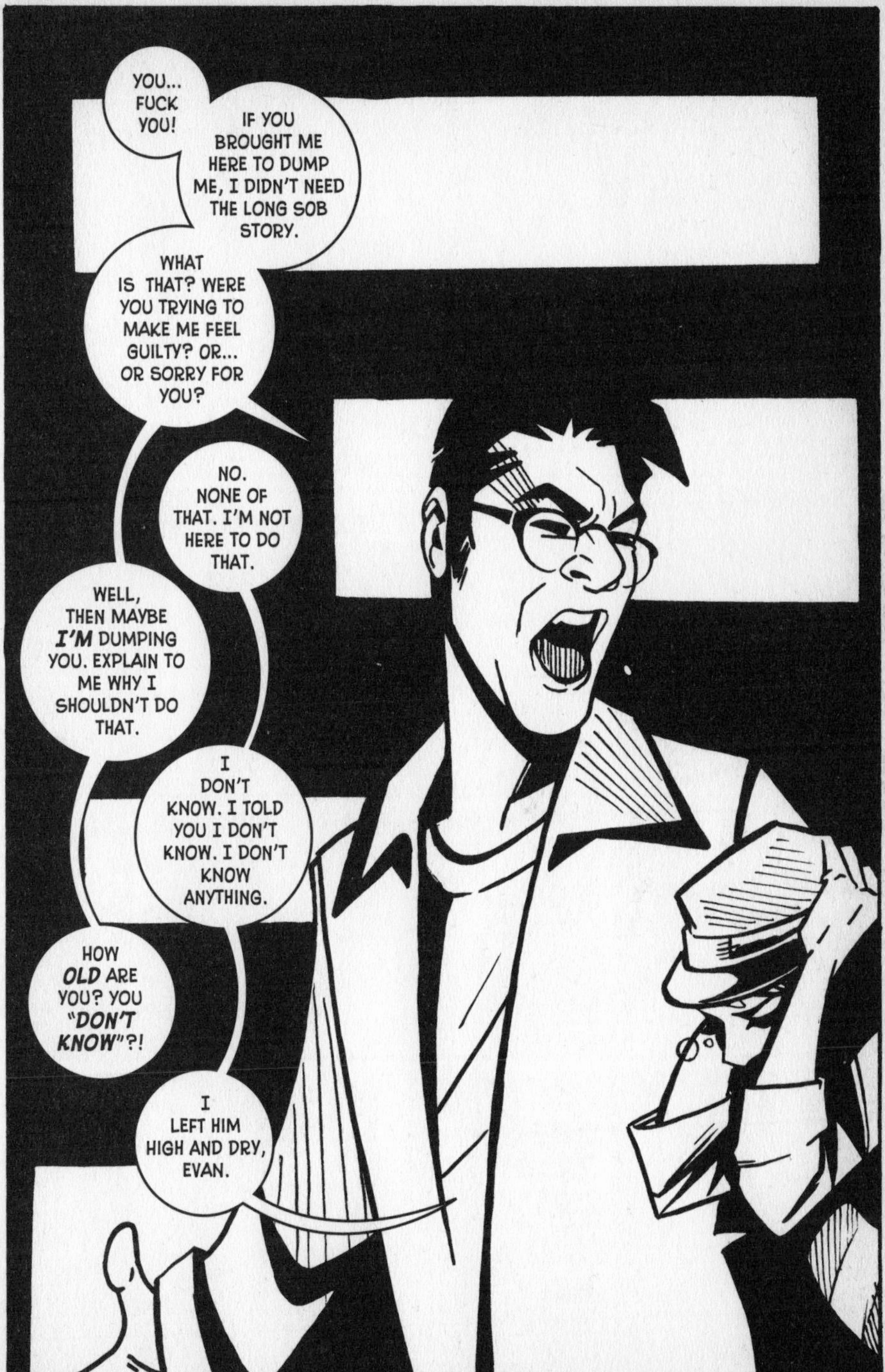
YOU... FUCK YOU!
IF YOU BROUGHT ME HERE TO DUMP ME, I DIDN'T NEED THE LONG SOB STORY.
WHAT IS THAT? WERE YOU TRYING TO MAKE ME FEEL GUILTY? OR... OR SORRY FOR YOU?
NO. NONE OF THAT. I'M NOT HERE TO DO THAT.
WELL, THEN MAYBE *I'M* DUMPING YOU. EXPLAIN TO ME WHY I SHOULDN'T DO THAT.
I DON'T KNOW. I TOLD YOU I DON'T KNOW. I DON'T KNOW ANYTHING.
HOW *OLD* ARE YOU? YOU *"DON'T KNOW"*?!
I LEFT HIM HIGH AND DRY, EVAN.

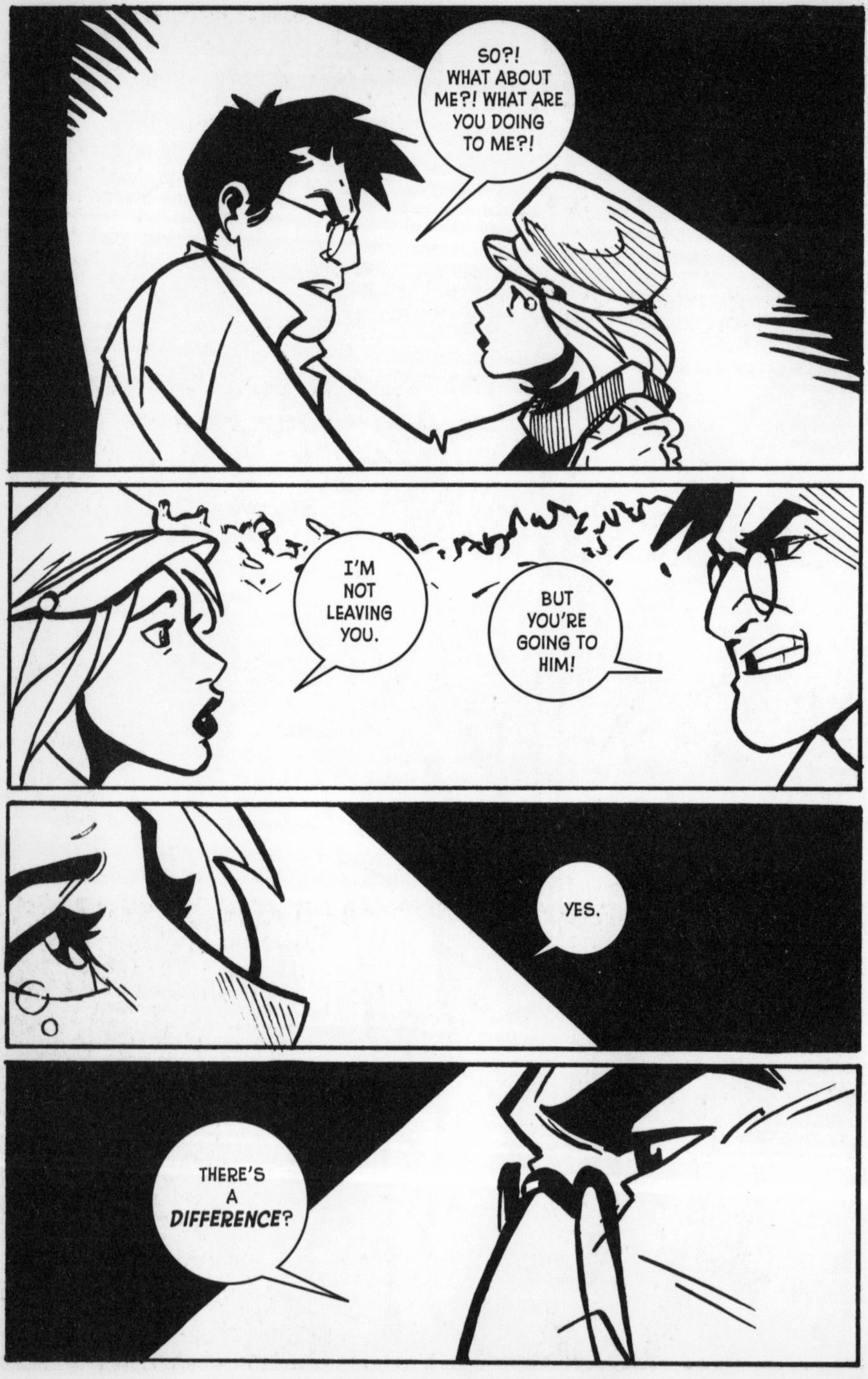
SO?! WHAT ABOUT ME?! WHAT ARE YOU DOING TO ME?!
I'M NOT LEAVING YOU.
BUT YOU'RE GOING TO HIM!
YES.
THERE'S A *DIFFERENCE*?

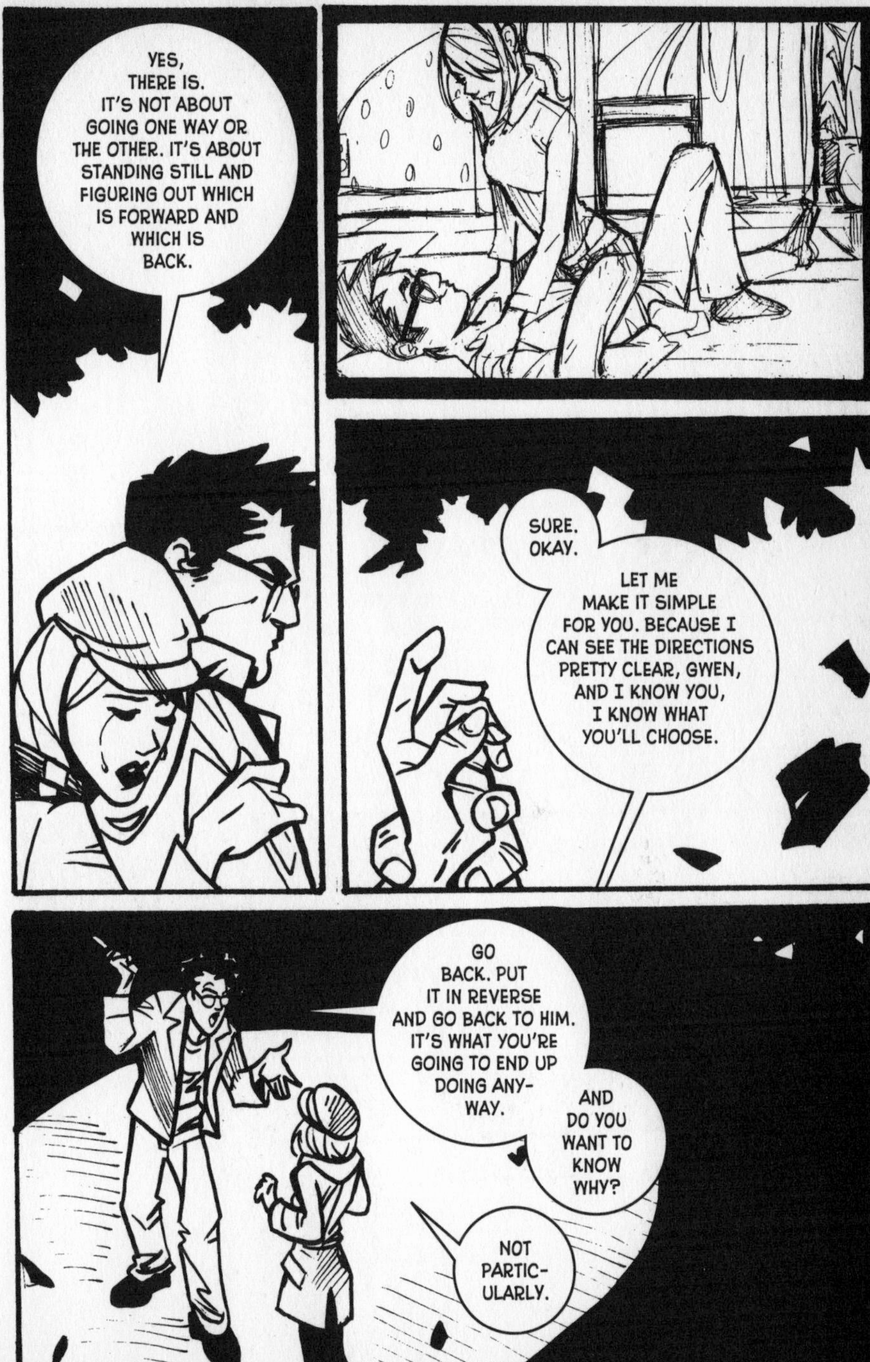
YES, THERE IS. IT'S NOT ABOUT GOING ONE WAY OR THE OTHER. IT'S ABOUT STANDING STILL AND FIGURING OUT WHICH IS FORWARD AND WHICH IS BACK.
SURE. OKAY.
LET ME MAKE IT SIMPLE FOR YOU. BECAUSE I CAN SEE THE DIRECTIONS PRETTY CLEAR, GWEN, AND I KNOW YOU, I KNOW WHAT YOU'LL CHOOSE.
GO BACK. PUT IT IN REVERSE AND GO BACK TO HIM. IT'S WHAT YOU'RE GOING TO END UP DOING ANY-WAY.
AND DO YOU WANT TO KNOW WHY?
NOT PARTIC-ULARLY.

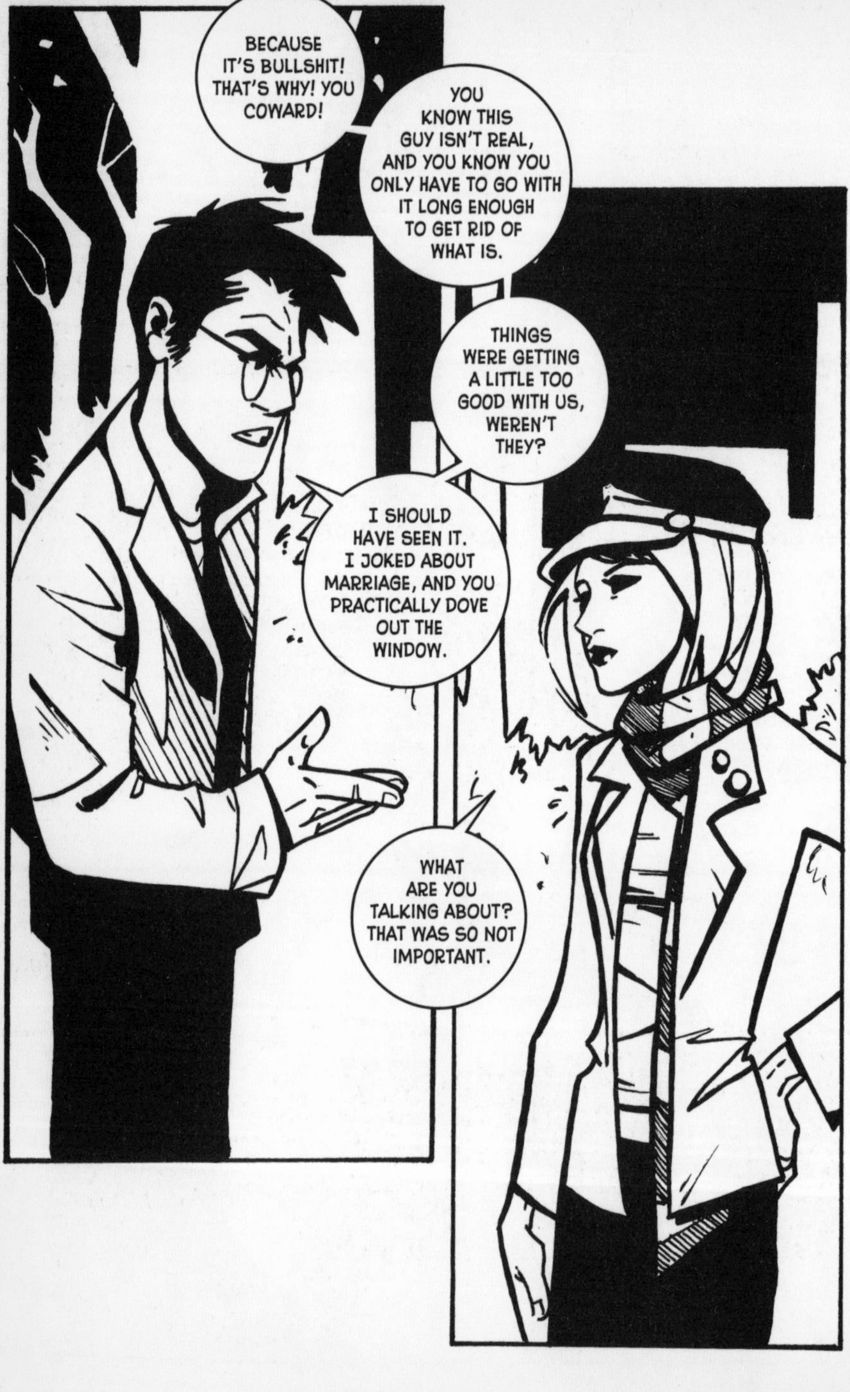
BECAUSE IT'S BULLSHIT! THAT'S WHY! YOU COWARD!
YOU KNOW THIS GUY ISN'T REAL, AND YOU KNOW YOU ONLY HAVE TO GO WITH IT LONG ENOUGH TO GET RID OF WHAT IS.
THINGS WERE GETTING A LITTLE TOO GOOD WITH US, WEREN'T THEY?
I SHOULD HAVE SEEN IT. I JOKED ABOUT MARRIAGE, AND YOU PRACTICALLY DOVE OUT THE WINDOW.
WHAT ARE YOU TALKING ABOUT? THAT WAS SO NOT IMPORTANT.

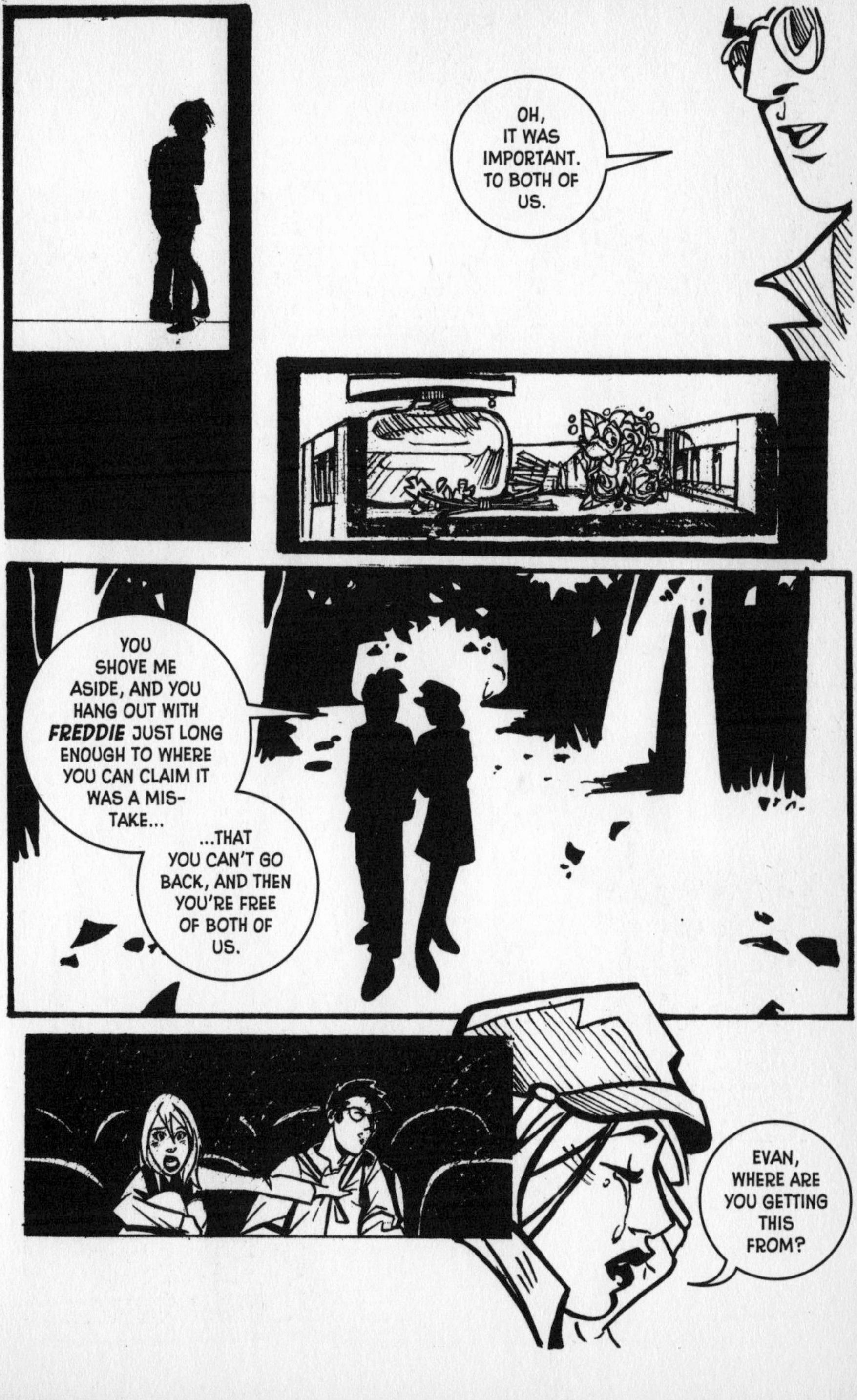
OH, IT WAS IMPORTANT. TO BOTH OF US.
YOU SHOVE ME ASIDE, AND YOU HANG OUT WITH FREDDIE JUST LONG ENOUGH TO WHERE YOU CAN CLAIM IT WAS A MIS-TAKE...
...THAT YOU CAN'T GO BACK, AND THEN YOU'RE FREE OF BOTH OF US.
EVAN, WHERE ARE YOU GETTING THIS FROM?

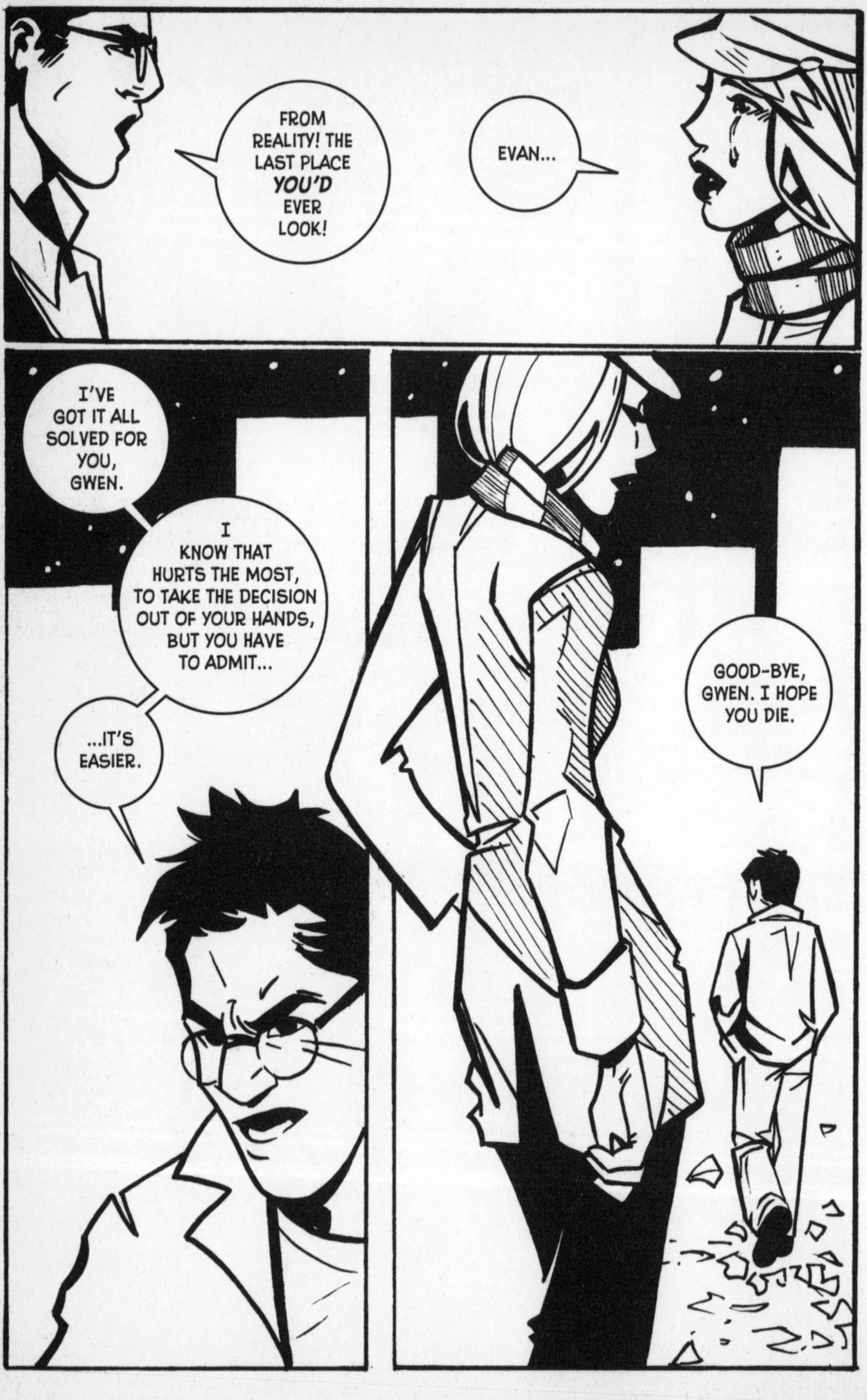
FROM REALITY! THE LAST PLACE *YOU'D* EVER LOOK!
EVAN...
I'VE GOT IT ALL SOLVED FOR YOU, GWEN.
I KNOW THAT HURTS THE MOST, TO TAKE THE DECISION OUT OF YOUR HANDS, BUT YOU HAVE TO ADMIT...
...IT'S EASIER.
GOOD-BYE, GWEN. I HOPE YOU DIE.

Twelve

SONG

John Lennon
"Real Love (acoustic)"

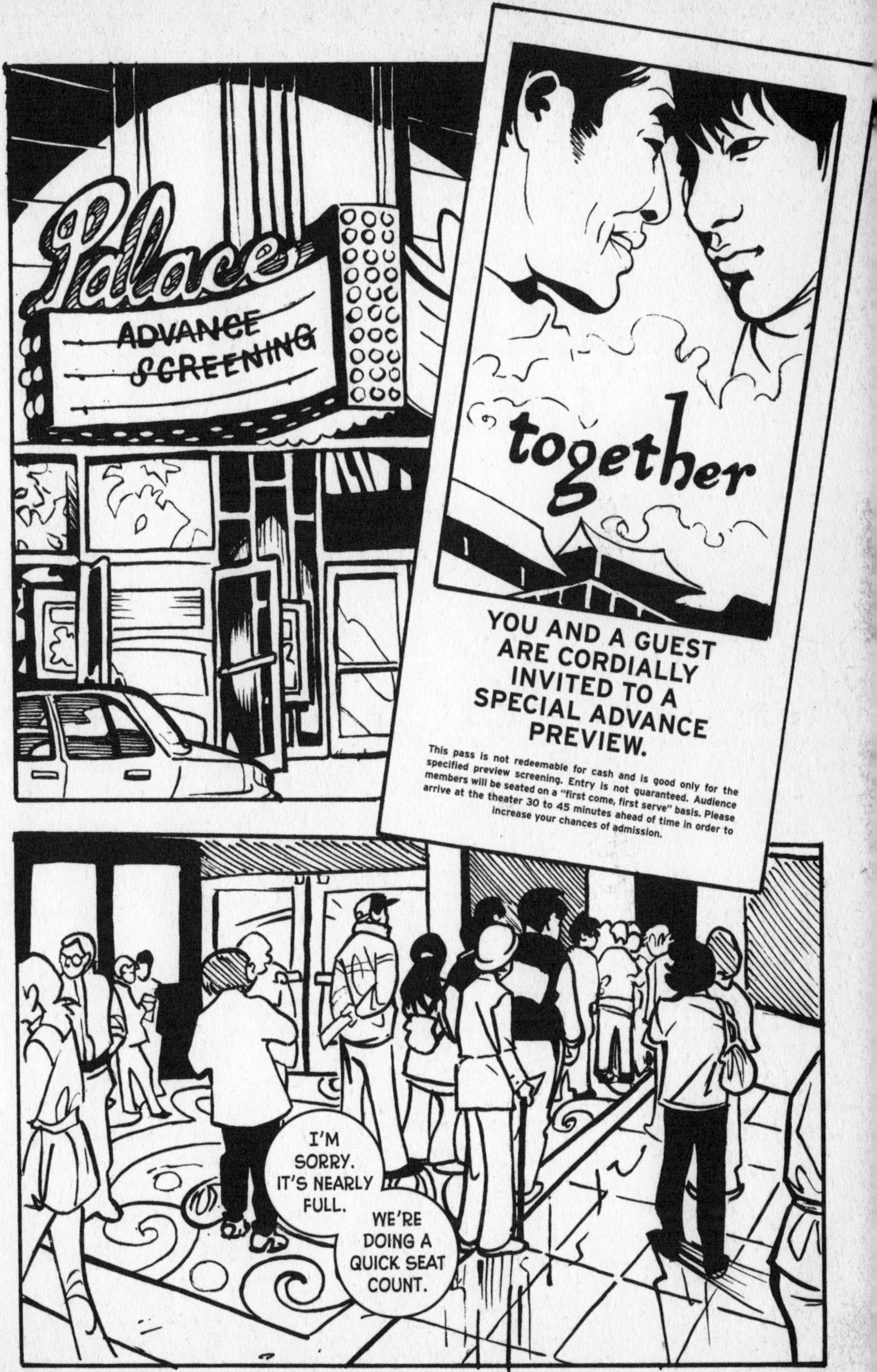
Palace
ADVANCE SCREENING
together
YOU AND A GUEST ARE CORDIALLY INVITED TO A SPECIAL ADVANCE PREVIEW.
This pass is not redeemable for cash and is good only for the specified preview screening. Entry is not guaranteed. Audience members will be seated on a "first come, first serve" basis. Please arrive at the theater 30 to 45 minutes ahead of time in order to increase your chances of admission.
I'M SORRY. IT'S NEARLY FULL.
WE'RE DOING A QUICK SEAT COUNT.

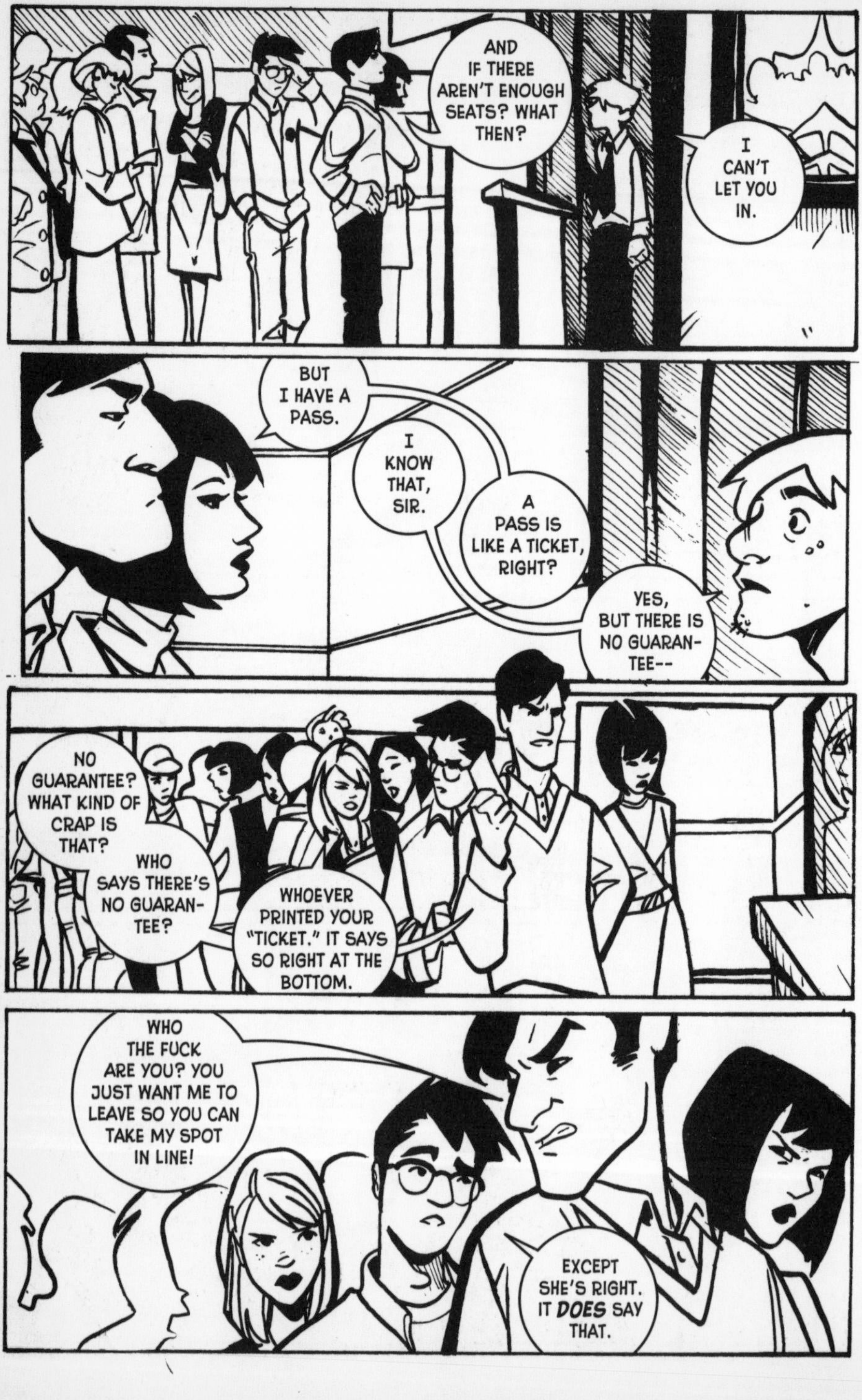
AND IF THERE AREN'T ENOUGH SEATS? WHAT THEN?
I CAN'T LET YOU IN.
BUT I HAVE A PASS.
I KNOW THAT, SIR.
A PASS IS LIKE A TICKET, RIGHT?
YES, BUT THERE IS NO GUARANTEE--
NO GUARANTEE? WHAT KIND OF CRAP IS THAT?
WHO SAYS THERE'S NO GUARANTEE?
WHOEVER PRINTED YOUR "TICKET." IT SAYS SO RIGHT AT THE BOTTOM.
WHO THE FUCK ARE YOU? YOU JUST WANT ME TO LEAVE SO YOU CAN TAKE MY SPOT IN LINE!
EXCEPT SHE'S RIGHT. IT *DOES* SAY THAT.

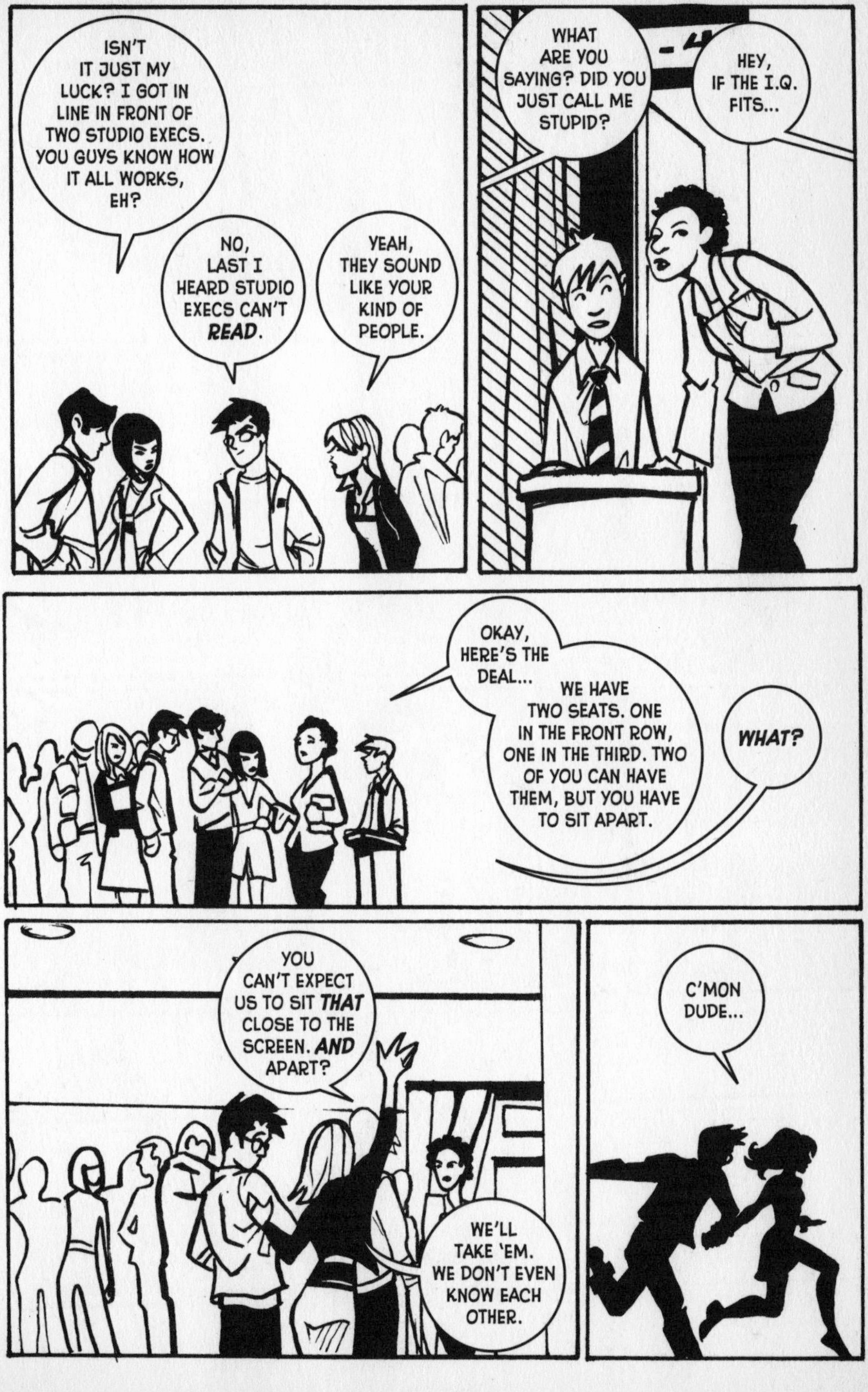
ISN'T IT JUST MY LUCK? I GOT IN LINE IN FRONT OF TWO STUDIO EXECS. YOU GUYS KNOW HOW IT ALL WORKS, EH?
NO, LAST I HEARD STUDIO EXECS CAN'T *READ*.
YEAH, THEY SOUND LIKE YOUR KIND OF PEOPLE.
WHAT ARE YOU SAYING? DID YOU JUST CALL ME STUPID?
HEY, IF THE I.Q. FITS...
OKAY, HERE'S THE DEAL...
WE HAVE TWO SEATS. ONE IN THE FRONT ROW, ONE IN THE THIRD. TWO OF YOU CAN HAVE THEM, BUT YOU HAVE TO SIT APART.
WHAT?
YOU CAN'T EXPECT US TO SIT *THAT* CLOSE TO THE SCREEN. *AND* APART?
WE'LL TAKE 'EM. WE DON'T EVEN KNOW EACH OTHER.
C'MON DUDE...

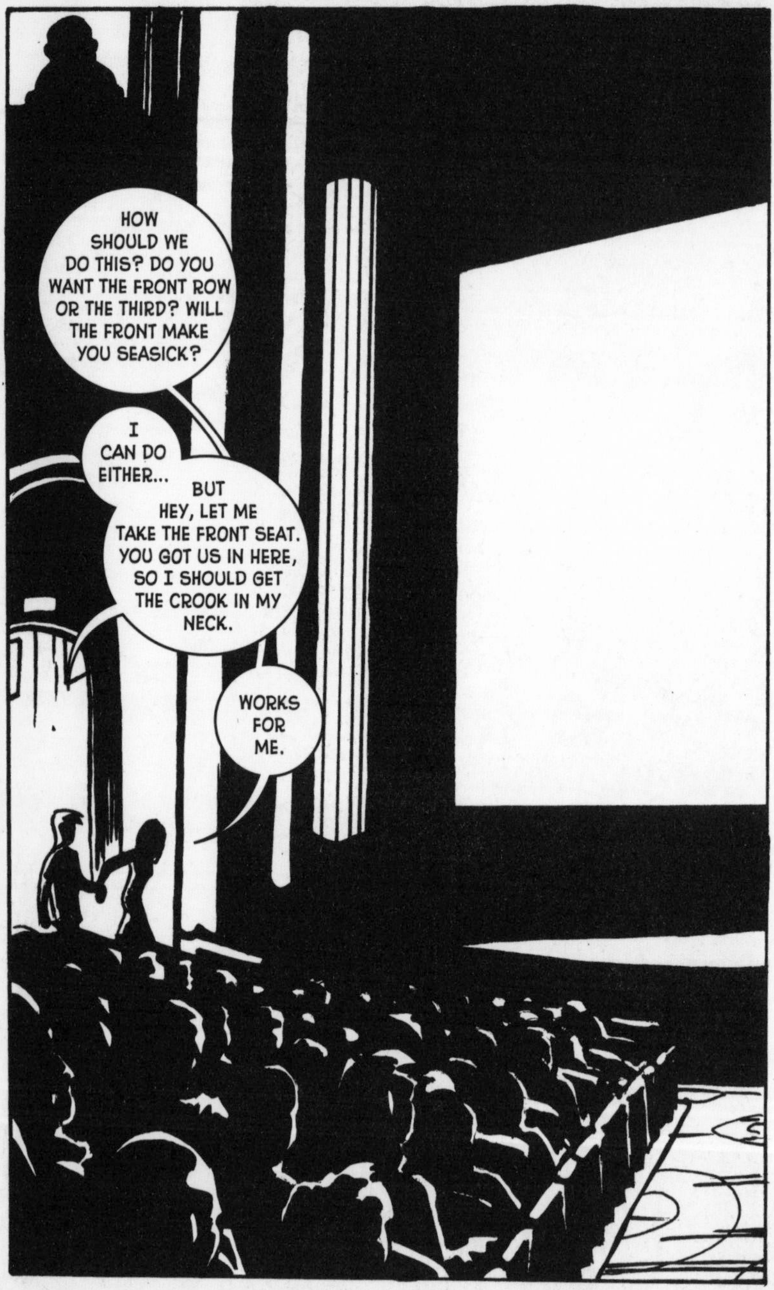
HOW SHOULD WE DO THIS? DO YOU WANT THE FRONT ROW OR THE THIRD? WILL THE FRONT MAKE YOU SEASICK?
I CAN DO EITHER...
BUT HEY, LET ME TAKE THE FRONT SEAT. YOU GOT US IN HERE, SO I SHOULD GET THE CROOK IN MY NECK.
WORKS FOR ME.

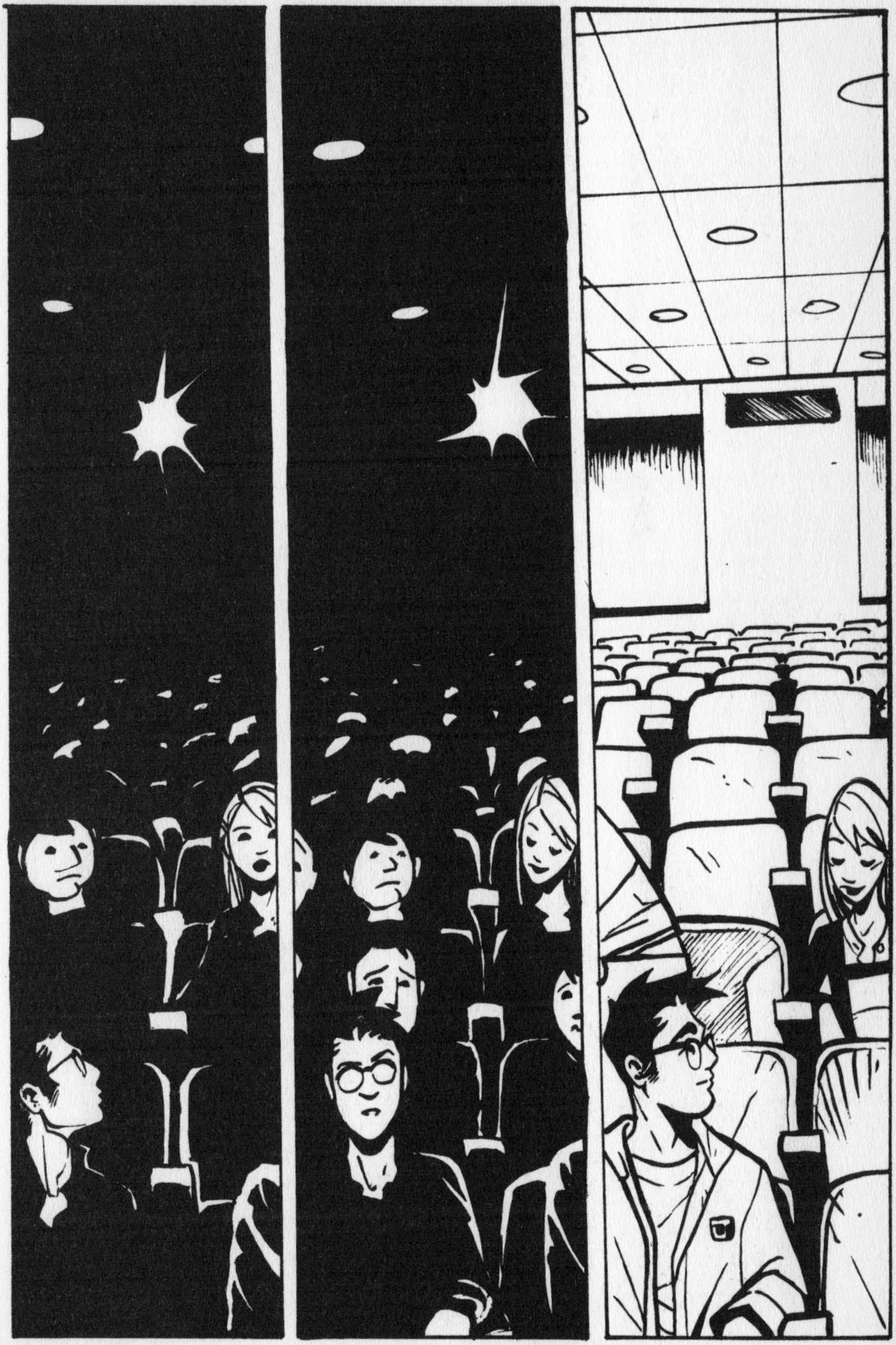

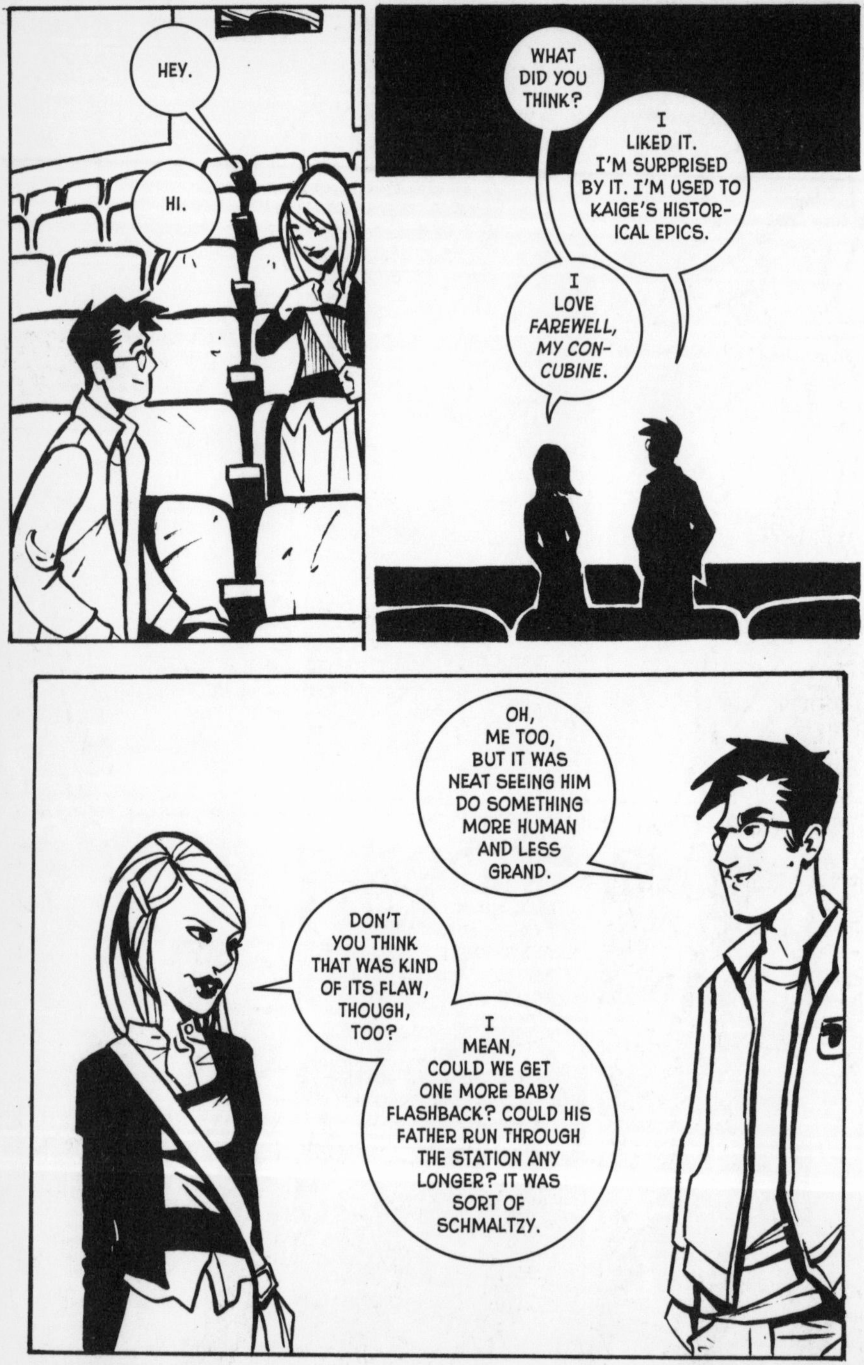

HEY.
HI.
WHAT DID YOU THINK?
I LOVE *FAREWELL, MY CONCUBINE*.
I LIKED IT. I'M SURPRISED BY IT. I'M USED TO KAIGE'S HISTORICAL EPICS.
OH, ME TOO, BUT IT WAS NEAT SEEING HIM DO SOMETHING MORE HUMAN AND LESS GRAND.
DON'T YOU THINK THAT WAS KIND OF ITS FLAW, THOUGH, TOO?
I MEAN, COULD WE GET ONE MORE BABY FLASHBACK? COULD HIS FATHER RUN THROUGH THE STATION ANY LONGER? IT WAS SORT OF SCHMALTZY.

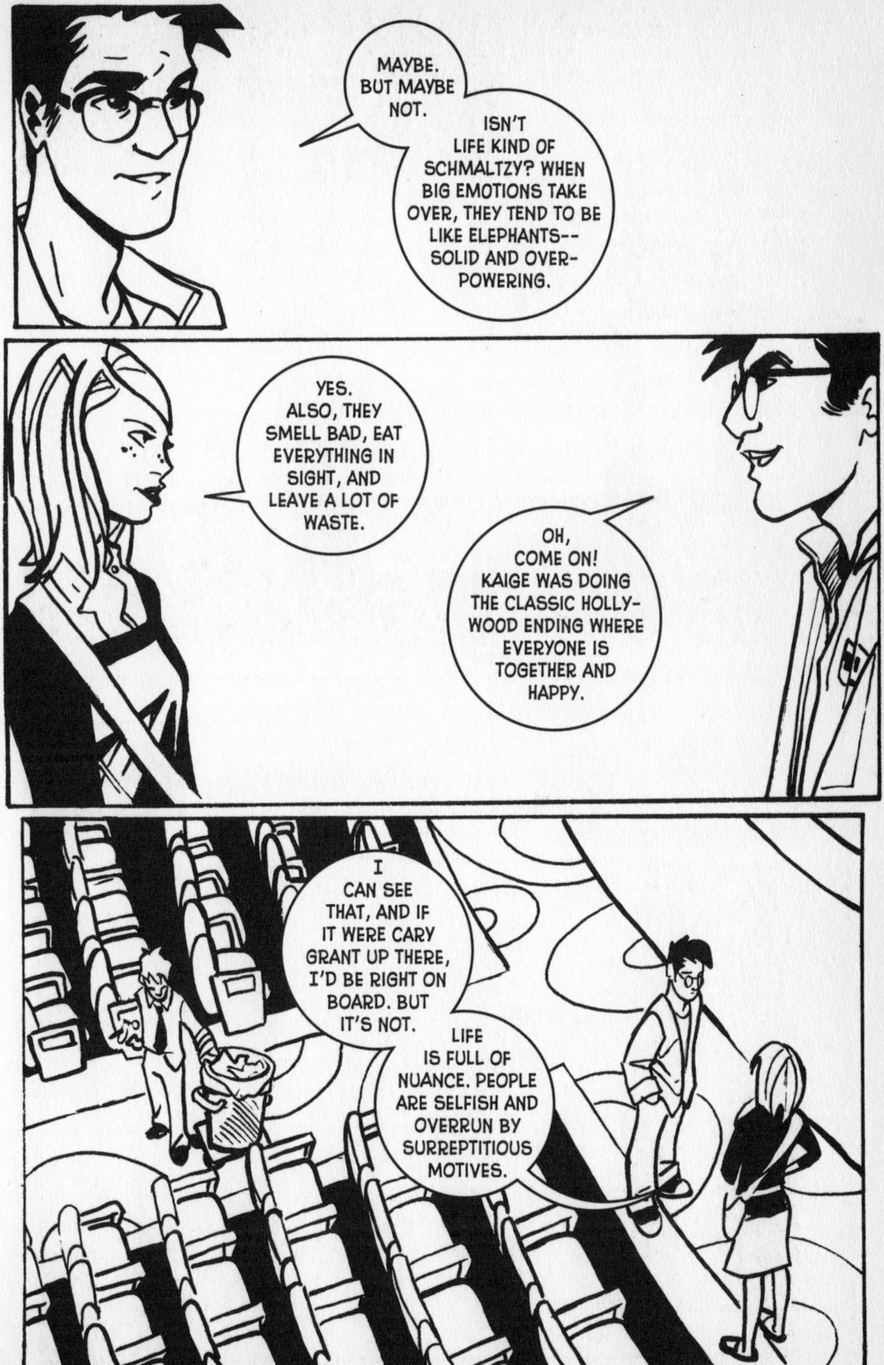
MAYBE. BUT MAYBE NOT.
ISN'T LIFE KIND OF SCHMALTZY? WHEN BIG EMOTIONS TAKE OVER, THEY TEND TO BE LIKE ELEPHANTS-- SOLID AND OVER-POWERING.
YES. ALSO, THEY SMELL BAD, EAT EVERYTHING IN SIGHT, AND LEAVE A LOT OF WASTE.
OH, COME ON! KAIGE WAS DOING THE CLASSIC HOLLY-WOOD ENDING WHERE EVERYONE IS TOGETHER AND HAPPY.
I CAN SEE THAT, AND IF IT WERE CARY GRANT UP THERE, I'D BE RIGHT ON BOARD. BUT IT'S NOT.
LIFE IS FULL OF NUANCE. PEOPLE ARE SELFISH AND OVERRUN BY SURREPTITIOUS MOTIVES.

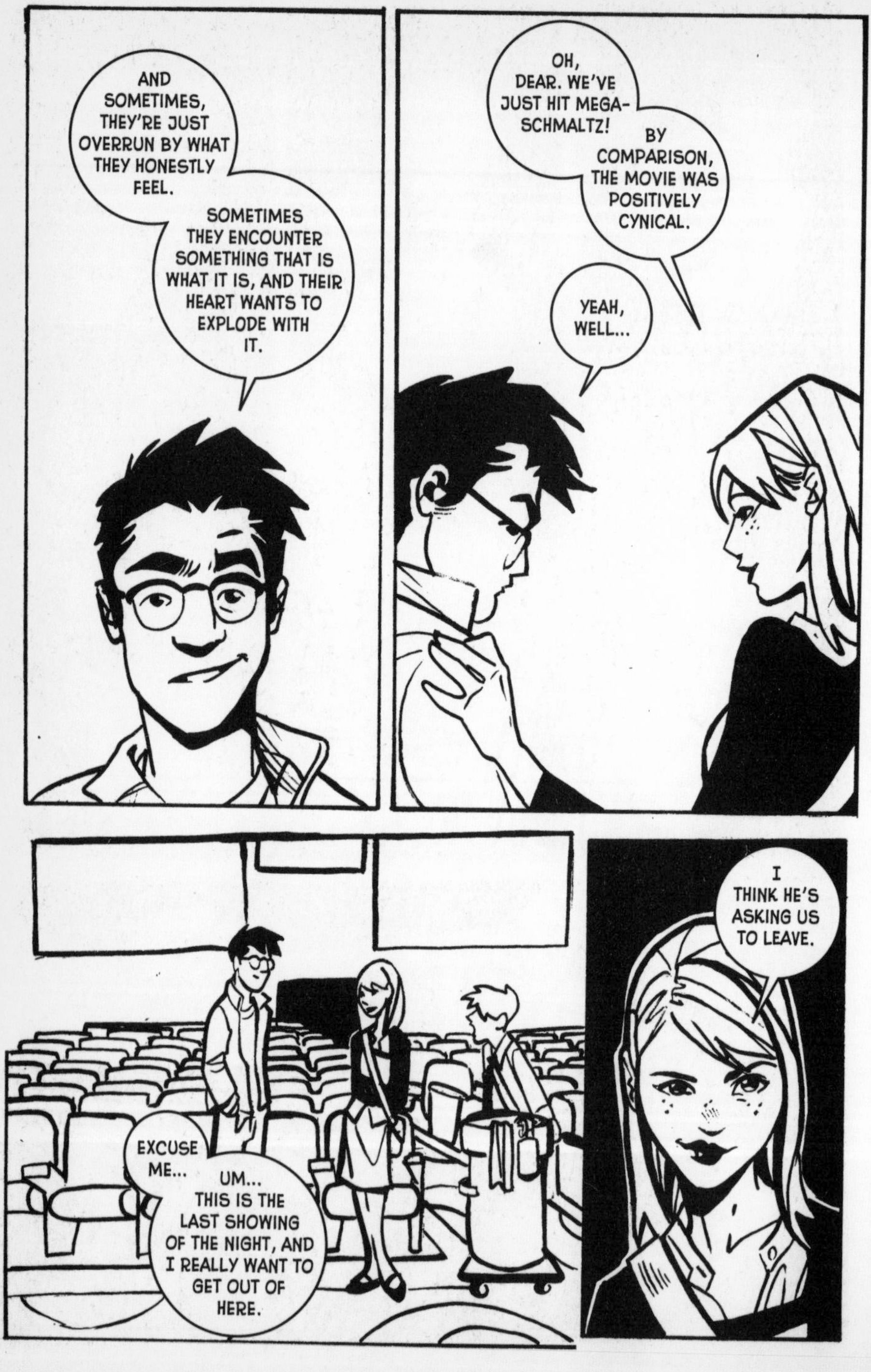
AND SOMETIMES, THEY'RE JUST OVERRUN BY WHAT THEY HONESTLY FEEL.
SOMETIMES THEY ENCOUNTER SOMETHING THAT IS WHAT IT IS, AND THEIR HEART WANTS TO EXPLODE WITH IT.
OH, DEAR. WE'VE JUST HIT MEGA-SCHMALTZ!
BY COMPARISON, THE MOVIE WAS POSITIVELY CYNICAL.
YEAH, WELL...
EXCUSE ME...
UM... THIS IS THE LAST SHOWING OF THE NIGHT, AND I REALLY WANT TO GET OUT OF HERE.
I THINK HE'S ASKING US TO LEAVE.

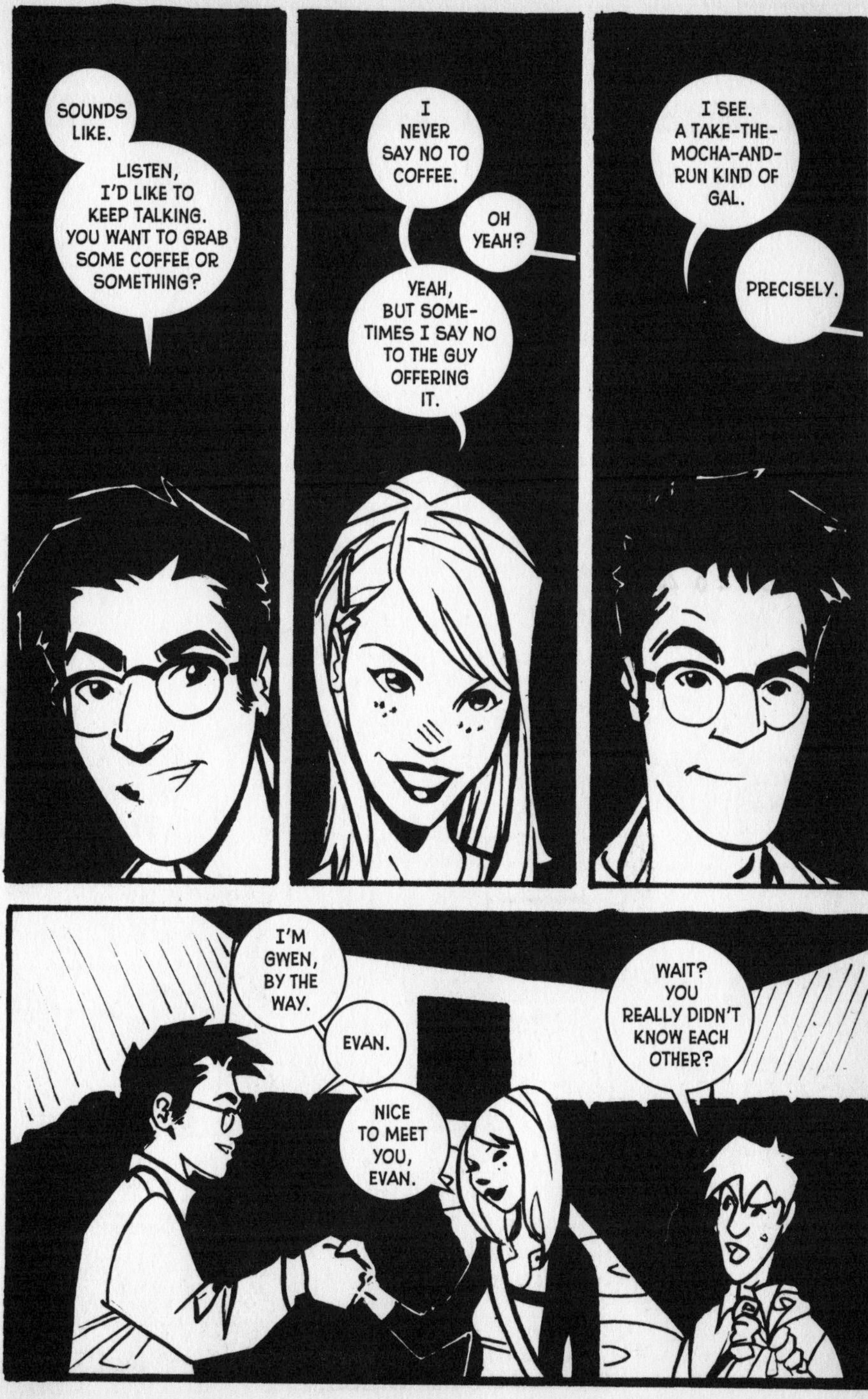
SOUNDS LIKE.
LISTEN, I'D LIKE TO KEEP TALKING. YOU WANT TO GRAB SOME COFFEE OR SOMETHING?
I NEVER SAY NO TO COFFEE.
OH YEAH?
YEAH, BUT SOME-TIMES I SAY NO TO THE GUY OFFERING IT.
I SEE. A TAKE-THE-MOCHA-AND-RUN KIND OF GAL.
PRECISELY.
I'M GWEN, BY THE WAY.
EVAN.
NICE TO MEET YOU, EVAN.
WAIT? YOU REALLY DIDN'T KNOW EACH OTHER?

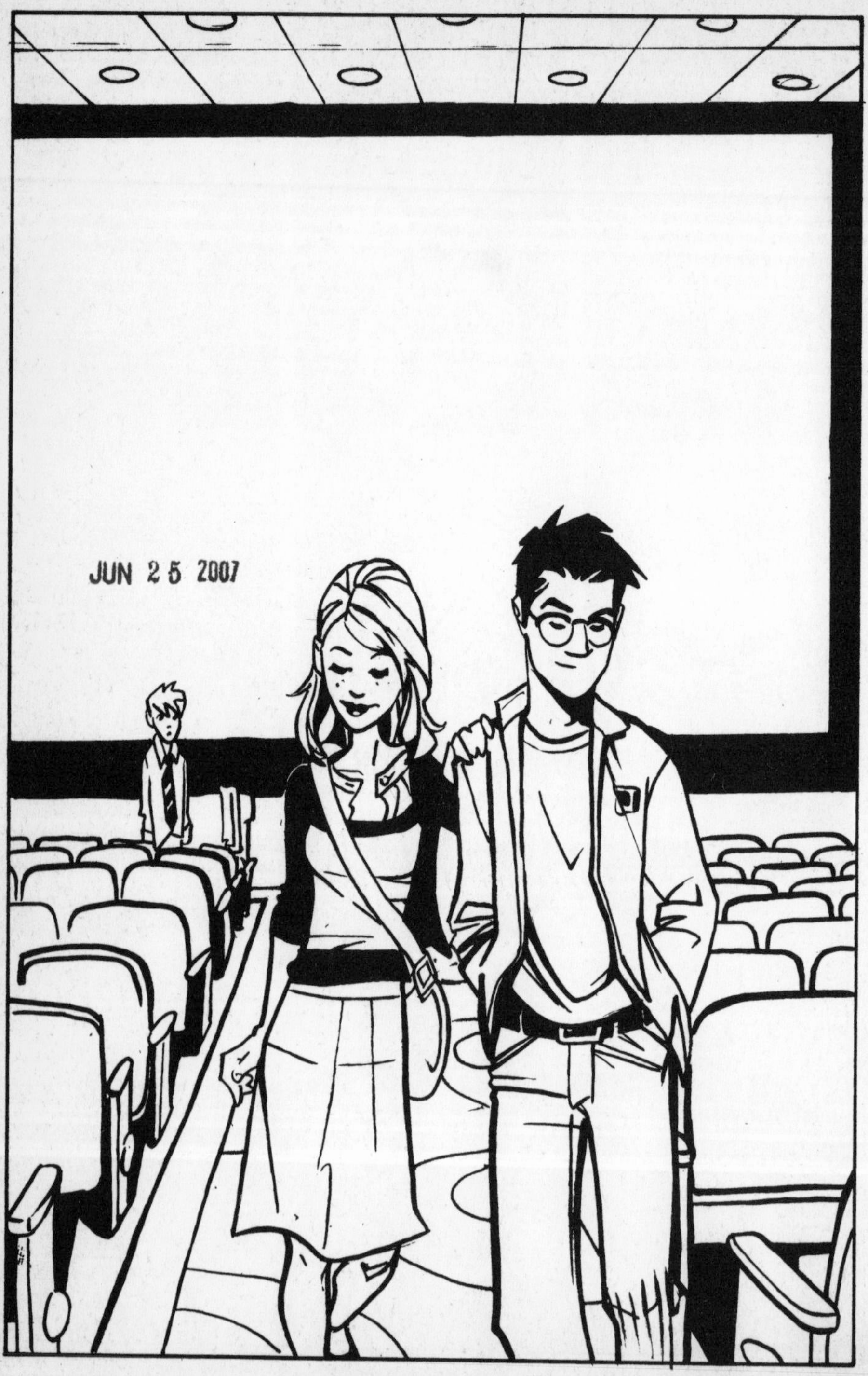

Fin

SONG

My Life Story
"12 Reasons Why I Love Her"

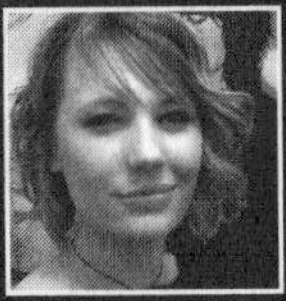

Photos by Terry Blas

Joëlle Jones spends her nights serving drinks and filling her sketchbook with images destined for future comics. Her work has appeared in Dark Horse's *Sexy Chix* anthology, as well as the Viz magazine *Shojo Beat*. *12 Reasons Why I Love Her* is her first full-length comic book.

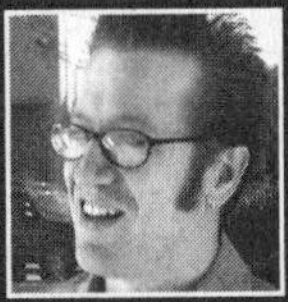

Jamie S. Rich is an author of both prose (*Cut My Hair*, *I Was Someone Dead*, and *The Everlasting*) and comics (the ongoing series *Love the Way You Love*). He has worked for publishers as diverse as Image Comics, Tokyopop, Ice Kunion, and Dark Horse. He is hard at work on *Have You Seen the Horizon Lately?*, his third full-length novel.

Both creators live in Portland, OR, each with a grouchy, headstrong feline. They are collaborating on a graphic novel for 2007, the hardboiled crime story *You Have Killed Me*.

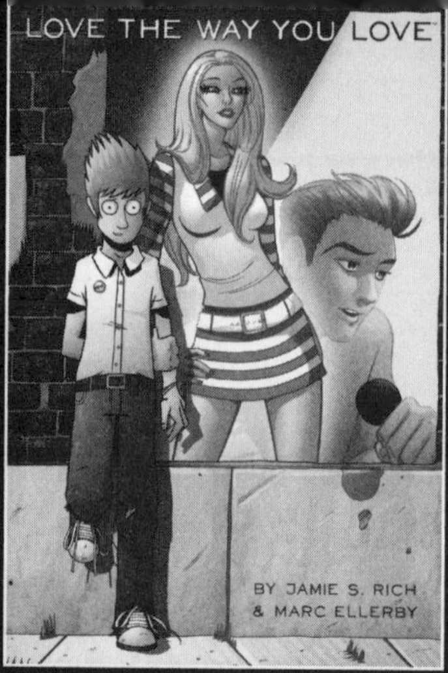
LOVE THE WAY YOU LOVE
BY JAMIE S. RICH
& MARC ELLERBY

LOVE THE WAY YOU LOVE™ #1
by Jamie S. Rich & Marc Ellerby
72 pages
$5.95 US
ISBN 1-932664-52-1

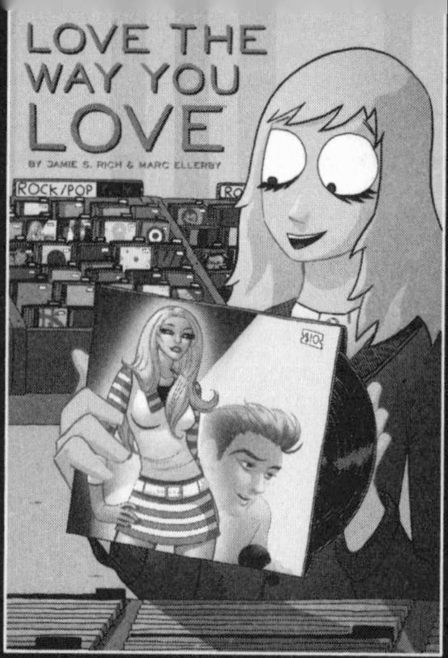
LOVE THE WAY YOU LOVE
BY JAMIE S. RICH & MARC ELLERBY
ROCK/POP

LOVE THE WAY YOU LOVE™ #2
by Jamie S. Rich & Marc Ellerby
72 pages
$5.95 US
ISBN 1-932664-53-X

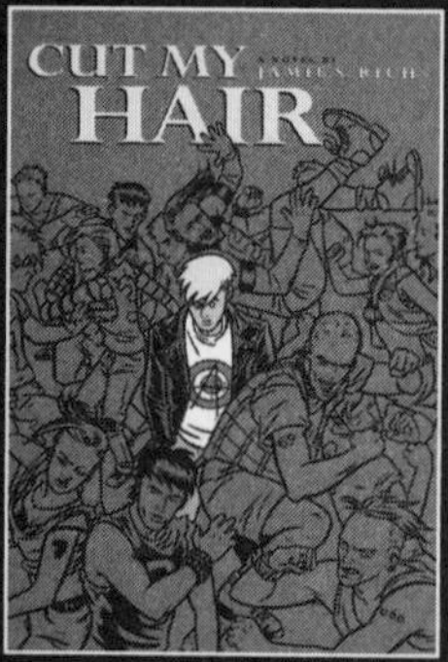
CUT MY HAIR

CUT MY HAIR™
by Jamie S. Rich
cover by Mike Allred
illustrations by Chynna Clugston, Renee French, Scott Morse, Andi Watson & Judd Winick
236 pages
prose w/black-&-white illustrations
$15.95 US
ISBN 0-9700387-0-4

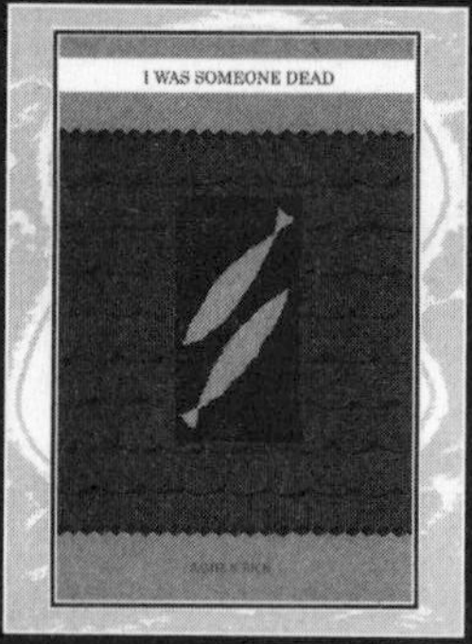
I WAS SOMEONE DEAD

I WAS SOMEONE DEAD™
illustrated prose novella
by Jamie S. Rich
cover & illustrations by Andi Watson
136 pages
prose w/black-&-white illustrations
$9.95 US
ISBN 1-932664-26-2

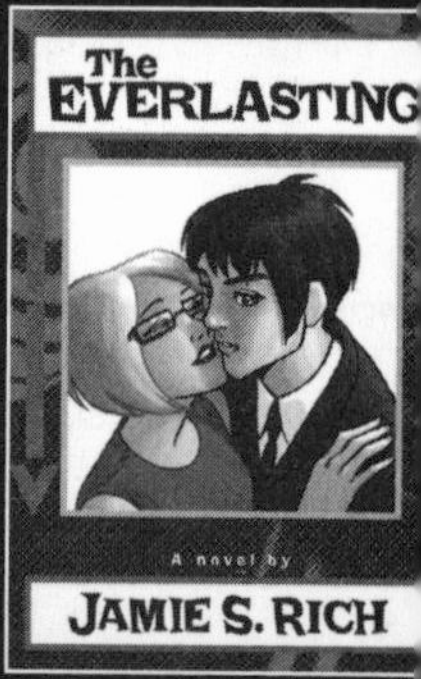
The EVERLASTING
A novel by
JAMIE S. RICH

THE EVERLASTING™
by Jamie S. Rich
cover by Chynna Clugston
504 pages, prose
$19.95 US
ISBN 1-932664-54-8

Available at finer comics shops everywhere. For a comics store near you, call 1-888-COMIC-BOOK or visit www.the-master-list.com.
For more Oni Press titles and information visit www.onipress.com